Light of Faith

The Compendium of Theology

St. Thomas Aquinas

Light of Faith

The Compendium of Theology

Mr & Mrs William R Campbell
91 Bay Avenue
Atlantic Highlands, NJ 07716

SOPHIA INSTITUTE PRESS
Manchester, New Hampshire

LIGHT OF FAITH: THE COMPENDIUM OF THEOLOGY was first published in English in 1947 as THE COMPENDIUM OF THEOLOGY by B. Herder Book Company and was reprinted by Herder in 1958. This 1993 edition contains many new headings and numerous editorial revisions to eliminate awkward, obscure, or archaic language, and to correct errors in the text and in the references.

Sophia Institute Press
Box 5284, Manchester, NH 03108
1-800-888-9344

Nihil obstat: G. H. Guyot, C.M., *Censor Librorum*
Imprimatur: Joseph E. Ritter, S.T.D., Archbishop of St. Louis
November 18, 1947

Library of Congress Cataloging-in-Publication Data

Thomas, Aquinas, Saint, 1225?-1274.
[*Compendium theologiae*. English]
Light of faith : the Compendium of theology / St. Thomas Aquinas.
  p. cm.
Originally published: Compendium of theology. St. Louis : B. Herder Book Co., 1947
Includes bibliographical references and index.
ISBN 0-918477-15-8 : $19.95
1. Theology, Doctrinal—Early works to 1800. 2. Catholic Church—Doctrines—Early works to 1800.   I. Title.
BX1749.T36   1993
230'.2—dc20   93-6793 CIP

4 6 8 10 9 7 5 3

Dedicated by the author
to Brother Reginald,
his friend and companion,

and by the translator
to his mother and father

TABLE OF CONTENTS

Editor's Note (1993)

The *Compendium of Theology* breaks off abruptly with the words "attainment of the kingdom is possible." At this point, death summoned St. Thomas to the heavenly kingdom and his book remained unfinished. We are left, nonetheless, with this rich text, immensely helpful in our own quest for the heavenly kingdom.

I have renamed it *Light of Faith*, a title less ponderous than *The Compendium of Theology*, seeking thereby to draw to its wisdom more of the laymen for whom it was intended.

For this edition, I have retained the essential content and structure of Fr. Vollert's excellent 1947 translation, as well as his numerous helpful footnotes. Where possible, I have given more precise references than were found in the earlier edition.

I have also preserved the chapter numbering of Father Vollert's edition, but, for greater ease of use, I have added general topical headings to guide readers. These new topical headings also serve as the Table of Contents at the front of this edition; the hundreds of original chapter headings appear at the beginning of each chapter as well as in the Detailed List of Topics found just before the Index.

Light of Faith

The English Scripture quotations in this edition are based on the Douay-Rheims translation of the Bible because the text of that translation closely approximates the text that St. Thomas seems to have been working from. However, the Douay translation sometimes employs archaic names of books of the Bible or does not use currently accepted enumerations. Where this occurs, I have indicated in parentheses the modern names and numbers as found in the Revised Standard Version (RSV) of the Bible according to the *New Oxford Annotated Bible with the Apocrypha* (New York: Oxford University Press, 1977). Also, where passages from the Douay-Rheims translation are obscure in their meaning, I have sometimes replaced them with the same passages from the Revised Standard Version.

As you read these pages, it is important that you keep in mind that this is not a scholarly edition nor does it pretend to be. Scholars should read these pages in Latin! This edition is for the average person who seeks to know more about his Faith and to grow holy.

Read it slowly, attentively, and prayerfully. You will soon discover why St. Thomas Aquinas was proclaimed a Doctor of the Universal Church in 1567 and why he has been revered as a master theologian for seven centuries.

More importantly, you yourself will grow wise in your Faith and, if you persist in living by that wisdom, you will soon come to be like St. Thomas not only in wisdom, but in holiness.

Translator's Preface (1947)

This translation of the *Compendium theologiae* of St. Thomas was undertaken for the benefit of students and readers who are eager to acquaint themselves with the thought of the Angelic Doctor, but who do not feel that they have mastered Latin sufficiently to read his works comfortably in the original. The book should be especially useful for courses in religion or theology for the laity.

St. Thomas had such readers expressly in mind. As he says in the opening chapter, the work was written for those who might desire a convenient synopsis of Christian teaching. Since he composed it during the last two years of his life, that is, in 1272-73,[1] when he was at the height of his power and had already written the *Summa contra Gentiles* and most of the *Summa theologica*, the work possesses a sureness of mastery and an authority that endow it with extraordinary value. It is surpassed in importance only by

---

[1] No scholar questions the date or the authenticity of the *Compendium*. These matters are thoroughly discussed in P. Mandonnet, *Des écrits authentiques de saint Thomas d'Aquin* (2nd ed., Fribourg: Imprimérie de l'Oeuvre de Saint-Paul, 1910); M. Grabmann, *Die Werke des Hl. Thomas von Aquin* (2nd ed., Münster: Aschendorff, 1931).

the two treatises just mentioned and the *Scriptum super libros Sententiarum*.

Thus the *Compendium*, written by St. Thomas in his full maturity, indicates what, to his clear mind, with its comprehensive theological grasp, is most important in theology. Therefore the book can also serve as a key to a fruitful study of his more detailed and copious works.

Indeed, the remarkable lucidity and brevity of the numerous points treated in the *Compendium of Theology* enable us to follow the unfolding of the thought of St. Thomas more inerrantly than is possible in any of the larger treatises. Without difficulty we can trace the logical consecutiveness of his deductive processes and see how he infers truth from truth.

As planned by St. Thomas, the work was to have consisted of three parts, under the headings of faith, hope, and charity. His untimely death prevented him from realizing his plan; he got no farther than the tenth chapter of Part Two. Fortunately he was able to complete Part One, the most important from the theological point of view. This part, on faith, is subdivided into two sections or treatises. The first of these deals mainly with the Blessed Trinity, but opens with a discussion of the unity of the divine nature, and also treats of creation and the different classes of creatures. The second treatise of Part One, after a preliminary discussion of Original Justice and Original Sin, takes up the question of Christ's humanity.

In reading the *Compendium* — and the same is true in reading the *Summa theologica* — we shall do well to advert to the difference between the science of theology as envisaged by St. Thomas and theology as treated in modern manuals.[2] Modern theology,

---

[2] On this point, see the excellent article by E. Marcotte, "De saint Thomas à nos manuels," *Revue de l'Université d'Ottawa*, XVI (1946), 154-74.

that is, theology as it has developed since the Spanish revival in the sixteenth century, seeks less to explain the intimate nature of supernatural truth than to establish the fact of its existence. Such facts escape our experience; we can have contact with the supernatural world only through Revelation. The concern of modern theological treatises is to establish their theses by means of authentic texts painstakingly drawn from the sources of Revelation. Undoubtedly the progress of apologetics and positive theology has fixed the data of Revelation with greater precision than was the case in the Middle Ages. Undoubtedly, too, such progress is to be highly esteemed, especially in view of the widespread heresy and defection from God that have been striving for centuries to undermine the foundations of the Faith. Today we know more accurately than in the past what we are to believe, and have established with all the certitude of the most rigorous scientific method the truths that God has revealed.

But the danger is that, in our engrossing zeal to safeguard the deposit of Revelation, we may neglect to penetrate the truths of Revelation, to assimilate them, to invigorate our charity with them. The *fides quaerens intellectum* ("faith in search of understanding"), which was the ideal of medieval theology, may become a faith in search of the motives of credibility.

The theologian has had to interrupt his proper task, which is the contemplation of the supernatural universe in the light of God's own knowledge, in answer to the call of more pressing needs. He has had to descend to the level of God's enemies and take up battle against them on many fronts. Until completely victorious, theology must continue to engage in controversy. At the same time, it may not lose its high vision. It must replenish its strength in the only atmosphere healthy for it, the atmosphere of serene theological contemplation. Such, not exclusively but at any rate predominantly, is the atmosphere of Thomistic theology.

For St. Thomas, theology was a science: not merely an ascertaining of facts, but a knowledge of facts through their causes. Living in happier days, well called the *Ages of Faith* in spite of the sneers of modern scoffers, he had less need to demonstrate the facts of Revelation — which is the domain of positive theology — and so could turn his genius to an investigation of the *why* and *wherefore* of the supernatural world disclosed by God.

His chief endeavor was to explain, through their causes, the natures of beings already known, of facts whose existence, duly attested by faith, he could presuppose as already ascertained with certitude.

This being his task, he did not judge that he had to justify his principles by invoking, at every step, the testimony of the inspired writers and their authentic interpreters. Arguments drawn from authority, he held, convince us of the existence of a supernatural truth; they do not give us an intelligence of it. As he points out in *Quodlibet* IV, a. 18, sometimes we have to dispute with Jews, heretics, or schismatics. At such times, appeal to the authorities admitted by these adversaries is our proper procedure. But if the teacher's aim is not to remove error but to impart instruction that will lead to understanding, he should lay bare the ultimate reasons underlying the truth. "If the teacher settles the question by merely citing authorities, the student will, indeed, be assured that the matter is so; but he will gain nothing of science or understanding, and will depart empty-minded."

Since arguments from authority cannot convey understanding, theological science bases its conclusions on ontological considerations, drawn from the very nature of the subject investigated. It seeks answers to its questions, not in this or that testimony of Sacred Scripture or the Fathers, but in the very essence of supernatural realities and of the whole supernatural order, as described by Revelation. In the causes — especially the final cause — of supernatural realities, it will find the ultimate explanation of their being, their properties, and their actions.

If we bear in mind this distinction between the scope of medieval theology and that of modern theology, we shall not search the writings of St. Thomas for Christian evidences that are not there, but shall follow him as he gradually unfolds before our eyes the eternal designs of God who loves us in Christ and who has predestined us to be made conformable to the image of His Son. In this advance our faith will acquire some understanding of the sublime truths of Revelation. The value of the *Summa theologica* is the ultimate explanation it endeavors to impart of all things supernatural through their causal connection with God. To a lesser extent, the same is true of the *Compendium of Theology*.

The full title by which this work is generally known is *Compendium theologiae ad fratrem Reginaldum socium suum carissimum*. The original designation seems to have been *Brevis compilatio theologiae ad fratrem Raynaldum de Piperno*.[3] The title *De fide et spe* is a later addition designed to explain its content.[4] The work is sometimes referred to as *Opusculum II* from its serial number in the Piana edition.

The *Compendium theologiae* is found in the following standard editions of St. Thomas:

1. *Opera omnia*, iussu S. Pii V, 18 vols. in fol. (Rome, 1570-71). Vol. XVII. This is known as the Piana edition, or the first Roman edition, or the *editio Vaticana*.
2. *Opera omnia*, 25 Vols. (Parma, 1852-73). Vol. XVI.

---

[3] See P. Synave, "Le catalogue officiel des oeuvres de saint Thomas d'Aquin," Archives d'histoire doctrinale et littéraire du moyen age, III (1928), 27, 30.

[4] Ibid., p. 31.

3. *Opera omnia*, ed. E. Fretté and P. Maré, 34 vols. (Paris: Vivès, 1871-80). Vol. XXVII.

4. *Opuscula omnia*, ed. P. Mandonnet, 5 vols. (Paris: Lethielleux, 1927). Vol. II.

In making the translation, I have used the last three of these editions. In general, I preferred the Vivès text, which seemed to me the best. But in numbering the chapters I have followed Mandonnet's order, which is also that of the Piana edition, as books or articles that refer to the *Compendium* almost universally cite or quote chapters according to this order.

The footnotes have been supplied by me; the conventions of medieval scholarship did not impose on St. Thomas the rigors of exact ascertaining of references. In the arduous labor of locating references I found some help in the annotations of the Ottawa edition of the *Summa* and the Leonine edition of the *Contra Gentiles*, for which I wish to express my acknowledgments. But in every case I checked the sources cited for accuracy. I have also supplied the verses to scriptural references, generally incorporating them in the text without further indication, so as to avoid needless footnotes. Complete titles of collections and works referred to in the annotations will be found in the Bibliography.

Cyril Vollert, S.J.
St. Mary's College
St. Marys, Kansas

FAITH

The first part
of
LIGHT OF FAITH:
THE COMPENDIUM OF THEOLOGY

Author's Introduction

To restore man, who had been laid low by sin, to the heights of divine glory, the Word of the eternal Father, though containing all things within His immensity, willed to become small. This He did, not by putting aside His greatness, but by taking to Himself our littleness. No one can say that he is unable to grasp the teaching of heavenly wisdom; what the Word taught at great length, although clearly, throughout the various volumes of Sacred Scripture for those who have leisure to study, He has reduced to brief compass for the sake of those whose time is taken up with the cares of daily life. Man's salvation consists in knowing the truth, so that the human mind may not be confused by diverse errors; in making for the right goal, so that man may not fall away from true happiness by pursuing wrong ends; and in carrying out the law of justice, so that he may not besmirch himself with a multitude of vices.

Knowledge of the truth necessary for man's salvation is comprised within a few brief articles of Faith. The Apostle says in Romans 9:28: "A short word shall the Lord make upon the Earth" and in a later passage he adds: "This is the word of faith, which we preach."[5] In a short prayer Christ clearly marked out man's right course; and in teaching us to say this prayer, He showed us the goal of our striving and hope. In a single precept of charity He summed up that human justice which consists in observing the Law: "Love therefore is the fulfilling of the Law."[6] Hence the Apostle taught that the whole perfection of this present life consists in faith, hope, and charity, as in certain brief headings outlining our salvation: "Now there remain faith, hope, and charity."[7] These are the three virtues, as St. Augustine says, by which God is worshiped.[8]

Wherefore, my dearest son Reginald, receive from my hands this compendious treatise on Christian teaching to keep continually before your eyes. My whole endeavor in the present work is taken up with these three virtues. I shall treat first of faith, then of hope, and lastly of charity. This is the Apostle's arrangement which, for that matter, right reason imposes. Love cannot be rightly ordered unless the proper goal of our hope is established; nor can there be any hope if knowledge of the truth is lacking. Therefore the first thing necessary is faith, by which you may come to a knowledge of the truth. Secondly, hope is necessary, that your intention may be fixed on the right end. Thirdly, love is necessary, that your affections may be perfectly put in order.

2

Arrangement of topics concerning faith

Faith is a certain foretaste of that knowledge which is to make us happy in the life to come. The Apostle says in Hebrews 11:1 that

---

5   Rom. 10:8.

6   Rom. 13:10.

7   1 Corinthians 13:13.

8   Cf. *De doctrina christiana*, I, 35 (PL, XXXIV, 34).

faith is "the substance of things to be hoped for," as though implying that faith is already, in some preliminary way, inaugurating in us the things that are to be hoped for, that is, future beatitude. Our Lord has taught us that this beatific knowledge has to do with two truths, namely, the divinity of the Blessed Trinity and the humanity of Christ. That is why, addressing the Father, He says: "This is eternal life: that they may know Thee, the only true God, and Jesus Christ, whom Thou hast sent."[9] All the knowledge imparted by faith turns about these two points, the divinity of the Trinity and the humanity of Christ. This should cause us no surprise: the humanity of Christ is the way by which we come to the divinity. Therefore, while we are still wayfarers, we ought to know the road leading to our goal. In the heavenly fatherland adequate thanks would not be rendered to God if men had no knowledge of the way by which they are saved. This is the meaning of our Lord's words to His disciples: "And whither I go you know, and the way you know."[10] Three truths must be known about the divinity: first the unity of the divine essence, secondly the Trinity of persons, and thirdly the effects wrought by the divinity.

[9] John 17:3.
[10] John 14:4.

The Divine Trinity

_____

The First Treatise on Faith

God

3
The existence of God

Regarding the unity of the divine essence, we must first believe that God exists. This is a truth clearly known by reason. We observe that all things that move are moved by other things, the lower by the higher. The elements are moved by heavenly bodies; and among the elements themselves, the stronger moves the weaker; and even among the heavenly bodies, the lower are set in motion by the higher. This process cannot be traced back into infinity. For everything that is moved by another is a sort of instrument of the first mover. Therefore, if a first mover is lacking, all things that move will be instruments. But if the series of movers and things moved is infinite, there can be no first mover. In such a case, these infinitely many movers and things moved will all be instruments. But even the unlearned perceive how ridiculous it is to suppose that instruments are moved, unless they are set in motion by some principal agent. This would be like fancying that, when a chest or a bed is being built, the saw or the hatchet performs its functions without the carpenter. Accordingly, there must be a first mover that is above all the rest; and this being we call God.

4
The immobility of God

We clearly infer from this that God, who moves all things, must Himself be immovable. If He, being the first mover, were Himself moved, He would have to be moved either by Himself or by another. He cannot be moved by another, for then there would have to be some mover prior to Him, which is against the very idea of a first mover. If He is moved by Himself, this can be conceived in two ways: either that He is mover and moved according to the same respect, or that He is a mover according to one aspect of Him and is moved according to another aspect.

The first of these alternatives is ruled out. For everything that is moved is, to that extent, in potency, and whatever moves is in act. Therefore if God is both mover and moved according to the same respect, He has to be in potency and in act according to the same respect, which is impossible.

The second alternative is also impossible. If one part were moving and another were moved, there would be no first mover Himself as such, but only by reason of that part of Him which moves. But what is *per se* is prior to that which is not *per se*. Hence there cannot be a first mover at all, if this perfection is attributed to a being by reason of a part of that being. Accordingly, the first mover must be altogether immovable.

Among things that are moved and that also move, the following may also be considered. All motion is observed to proceed from something immobile, that is, from something that is not moved according to the particular species of motion in question. Thus we see that alterations, generations, and corruptions occurring in lower bodies are reduced, as to their first mover, to a heavenly body that is not itself moved according to this species of motion, since it is incapable of being generated, but rather is incorruptible and unalterable.[11] Therefore the first principle of all motion must be absolutely immobile.

5
The eternity of God

The further conclusion is evident that God is eternal. For everything that begins to be or that ceases to be, is affected in this way through motion or change. But we have just shown that God is absolutely immobile. Consequently He is eternal.[12]

6
Necessity of God's existence

The same line of reasoning clearly shows that God necessarily exists. For everything that has the possibility of being and of not being, is mutable. But God is absolutely immutable, as has been demonstrated.[13] Therefore it is impossible for God to be and not

---

[11] In scholastic terminology, *generation* is the acquisition of a form by a being and *corruption* is the loss of a form. Generation and corruption are *substantial* if the form acquired or lost is substantial, and are *accidental* if the form is accidental. The latter process is called *alteration*.

[12] Very likely St. Thomas did not intend to retain this chapter in the final form of the *Compendium theologiae*. The chapter is extraordinarily short, and gives but one briefly worded argument. This argument is not very satisfactory, for it excludes only beginning and end from God. It does not touch on the perfect simultaneity of God's existence, although such simultaneity is the essential characteristic of eternity. On the other hand, chapter 7, "The everlasting existence of God," and chapter 8, "Absence of succession in God," taken together, do demonstrate God's eternity in a cogent way. Hence it seems that chapter 5 does not belong to the work as definitively planned by St. Thomas. See A. R. Motte, O.P., "Un chapitre inauthentique dans le *Compendium Theologiae* de S. Thomas," *Revue Thomiste*, XLV (1939), 749-53.

[13] Cf. chap. 4.

to be. But anything that exists in such a way that it is impossible for it not to exist, is necessarily Being itself, *ipsum esse*. Necessary existence, and impossibility of non-existence, mean one and the same thing. Therefore God must necessarily exist.

Moreover, everything that has a possibility of being and of not being, needs something else to make it be, for, as far as it itself is concerned, it is indifferent with regard to either alternative. But that which causes another thing to be is prior to that thing. Hence something exists prior to that which has the possibility of being and of not being. However, nothing is prior to God. Therefore it is impossible for Him to be and not to be. Of necessity, He must be. And since there are some necessary things that have a cause of their necessity, a cause that must be prior to them, God, who is the first of all, has no cause of His own necessity. Therefore it is necessary for God to be through Himself.

7

The everlasting existence of God

From all this it is evident that God exists always. For whatever necessarily exists, always exists; it is impossible for a thing that has no possibility of not being, not to be. Hence such a thing is never without existence. But it is necessary for God to be, as has been shown.[14] Therefore God exists always.

Again, nothing begins to be or ceases to be except through motion or change. But God is absolutely immutable, as has been proved.[15] Therefore it is impossible for Him ever to have begun to be or to cease to be.

[14] Cf. chap. 6.
[15] Cf. chap. 4.

Likewise, if anything that has not always existed begins to be, it needs some cause for its existence. Nothing brings itself forth from potency to act or from non-being to being. But God can have no cause of His being, since He is the first Being; a cause is prior to what is caused. Of necessity, therefore, God must always have existed.

Furthermore, whatever pertains to anyone in some other way than by reason of an external cause, pertains to him of himself. But existence does not come to God from any external cause, since such a cause would have to be prior to Him. Therefore God has existence of Himself, *per se ipsum*. But what exists *per se* exists always and necessarily. Therefore God exists always.

8
Absence of succession in God

Clearly, therefore, no succession occurs in God. His entire existence is simultaneous. Succession is not found except in things that are in some way subject to motion; for prior and posterior in motion cause the succession of time. God, however, is in no sense subject to motion, as has been shown.[16] Accordingly, there is no succession in God. His existence is simultaneously whole.

Again, if a being's existence is not simultaneously whole, something can be lost to it and something can accrue to it. That which passes is lost, and what is expected in the future can be acquired. But nothing is lost to God and nothing accrues to Him since He is immutable. Therefore His existence is simultaneously whole.

From these two observations the proper meaning of eternity emerges. That is properly eternal which always exists, in such a

[16] Cf. chap. 4.

way that its existence is simultaneously whole. This agrees with the definition proposed by Boethius: "Eternity is the simultaneously whole and perfect possession of endless life.[17]

9
Simplicity of God

A similar course of reasoning clearly shows that the first mover must be simple. For any composite being must contain two factors that are related to each other as potency to act. But in the first mover, which is altogether immobile, all combination of potency and act is impossible, because whatever is in potency is, by that very fact, movable. Accordingly, the first mover cannot be composite.

Moreover, something has to exist prior to any composite, since composing elements are by their very nature antecedent to a composite. Hence the first of all beings cannot be composite. Even within the order of composite beings we observe that the simpler things have priority. Thus elements are naturally prior to mixed bodies.[18] Likewise, among the elements themselves, the first is fire, which is the simplest of all. Prior to all elements is the heavenly

---

[17] *De consolatione philosophiae*, V, *prosa* 6 (PL, LXIII, 858).

[18] Aristotle and St. Thomas, along with the medieval Scholastics in general, made their own the theory of Empedocles, who taught the existence of four elemental bodies: earth, air, fire, and water. All composite bodies, which they called mixed, were thought to result from a combination of the primary elements. These philosophers also believed that a special locality corresponded to each of the elements: fire and air naturally tended upward, water and earth tended downward. Cf. Aristotle, *Metaph.*, I, 8 (988 b 32); *De caelo*, I, 2 (269 a 17). St. Thomas likewise followed the curious view of Aristotle that heavenly bodies differ from terrestrial bodies in their nature, their movement, and their incorruptibility. Cf. *Summa*, Ia, q. 66, a.2; Aristotle, *De caelo*, I, 2 (269 a 12-b 17); 3 (270 a 12-35).

body, which has a simpler construction, since it is free from all contrariety. Hence the truth remains that the first of beings must be absolutely simple.

10
Identity of God with His essence

The further conclusion follows that God is His own essence. The essence of anything is that which its definition signifies. This is identical with the thing of which it is the definition, unless *per accidens* something is added to the thing defined over and above its definition. Thus whiteness is added to man, over and above the fact that he is a rational and mortal animal. Hence rational and mortal animal is the same as man; but whiteness, so far as it is white, is not the same as man.

In any being, therefore, in which there are not found two factors whereof one is *per se* and the other *per accidens*, its essence must be altogether identical with it. In God, however, since He is simple, as has been shown,[19] there are not found two factors whereof one is *per se* and the other *per accidens*. Therefore His essence must be absolutely the same as He Himself.

Moreover, whenever an essence is not absolutely identical with the thing of which it is the essence, something is discerned in that thing that has the function of potency and something else that has the function of act. For an essence is formally related to the thing of which it is the essence as humanity is related to man. In God, however, no potency and act can be discerned: He is pure act. Accordingly, He is His essence.

[19] Cf. chap. 9.

11
Identity of essence and existence in God

God's essence cannot be other than His existence. In any being whose essence is distinct from its existence, *what* it is must be distinct from that *whereby* it is. For in virtue of a thing's existence we say *that it is*, and in virtue of its essence we say *what it is*. This is why a definition that signifies an essence manifests what a thing is. In God, however, there is no distinction between what He is and that whereby He is, since there is no composition in Him, as has been shown.[20] Therefore God's essence is nothing else than His existence.

Likewise, we have proved that God is pure act without any admixture of potentiality.[21] Accordingly, His essence must be the ultimate act in Him; for any act that has a bearing on the ultimate act, is in potency to that ultimate act. But the ultimate act is existence itself, *ipsum esse*. For, since all motion is an issuing forth from potency to act, the ultimate act must be that toward which all motion tends; and since natural motion tends to what is naturally desired, the ultimate act must be that which all desire. This is existence. Consequently the divine essence, which is pure and ultimate act, must be existence itself, *ipsum esse*.

12
God not contained under any genus

We infer from the above that God is not contained as a species within any genus. Species is constituted by specific difference

---

[20] Cf. chap. 9.
[21] Ibid.

added to genus. Hence the essence of any species possesses something over and above its genus. But existence itself, *ipsum esse*, which is God's essence, does not comprise within itself any factor added to some other factor. Thus, God is not a species of any genus.

Furthermore, since genus potentially contains specific differences, in every being composed of genus and differences, act is commingled with potency. But we have shown that God is pure act without any commingling of potency.[22] Therefore His essence is not composed of genus and differences; and so He is not in any genus.

13
God is not a genus

We go on to show that God cannot be a genus. *What* a thing is, but not *that* it is, comes from its genus; the thing is established in its proper existence by specific differences. But *that* which God is, is very existence itself. Therefore He cannot be a genus.

Moreover, every genus is divided by some differences. But no differences can be apprehended in very existence itself. For differences do not share in genus except indirectly,[23] so far as the species

---

[22] Cf. chap. 9.

[23] The word *indirectly* here and elsewhere is sometimes used to translate *per accidens*. Thus, in the present case, a species participates in genus *per se*, or directly and of itself, since it is a logical division of a genus. A specific difference, however, pertains to genus, not *per se*, directly of itself, but only so far as it is the determining factor of a species, distinguishing it from other species of the same genus; that is, it pertains to genus only *per accidens*, indirectly, through the species it constitutes. Another instance of this same meaning of *per accidens* is discerned in the death of a brute animal (Cf. ch. 84). What perishes *per se* or directly is the animal. The vital principle or form of the animal also perishes, but only *per accidens*, that is, indirectly or incidentally, because of the destruction of the animal.

that are constituted by differences share in a genus. But there cannot be any difference that does not share in existence, since non-being is not the specific difference of anything. Accordingly, God cannot be a genus predicated of a number of species.

14
God is not a species predicated of individuals

God cannot be, as it were, a single species predicated of many individuals. Various individuals that come together in one essence of a species are distinguished by certain notes that lie outside the essence of the species. For example, men are alike in their common humanity but differ from one another in virtue of something that is outside the concept of humanity. This cannot occur in God, for God Himself is His essence, as has been shown.[24] Therefore God cannot be a species that is predicated of several individuals.

Again, a number of individuals comprised under one species differ in their existence, and yet are alike in their one essence. Accordingly, whenever a number of individuals are under one species, their existence must be different from the essence of the species. But in God existence and essence are identical, as has been demonstrated.[25] Therefore God cannot be a sort of species predicated of many individuals.

15
The unicity of God

Thus it is evident that there can be but one God. If there were many gods, they would be called by this name either equivocally

---

[24] Cf. chap. 10.
[25] Cf. chap. 11.

or univocally. If they are called gods equivocally, further discussion is fruitless; there is nothing to prevent other peoples from applying the name *god* to what we call a stone. If they are called gods univocally, they must agree either in genus or in species. But we have just shown that God can be neither a genus nor a species comprising many individuals under Himself. Accordingly, a multiplicity of gods is impossible.

Again, that whereby a common essence is individuated cannot pertain to many. Although there can be many men, it is impossible for this particular man to be more than one only. So if an essence is individuated by itself, and not by something else, it cannot pertain to many. But the divine essence is individuated by itself, since God's essence is not distinct from His existence; for we have shown that God is His essence.[26] Hence God cannot be more than one only.

Another consideration is the following. A form can be multiplied in two ways: first, by specific differences, as in the case of a generic form (in this way, color is differentiated into the various species of color); secondly, by the subjects in which it inheres (such as whiteness). Therefore any form incapable of being multiplied by specific differences cannot be multiplied at all, if it is a form that does not exist in a subject. Thus whiteness, if it were to subsist without a subject, would not be more than one. But the divine essence is very existence, *ipsum esse,* which does not admit of specific differences, as we have shown.[27] Since, therefore, the divine existence is a quasi-form subsisting by itself, seeing that God is His existence, the divine essence cannot be more than one. Accordingly, a plurality of gods is impossible.

[26] Cf. chap. 10.
[27] Cf. chap. 13.

16
God is not a body

It is evident, further, that God Himself cannot be a body. For in every body some composition is found, since a body has parts. Hence that which is absolutely simple cannot be a body.

Moreover, we find that a body does not move anything else unless it is first moved itself, as will appear clearly to anyone who examines the matter fully. So if the first mover is absolutely immovable, that being cannot be a body.

17
God is neither the form of a body nor a force in a body

God cannot be the form of a body or any kind of force existing in a body. For, since all bodies are found to be mobile, whatever is present in a body must be moved, at least *per accidens* or concomitantly, if the body itself is moved. The first mover, however, cannot be moved either *per se* or *per accidens*, for it must be absolutely immobile, as has been shown.[28] Therefore God cannot be a body or a force in a body.

Again, in order to move an object, every mover must have dominion over the thing that is moved. For we observe that motion is more rapid in proportion as the motive force exceeds the resisting force of the mobile object. Therefore that which is the very first among all movers, must predominate supremely over all the things moved. But this would be impossible if the mover were in any way attached to the mobile object, as it would have to be if it were the form or motive power of the latter. Consequently the

[28] Cf. chap. 4.

first mover cannot be a body or a force in a body or a form in a body. This is why Anaxagoras postulated an intelligence liberated from matter, that it might rule and move all things.[29]

18
The infinity of God according to essence

This leads to the question of God's infinity. God is not infinite by way of privation, according to which infinity is a passion of quantity; in this sense whatever lacks limits, but is nevertheless capable of having limits by reason of its genus, is said to be infinite. Rather, God is infinite negatively, in the sense that a being that is unlimited in every way is infinite. No act is found to be limited except by a potency that is receptive of the act; thus we observe that forms are limited in accordance with the potency of matter. Hence, if the first mover is an act without any admixture of potency, as not being the form of any body or a force inhering in a body, it must be infinite.

The very order perceived in things is a proof of this. The higher the position occupied in the scale of being, the greater are things found to be in their own way. Among the elements, nobler things are found to be greater in quantity, as also in simplicity. Their generation demonstrates this: as the proportion of the respective elements is increased, fire is generated from air, air from water, and water from earth. And a heavenly body clearly exceeds the total quantity of the elements. Necessarily, therefore, that which is the first among beings and which has nothing above it, must in its own fashion be of infinite quantity.

[29] See Anaxagoras, fragment 12 in H. Diels, *Die Fragmente der Vorsokratiker* (Berlin: Weidmann, 1922), I, 404; cf. Aristotle, *Metaph.*, I, 3; 8 (984 b 15-22; 989 b 15).

Nor is there anything to wonder at if what is simple and lacks corporeal quantity is said to be infinite and to exceed in its immensity all quantity of body. For our own intellect, which is incorporeal and simple, exceeds the quantity of all bodies in virtue of its knowledge, and embraces all things.

Much more, then, that which is the very first of all exceeds the universe of beings in its immensity, and embraces them all.

19
The infinite power of God

The further inference is drawn that God is infinite in power. For power is consequent upon a thing's essence; anything whatever possesses a power of activity consonant with its manner of being. Therefore, if God is infinite in His essence, His power must be infinite.

This is clear to anyone who will inspect the order of things. Whatever is in potency, is thereby endowed with receptive and passive power; and so far as a thing is in act, it possesses active power. Hence what is exclusively in potency, namely, prime matter, has an unlimited power of receptivity, but has no part in active power. And in the scale of being above matter, the more a thing has of form, the more it abounds in the power of acting. This is why fire is the most active of all the elements. Therefore God, who is pure act without any admixture of potency, infinitely abounds in active power above all things.

20
Absence of imperfection in God's infinity

Although the infinity discerned in quantities is imperfect, the infinity predicated of God indicates supreme perfection in Him.

The infinity that is in quantities pertains to matter, in the sense that matter lacks limits. Imperfection occurs in a thing for the reason that matter is found in a state of privation. On the other hand, perfection comes exclusively from form. Consequently, since God is infinite because He is exclusively form or act and has no admixture of matter or potentiality, His infinity pertains to His supreme perfection.

This can also be gathered from a consideration of other things. Although in one and the same being that evolves from imperfect to perfect, something imperfect precedes the perfect stage (as, for example, the boy is prior to the man), everything imperfect must derive its origin from what is perfect. The child is not begotten except by a man and the seed does not receive existence except from an animal or a plant. Accordingly, that which is by nature prior to all other things and sets them all in motion, must be more perfect than all the rest.

21
Eminent existence in God of all perfections found in creatures

The further inference clearly follows that all perfections found in anything at all must originally and superabundantly be present in God. Whatever moves something toward perfection, must first possess in itself the perfection it confers on others. Thus a teacher has in his own mind the knowledge he hands on to others.

Therefore, since God is the first mover and moves all other beings toward their perfections, all perfections found in things must pre-exist in Him superabundantly.

Besides, whatever has a particular perfection but lacks another perfection, is contained under some genus or species. For each thing is classed under a genus or a species by its form, which is the thing's perfection.

But what is placed under species and genus cannot be infinite in essence; for the ultimate difference whereby it is placed in a species necessarily closes off its essence. Hence the very *ratio* or description that makes a species known is called its definition, or even *finis*. Therefore, if the divine essence is infinite, it cannot possess merely the perfection of some genus or species and be lacking in other perfections; the perfections of all genera or species must be in God.

22
Unity of all perfections in God

If we gather together the various points established thus far, we perceive that all perfections in God are in reality one. We have shown above that God is simple.[30] But where there is simplicity, there can be no distinction among the perfections that are present. Hence, if the perfections of all things are in God, they cannot be distinct in Him. Accordingly, they are all one in Him.

This will become evident to anyone who reflects on our cognitive powers. A higher faculty has a unified knowledge of all that is known through the lower faculties according to diverse aspects. All that the sight, the hearing, and the other senses perceive, the intellect judges with the one, simple power that belongs to it. Something similar appears in the sciences. The lower sciences are multiplied in accord with the various classes of beings that constitute their objects. Yet one science which holds the primacy among them is interested in all classes of beings. This is known as *first philosophy*. The same situation is observed in civil power: in the royal power, which is but one, are included all the powers that are

[30] Cf. chap. 9.

distributed through various offices within the jurisdiction of the kingdom. In the same way perfections, which in lower things are multiplied according to the diversity of these things, must be united in the pinnacle of being, that is, in God.

23
Absence of accidents in God

It is also clear there can be no accident in God. If all perfections are one in Him, and if existence, power, action, and all such attributes pertain to perfection, they are necessarily identical with His essence. Thus none of these perfections is an accident in God.

Furthermore, a being to whose perfection something can be added, cannot be infinite in perfection. But if a being has some perfection that is an accident, a perfection can be added to its essence, since every accident is superadded to essence. Hence infinite perfection will not be found in its essence. But, as we have shown, God is of infinite perfection according to essence.[31] Consequently there can be in Him no accidental perfection: whatever is in Him, is His substance.

The same truth can be easily inferred from God's supreme simplicity, and from the fact that He is pure act and is the first among beings. For some sort of composition obtains between an accident and its subject. Likewise, that which is a subject of this kind cannot be pure act, since an accident is a certain form or act of the subject. Similarly, what is *per se* always precedes what is *per accidens*. From this we can infer, in keeping with the truths shown above, that nothing can be predicated of God as an accident.

[31] Cf. chap. 18.

24

God's simplicity is not contradicted by the
multiplicity of names applied to Him

This enables us to perceive the reason for the many names that are
applied to God, even though in Himself He is absolutely simple.
Since our intellect is unable to grasp His essence as it is in itself,
we rise to a knowledge of that essence from the things that surround
us. Various perfections are discerned in these things, the root and
origin of them all being one in God, as has been shown.[32] Since we
cannot name an object except as we understand it (for names are
signs of things understood), we cannot give names to God except
in terms of perfections perceived in other things that have their
origin in Him. And since these perfections are multiple in such
things, we must assign many names to God. If we saw His essence
as it is in itself, a multiplicity of names would not be required; our
idea of it would be simple, just as His essence is simple. This vision
we hope for in the day of our glory; for, according to Zechariah 14:9,
"In that day there shall be one Lord, and His name shall be one."

25

The names of God are not synonymous

In this connection three observations are in order. The first is that
the various names applied to God are not synonymous, even
though they signify what is in reality the same thing in God. In
order to be synonymous, names must signify the same thing, and
besides must stand for the same intellectual conception. But when
the same object is signified according to diverse aspects (that is,

---

[32] Cf. chap. 22.

according to notions which the mind forms of that object), the names are not synonymous. For then the meaning is not quite the same, since names directly signify intellectual conceptions, which are likenesses of things.

Therefore, since the various names predicated of God signify the various conceptions that our mind forms of Him, they are not synonymous, even though they signify absolutely the same thing.

26
Impossibility of defining God

A second point is this: since our intellect does not adequately grasp the divine essence in any of the conceptions which the names applied to God signify, the definitions of these terms cannot define what is in God. That is, any definition we might formulate of the divine *wisdom* would not be a definition of the divine *power* (and so on regarding other attributes).

The same is clear for another reason. A definition is made up of genus and specific differences, for what is properly defined is the species. But earlier we have shown that the divine essence is not included under any genus or species.[33] Therefore it cannot be defined.

27
Analogy of terms predicated of God and of other beings

The third point is that names applied to God and to other beings are not predicated either quite univocally or quite equivocally. They cannot be predicated univocally because the definition of

---

[33] Cf. chaps. 12, 14, 15.

what is said of a creature is not a definition of what is said of God. Things predicated univocally must have the same definition.

Nor are these names predicated in all respects equivocally. In the case of fortuitous equivocation, a name is attached to an object that has no relation to another object bearing the same name. Hence the reasoning in which we engage about one cannot be transferred to the other. But the names predicated of God and of other things are attributed to God according to some relation He has to those things; and in their case, the mind ponders what the names signify. This is why we can transfer our reasoning about other things to God.

Therefore such terms are not predicated altogether equivocally about God and other things, as happens in the case of fortuitous equivocation. Thus they are predicated according to analogy, that is, according to their proportion to one thing. For, from the fact that we compare other things with God as their first origin, we attribute to God such names as signify perfections in other things. This clearly shows that, as regards the assigning of the names, such names are primarily predicated of creatures, inasmuch as the intellect that assigns the names ascends from creatures to God. But as regards the thing signified by the name, they are primarily predicated of God, from whom the perfections descend to other beings.

28
The intelligence of God

We must now demonstrate that God is intelligent. We have already proved that all perfections of all beings whatsoever preexist in God superabundantly.[34] Among all the perfections found in beings,

---

[34] Cf. chap. 21.

intelligence is deemed to possess a special preeminence, for the reason that intellectual beings are more powerful than all others. Therefore God must be intelligent.

Moreover, we pointed out above that God is pure act without any admixture of potentiality.[35] On the other hand, matter is being in potency. Consequently God must be utterly free from matter. But freedom from matter is the cause of intellectuality. An indication of this is that material forms are rendered intelligible in act by being abstracted from matter and from material conditions. Therefore God is intelligent.

We proved, further, that God is the first mover.[36] This very perfection appears to be a property of intellect, for the intellect, we observe, uses all other things as instruments, so to speak, in producing movement. Thus man, through his intellect, uses animals and plants and inanimate objects as instruments, of a sort, to cause motion. Consequently God, the first mover, must be intelligent.

29
God's intelligence is not potential or habitual but actual

Since in God nothing is in potency but all is in act, as has been shown,[37] God cannot be intelligent either potentially or habitually but only actually. An evident consequence of this is that He undergoes no succession in understanding. The intellect that understands a number of things successively is able, while actually understanding one thing, to understand another only potentially. But there is no succession among things that exist simultaneously. So, if God understands nothing in potency, His understanding is

[35] Cf. chap. 4.
[36] Cf. chap. 3.
[37] Cf. chap. 4.

free from all succession. Accordingly, whatever He understands, He understands simultaneously. Furthermore, He does not begin to understand anything. For the intellect that begins to understand something, was previously in potency to understanding.

It is likewise evident that God's intellect does not understand in discursive fashion, proceeding from one truth to a knowledge of another, as is the case with our intellect in reasoning. A discursive process of this sort takes place in our intellect when we advance from the known to a knowledge of the unknown, or to that which previously we had not actually thought of. Such processes cannot occur in the divine intellect.

30

God's essence is the only species in His understanding

The foregoing exposition makes it clear that God understands through no other species than through His essence.

The reason is, that any intellect which understands through a species other than itself, is related to that intelligible species as potency to act. For an intelligible species is a perfection of the intellect, causing it to understand in act. Therefore, if nothing in God is in potency, but He is pure act, He must understand through His own essence, and not through any other kind of species.

In consequence of this, He directly and principally understands Himself. For the essence of a thing does not properly and directly lead to the knowledge of anything else than of that being whose essence it is.

Thus man is properly known through the definition of man, and horse is known through the definition of horse. Therefore, if God understands through His essence, that which is directly and principally understood by Him must be God Himself. And, since God is His own essence, it follows that, in Him, *understanding* and *that whereby He understands* and *that which is understood* are absolutely identical.

31
Identity between God and His intelligence

God must be His own intelligence. Since *to understand* is second act[38] (for example, to consider), whereas the corresponding first act is the intellect or knowledge, any intellect that is not its own understanding is related to its understanding as potency to act. For in the order of potencies and acts, that which is first is always potential with respect to what follows, and that which is last is perfective.

This is true only with reference to one and the same being, for among different beings the converse obtains. Thus a mover and an agent are related to the thing moved and actuated as act to potency. In God, however, who is pure act, there is nothing that is related to anything else as potency to act. Accordingly, God must be His own intelligence.

Furthermore, the intellect is related to its act of understanding as essence is related to existence. But God understands through His essence, and His essence is His existence.

Therefore His intellect is His act of understanding. And thus no composition is attributed to Him by the fact that He understands, since in Him intellect and understanding and intelligible species are not distinct; and these in turn are nothing else than His essence.

---

[38] In scholastic usage, *first act* (*actus primus*) designates the prime form of a thing, a faculty (such as intellect or will), or even a habit (such as habitual knowledge). *Second act* (*actus secundus*) denotes activity or operation. In general, first act may be said to be entitative and second act is operative.

32
The volition of God

We perceive, further, that God must have volition. For He under-stands Himself, who is perfect good, as is clear from all that has been hitherto established. But good as apprehended is necessarily loved, and love operates through the will. Consequently, God must have volition.

Moreover, we showed above that God is the first mover.[39] But the intellect, assuredly, does not move except through the inter-mediacy of appetite, and the appetite that follows intellectual apprehension is the will. Therefore God must have volition.

33
Identity of God's will with His intellect

Evidently God's will cannot be anything other than His intellect. For, since a good that is apprehended by the intellect is the object of the will, it moves the will and is the will's act and perfection. In God, however, there is no distinction between mover and moved, act and potency, perfection and perfectible, as is clear from the truths we have already gained. Also, the divine intellect and the divine essence are identical. Therefore the will of God is not distinct from the divine intellect and God's essence.

Another consideration is that among the various perfections of things, the chief are intellect and will. A sign of this is that they are found in the nobler beings. But the perfections of all things are one in God, and this is His essence, as we showed above.[40] In God, therefore, intellect and will are identical with His essence.

---

[39] Cf. chap. 3.
[40] Cf. chap. 22.

34
Identity between God's will and His willing

Hence it is also clear that the divine will is the very act of willing in God. As has been pointed out,[41] God's will is identical with the good willed by Him. But this would be impossible if His willing were not the same as His will; for willing is in the will because of the object willed. Accordingly, God's will is His willing.

Again, God's will is the same as His intellect and His essence. But God's intellect is His act of understanding, and His essence is His existing. Therefore His will must be His act of willing. And so we see clearly that God's will is not opposed to His simplicity.

35
The foregoing truths are embraced in one article of Faith

From all the details of doctrines thus far discussed, we can gather that God is one, simple, perfect, and infinite, and that He understands and wills. All these truths are assembled in a brief article of our Creed, wherein we profess to believe "in one God, almighty." For, since this name *God* (*Deus*), is apparently derived from the Greek name *Theos*, which comes from *theasthai*, meaning "to see or to consider," the very name of God makes it clear that He is intelligent and consequently that He wills.

In proclaiming that He is one, we exclude a plurality of gods, and also all composition; for a thing is not simply one unless it is simple.

The assertion that He is almighty is evidence of our belief that He possesses infinite power, from which nothing can be taken

---

[41] Cf. chap. 32.

away. And this includes the further truth that He is infinite and perfect; for the power of a thing follows the perfection of its essence.

The Holy Trinity

36
Philosophical character of this doctrine

The truths about God thus far proposed have been subtly discussed by a number of pagan philosophers, although some of them erred concerning these matters. And those who propounded true doctrine in this respect were scarcely able to arrive at such truths even after long and painstaking investigation.

But there are other truths about God revealed to us in the teaching of the Christian religion, which were beyond the reach of the philosophers. These are truths about which we are instructed, in accord with the norm of Christian faith, in a way that transcends human perception.

The teaching is that although God is one and simple, as has been explained above,[42] God is Father, God is Son, and God is Holy Spirit. And these three are not three gods, but are one God. We now turn to a consideration of this truth, so far as is possible to us.

---

[42] Cf. chaps. 9, 15.

37
The Word in God

We take from the doctrine previously laid down that God understands and loves Himself; likewise, that understanding and willing
in Him are not something distinct from His essence. Since God
understands Himself, and since all that is understood is in the
person who understands, God must be in Himself as the object
understood is in the person understanding.

But the object understood, so far as it is in the one who
understands, is a certain word of the intellect. We signify by an
exterior word what we comprehend interiorly in our intellect. For
words, according to the Philosopher, are signs of intellectual con-
cepts.[43] Hence we must acknowledge in God the existence of His
Word.

38
The word as conception

What is contained in the intellect, as an interior word, is by
common usage said to be a conception of the intellect. A being is
said to be conceived in a corporeal way if it is formed in the womb
of a living animal by a life-giving energy, in virtue of the active
function of the male and the passive function of the female in
whom the conception takes place. The being thus conceived shares
in the nature of both parents and resembles them in species.

In a similar manner, what the intellect comprehends is formed
in the intellect, the intelligible object being, as it were, the active
principle, and the intellect the passive principle. That which is

---

[43] Aristotle, De interpretatione, I, 1 (16 a 3).

thus comprehended by the intellect, existing as it does within the intellect, is conformed both to the moving intelligible object (of which it is a certain likeness) and to the quasi-passive intellect (which confers on it intelligible existence). Hence what is comprehended by the intellect is not unfittingly called the conception of the intellect.

39
Relation of the Word to the Father

But here a point of difference must be noted. What is conceived in the intellect is a likeness of the thing understood and represents its species; and so it seems to be a sort of offspring of the intellect. Therefore, when the intellect understands something other than itself, the thing understood is, so to speak, the father of the word conceived in the intellect, and the intellect itself resembles rather a mother, whose function is such that conception takes place in her. But when the intellect understands itself, the word conceived is related to the understanding person as offspring to father. Consequently, since we are using the term *word* in the latter sense (that is, according as God understands Himself), the word itself must be related to God, from whom the word proceeds, as Son to Father.

40
Generation in God

Hence in the rule of the Catholic Faith we are taught to profess belief in the Father and Son in God by saying: "I believe in God the Father, and in His Son." And lest anyone, on hearing Father and Son mentioned, should have any notion of carnal generation, by which among us men father and son receive their designation, John the Evangelist, to whom were revealed heavenly mysteries, substitutes *Word* for *Son*,[44] so that we may understand that the generation is intellectual.

41
The Son is equal to the Father in existence and essence

Since natural existence and the action of understanding are distinct in us, we should note that a word conceived in our intellect, having only intellectual existence, differs in nature from our intellect, which has natural existence. In God, however, *to be* and *to understand* are identical. Therefore, the divine Word that is in God, whose Word He is according to intellectual existence, has the same existence as God, whose Word He is. Consequently the Word must be of the same essence and nature as God Himself, and all attributes whatsoever that are predicated of God, must pertain also to the Word of God.

42
This teaching in the Catholic Faith

Hence we are instructed in the rule of the Catholic Faith to profess that the Son is "consubstantial with the Father," a phrase that excludes two errors. First, the Father and the Son may not be thought of according to carnal generation, which is effected by a certain separation of the son's substance from the father. If this were so in God, the Son could not be consubstantial with the Father. Secondly, we are taught not to think of the Father and the Son according to intellectual generation in the way that a word is conceived in our mind. For such a word comes to our intellect by

[44] John 1:14

a sort of accidental accretion, and does not exist with the existence proper to the essence of the intellect.

43

The Word is not distinct from the Father in time, species, or nature

Among things that are not distinct in essence, there can be no distinction according to species, time, or nature. Therefore, since the Word is consubstantial with the Father, He cannot differ from the Father in any of these respects.

There can be no difference according to time. The divine Word is present in God for the reason that God understands Himself, thereby conceiving His intelligible Word. Hence, if at any time there were no Word of God, during that period God would not understand Himself. But God always understood Himself during His whole existence, because His understanding is His existence. Therefore His Word, also, existed always. And so in the rule of the Catholic Faith we say that the Son of God "is born of the Father before all ages."

According to species, too, it is impossible for the Word of God to differ from God, as though He were inferior; for God does not understand Himself to be less than He is. The Word has a perfect likeness to the Father, because that whereof He is the Word is perfectly understood. Therefore the Word of God must be absolutely perfect according to the species of divinity.

Some beings, it is true, that proceed from others, are found not to inherit the perfect species of those from whom they proceed. One way in which this can happen is in equivocal generations: the sun does not generate a sun, but an animal of some kind.[45] In order

---

[45] Ancient and medieval philosophers commonly admitted the possibility of "equivocal generation," according to which some organisms were thought

to exclude imperfection of this sort from divine generation, we proclaim that the Word is born "God from God."

The same thing occurs in another way when that which proceeds from another differs from the latter because of a defect in purity; that is, when something is produced from what is simple and pure in itself by being applied to extraneous matter, and so turns out to be inferior to the original species. Thus, from a house that is in the architect's mind, a house is fashioned in various materials; and from light received in the surface of a body, color results; and from fire, by adding other elements, a mixture is produced; and from a beam of light, by interposing an opaque body, shadow is caused. To exclude any imperfection of this kind from divine generation, we add: "Light from Light."

In yet a third way, what proceeds from another can fail to equal the latter's species, because of a deficiency in truth. That is, it does not truly receive the nature of its original, but only a certain likeness thereof (for example, an image in a mirror or in a picture or in a statue; also, the likeness of a thing in the intellect or in one of the senses). For the image of a man is not said to be a true man, but is a likeness of a man; and a stone is not in the soul, as the Philosopher notes, but a likeness of the stone is in the soul.[46] To

to be produced from inorganic matter, especially such as had previously been alive, under the influence of heavenly bodies, which were believed to be of a superior nature. Thus St. Thomas, *Summa*, Ia, q. 71, a. un.: "In the natural generation of animals begotten of seed, the active principle is the formative power that is in the seed; but in animals generated from putrefaction, the formative power is the influence of a heavenly body"; Ia., q. 91, a.2 ad 2: "The power of a heavenly body may cooperate in the work of natural generation, as the Philosopher says: 'Man is begotten from matter by man, and by the sun as well' (Aristotle, *Phys.*, II, 2 [194 b 131]). . . . But the power of the heavenly bodies suffices for the generation of certain imperfect animals from properly disposed matter."

[46] Aristotle, *De anima*, III, 8 (431 b 29).

exclude all this from divine generation, we subjoin: "True God from true God."

Lastly it is impossible for the Word to differ from God according to nature, since it is natural for God to understand Himself. Every intellect has some objects which it naturally understands. Thus, our intellect naturally understands first principles. Much more does God, whose intellectual activity is His existence, naturally understand Himself.

Therefore His Word proceeds from Him naturally, not in the way that things proceed otherwise than by natural origin (that is, not in the way that artificial objects, which we are said to make, take shape from us). On the other hand, whatever proceeds from us naturally we are said to generate (for example, a son). Accordingly, to preclude the error of thinking that the Word of God proceeds from God, not by way of nature, but by the power of His will, the phrase is added: "begotten, not made."

44
Conclusion from the foregoing

As is clear from the foregoing, all the characteristics of divine generation we have been discussing lead to the conclusion that the Son is consubstantial with the Father. Therefore, by way of summing up all these points, the words, "consubstantial with the Father," are subjoined.

45
God in Himself as beloved in lover

As the object known is in the knower to the extent that it is known, so the beloved must be in the lover, as loved. The lover is, in some way, moved by the beloved with a certain interior impulse.

Therefore, since a mover is in contact with the object moved, the beloved must be intrinsic to the lover. But God, just as He understands Himself, must likewise love Himself; for good, as apprehended, is in itself lovable. Consequently God is in Himself as beloved in lover.

46
Love in God as Spirit

Since the object known is in the knower and the beloved is in the lover, the different ways of existing in something must be considered in the two cases before us. The act of understanding takes place by a certain assimilation of the knower to the object known; and so the object known must be in the knower in the sense that a likeness of it is present in him.

But the act of loving takes place through a sort of impulse engendered in the lover by the beloved: the beloved draws the lover to himself. Accordingly, the act of loving reaches its perfection not in a likeness of the beloved (in the way that the act of understanding reaches perfection in a likeness of the object understood); rather the act of loving reaches its perfection in a drawing of the lover to the beloved in person.

The transferring of the likeness of the original is effected by univocal generation whereby, among living beings, the begetter is called father, and the begotten is called son. Among such beings, moreover, the first motion occurs conformably to the species. Therefore, as within the Godhead the way whereby God is in God as the known in the knower, is expressed by what we call *Son*, who is the Word of God, so the way by which God is in God as the beloved is in the lover is brought out by acknowledging in God a Spirit, who is the love of God. And so, according to the rule of the Catholic Faith, we are directed to believe in the Spirit.

47
Holiness of the Spirit in God

Another point to consider is this. Since good that is loved has the nature of an end, and since the motion of the will is designated good or evil in terms of the end it pursues, the love whereby the supreme good that is God is loved must possess the supereminent goodness that goes by the name of holiness. This is true whether *holy* is taken as equivalent to "pure," according to the Greeks (the idea being that in God there is purest goodness free from all defect) or whether *holy* is taken to mean "firm," in the view of the Latins (on the score that in God there is unchangeable goodness). In either case, everything dedicated to God is called holy, such as a temple and the vessels of the temple and all objects consecrated to divine service. Rightly, then, the Spirit, who represents to us the love whereby God loves Himself, is called the Holy Spirit. For this reason the rule of the Catholic Faith proclaims that the Spirit is holy, in the clause, "I believe in the Holy Spirit."

48
Love in God is not accidental

Just as God's understanding is His existence, so likewise is His love. Accordingly, God does not love Himself by any act that is over and above His essence; He loves Himself by His very essence. Since God loves Himself because He is in Himself as the beloved in the lover, God the beloved is not in God the lover in any accidental fashion (in the way that the objects of our love are in us who love them — that is, *accidentally*). No, God is substantially in Himself as beloved in lover. Therefore the Holy Spirit, who represents the divine love to us, is not something accidental in God, but subsists in the divine essence just as the Father and the Son do. And so in the rule of the Catholic Faith He is exhibited as no less worthy of adoration and glorification than the Father and the Son are.

49
Procession of the Holy Spirit from the Father and the Son

We should recall that the act of understanding proceeds from the intellectual power of the mind. When the intellect actually understands, the object it understands is in it. The presence of the object known in the knower results from the intellectual power of the mind, and is its word, as we said above.[47] Likewise, what is loved is in the lover, when it is actually loved. The fact that an object is actually loved, results from the lover's power to love and also from the lovable good as actually known. Accordingly, the presence of the beloved object in the lover is brought about by two factors: the appetitive principle and the intelligible object as apprehended (that is, the word conceived about the lovable object). Therefore, since the Word in God who knows and loves Himself is the Son, and since He to whom the Word belongs is the Father of the Word, as is clear from our exposition, the necessary consequence is that the Holy Spirit, who pertains to the love whereby God is in Himself as beloved in lover, proceeds from the Father and the Son. And so we say in the Creed: "who proceeds from the Father and the Son."

50
The Trinity of divine persons and the unity of the divine essence

We must conclude from all we have said that in the Godhead there is something threefold which is not opposed to the unity and

[47] Cf. chap. 37.

simplicity of the divine essence. We must acknowledge that God is, as existing in His nature, and that He is known and loved by Himself.

But this occurs otherwise in God than in us. Man, to be sure, is a substance in his nature; but his actions of knowing and loving are not his substance. Considered in his nature, man is indeed a subsisting thing; as he exists in his mind, however, he is not a subsisting thing, but a certain representation of a subsisting thing; and similarly with regard to his existence in himself as beloved in lover. Thus man may be regarded under three aspects: that is, man existing in his nature, man existing in his intellect, and man existing in his love. Yet these three are not one, for man's knowing is not his existing, and the same is true of his loving. Only one of these three is a subsisting thing, namely, man existing in his nature.

In God, on the contrary, to be, to know, and to love are identical. Therefore God existing in His natural being and God existing in the divine intellect and God existing in the divine love are one thing. Yet each of them is subsistent. And, as things subsisting in intellectual nature are usually called persons in Latin, or *hypostases* in Greek, the Latins say that there are three persons in God, and the Greeks say that there are three *hypostases*, namely, the Father, the Son, and the Holy Spirit.

51
A seeming contradiction in the Trinity

A certain contradiction, arising from truths previously established, seemingly appears at this point. If threefold personality is assumed in God, then, since number always follows division, some division will have to be acknowledged in God whereby the three may be distinguished from one another. Thus supreme simplicity will be lacking in God. If three agree in some respect and differ in another, composition must be present — which is contrary to what was set forth above.[48] Again, if God must be strictly one, as has been shown above,[49] and if one and the same thing cannot originate or proceed from itself, it therefore seems impossible for God to be begotten or to proceed. Wrongly, therefore, the names of Father, Son, and proceeding Spirit are given place in the Godhead.

52
Solution of the difficulty: distinction in God according to relations

The principle for solving this difficulty must be derived from the fact that, among different classes of beings, the various ways in which one thing may arise or proceed from another depend on the diversity of their natures. Among lifeless beings, which do not move themselves and are capable of being moved only from outside, one thing arises from another by being, as it were, outwardly altered and changed. In this way fire is generated from fire and air from air.

But among living beings (which have the property of moving themselves), something is generated within the parent (for example, the young of animals and the fruits of plants). Moreover, the different manner of procession in living beings must be viewed according to their different powers and their different kinds of proceeding.

Among such beings, there are certain powers whose operations extend only to bodies, so far as they are material. This is clear with regard to the powers of the vegetative soul, which serve nutrition, growth, and generation. In virtue of this class of the soul's powers,

[48] Cf. chap. 9.
[49] Cf. chap. 15.

there proceeds only what is corporeal and what is bodily distinct although, in the case of living beings, it is somehow joined to that from which it proceeds.

There are other powers whose operations do not transcend the limits of bodies and yet extend to the species of bodies, receiving them without their accompanying matter. This is the case with all the powers of the sensitive soul. For sense is capable of receiving species without matter, as the Philosopher says.[50] But such faculties, although they are receptive of the forms of things in a sort of immaterial way, do not receive them without a bodily organ. If procession takes place within these powers of the soul, that which proceeds will not be something corporeal, nor will it be distinct or joined to that faculty whence it proceeds in a corporeal way, but rather in a certain incorporeal and immaterial fashion, although not entirely without the help of a bodily organ.

Thus the representations of things imagined, which exist in the imagination not as a body in a body, but in a certain spiritual way, proceed in animals. This is why imaginary vision is called spiritual by Augustine.[51]

But if something proceeds in a way that is not corporeal when the imagination is in action, this will be the case much more in the operation of the intellectual faculty, which can act without any bodily organ at all; its operation is strictly immaterial. For in intellectual operation a word proceeds in such a way that it exists in the very intellect of the speaker, not as though contained therein locally, nor as bodily separated therefrom, but as present there in a manner that is conformable to its origin. The same is true in that procession which is observed to take place in the operation of the will, so far as the thing loved exists in the lover,

---

[50] Aristotle, De anima, III, 4 (429 b 21).
[51] De Genesi ad litteram, XII, vii, 16; xxiv, 50 (PL, XXXIV, 459, 474).

in the sense described above.[52] However, although the intellectual and sensitive powers are nobler in their own scale of being than the powers of the vegetative soul, nothing that subsists in the nature of the same species proceeds either in men or in other animals according to the procession of the imaginative or sensitive faculties. This occurs only in that procession which takes place through the operation of the vegetative soul.

The reason for this is that in all beings composed of matter and form, the multiplication of individuals in the same species is effected by a division of matter. Hence among men and other animals, composed as they are of form and matter, individuals are multiplied in the same species by the bodily division which ensues in the procession that is proper to the operation of the vegetative soul, but that does not take place in other operations of the soul. In beings that are not composed of matter and form, no distinction can be discerned other than that of the forms themselves. But if the form, which is the reason for the distinction, is the substance of a thing, the distinction must obtain between subsistent things. Of course, this is not the case if the form in question is not the substance of the thing.

As is clear from our discussion, every intellect has this in common, that what is conceived in the intellect must in some way proceed from the knower, so far as he is knowing; and in its procession it is to some extent distinct from him, just as the conception of the intellect, which is the intellectual likeness,[53] is

---

[52] Cf. chap. 46.

[53] The term here used by St. Thomas, *intentio intellecta*, cannot well be translated literally. For our purposes we may translate it as "intellectual likeness," as "intellectual representation," or as "mental word." Regardless, the meaning itself is clear, for St. Thomas defines the term in his *Summa Contra Gentiles*, IV, 11: "*Dico autem intentionem intellectam id quod intellectus in seipso concipit de re intellecta*"; that is: "By *intentio intellecta*

distinct from the knowing intellect. Similarly the affection of the lover, whereby the beloved is in the lover, must proceed from the will of the lover so far as he is loving. But the divine intellect has this exclusive perfection: since God's understanding is His existence, His intellectual conception, which is the intelligible likeness, must be His substance; and the case is similar with affection in God, regarded as loving. Consequently the representation of the divine intellect, which is God's Word, is distinct from Him who produces the Word, not with respect to substantial existence, but only according to the procession of one from the other. And in God considered as loving, the same is true of the affection of love, which pertains to the Spirit.

Thus it is plain that nothing prevents God's Word, who is the Son, from being one with the Father in substance, and that, nevertheless, the Word is distinct from the Father according to the relation of procession, as we have said. Hence it is also evident that the same thing does not arise or proceed from itself; for the Son, as proceeding from the Father, is distinct from Him. And the same observation holds true of the Holy Spirit, relative to the Father and the Son.

53
Nature of the relations whereby the Father, the Son, and the Holy Spirit are distinguished

The relations by which the Father, the Son, and the Holy Spirit are distinguished from one another are real relations, and not merely mental relations. Those relations are purely mental which do not correspond to anything found in the nature of things, but

---

I mean that which the intellect conceives within itself of the thing understood."

depend on intellectual apprehension alone. Thus right and left in a stone are not real relations, but only mental relations; they do not correspond to any real disposition present in the stone, but exist only in the mind of one who apprehends the stone as left, because it is, for instance, to the left of some animal. On the other hand, left and right in an animal are real relations, because they correspond to certain dispositions found in definite parts of the animal. Therefore, since the relations which distinguish the Father, the Son, and the Holy Spirit really exist in God, the relations in question must be real relations, and are not merely mental relations.

54
Relations in God are not accidental

These relations cannot inhere in God accidentally, because the operations on which the relations follow directly are the very substance of God, and also because, as was shown above,[54] there can be no accident in God. Hence, if the relations are really in God, they cannot be accidentally inherent, but must be subsistent. How it is that what is an accident in other things, can exist substantially in God, is clear from the doctrine previously set forth.[55]

55
Personal distinction in God through the relations

Since distinction in the Godhead is accounted for by relations that are not accidental but are subsistent, and since among beings

---

[54] Cf. chap. 23.
[55] Cf., e.g., chaps. 4, 6, 9-11, 21.

subsisting in an intellectual nature personal distinction is discerned, it necessarily follows that personal distinction in God is constituted by the relations in question. Therefore the Father and the Son and the Holy Spirit are three persons, and also three *hypostases*, since *hypostasis* means "that which is subsistent and complete."

56
Impossibility of more than three persons in God

There cannot be more than three persons in God. For the divine persons cannot be multiplied by a division of their substance, but solely by the relation of some procession; and not by any sort of procession, but only by such as does not have its term in something outside of God. If the relation had something external as its term, this would not possess the divine nature, and so could not be a divine person or *hypostasis*. But procession in God that does not terminate outside of God, must be either according to the operation of the intellect, whereby the Word proceeds, or according to the operation of the will, whereby love proceeds, as is clear from our exposition.[56] Therefore no divine person can proceed unless He proceeds as the Word, whom we call the Son, or as love, whom we call the Holy Spirit.

Moreover, since God comprehends everything in His intellect by a single act of intuition and similarly loves everything by a single act of His will, there cannot be several words or several loves in God. If, then, the Son proceeds as Word, and if the Holy Spirit proceeds as love, there cannot be several Sons or several Holy Spirits in God.

[56] Cf. chaps. 37, 46.

Again: the perfect is that beyond which there is nothing. Hence a being that would tolerate anything of its own class to be outside itself, would fall short of absolute perfection. This is why things that are simply perfect in their natures are not numerically multiplied; thus God, the sun, the moon, and so on.[57] But both the Son and the Holy Spirit must be simply perfect, since each of them is God, as we have shown.[58] Therefore several Sons or several Holy Spirits are impossible.

Besides, that whereby a subsistent thing is *this* particular thing, distinct from other things, cannot be numerically multiplied, for the reason that an individual cannot be predicated of many. But the Son is *this* divine person, subsisting in Himself and distinct from the other divine persons by sonship just as Socrates is constituted *this* human person by individuating principles. Accordingly, as the individuating principles whereby Socrates is this man cannot pertain to more than one man, so sonship in the Godhead cannot pertain to more than one divine person. Similar is the case with the relation of the Father and the Holy Spirit. Hence there cannot be several Fathers in God or several Sons or several Holy Spirits.

Lastly, whatever is one by reason of its form, is not numerically multiplied except through matter (thus, whiteness is multiplied by existing in many subjects). But there is no matter in God. Consequently, whatever is one in species and form in the Godhead cannot be multiplied numerically. Such are paternity and filiation

---

[57] St. Thomas and the Scholastics of his time thought that the stars were incorruptible and were constructed of matter essentially different from the matter of terrestrial bodies. Consequently the sun, the moon, and all the stars were held to be superior to the material objects of our Earth.

[58] Cf. chap. 50.

and the procession of the Holy Spirit. And thus there cannot be several Fathers or Sons or Holy Spirits in God.

57
Properties of the Father

Such being the number of persons in God, the properties whereby the persons are distinguished from one another must be of some definite number. Three properties are characteristic of the Father. The first is that whereby He is distinguished from the Son alone. This is *paternity*. The second is that whereby the Father is distinguished from the other two persons, namely, the Son and the Holy Spirit. And this is *innascibility;* for the Father is not God as proceeding from another person, whereas the Son and the Holy Spirit do proceed from another person. The third property is that whereby the Father along with the Son is distinguished from the Holy Spirit. This is called their common *spiration*. But a property whereby the Father may be distinguished from the Holy Spirit alone is not to be assigned, for the reason that the Father and the Son are a single principle of the Holy Spirit, as has been shown.[59]

58
Properties of the Son and the Holy Spirit

Two properties must pertain to the Son: one whereby He is distinguished from the Father, and this is *filiation;* another whereby, along with the Father, He is distinguished from the Holy Spirit; and this is their common *spiration*. But no property is to be assigned whereby the Son is distinguished from the Holy Spirit alone,

[59] Cf. chap. 49.

because, as we said above, the Son and the Father are a single principle of the Holy Spirit.[60] Similarly, no single property is to be assigned whereby the Holy Spirit and the Son together are distinguished from the Father. For the Father is distinguished from them by one property, namely, innascibility, inasmuch as He does not proceed. However, since the Son and the Holy Spirit proceed, not by one procession, but by several, they are distinguished from the Father by two properties. The Holy Spirit has only one property by which He is distinguished from the Father and the Son, and this is called *procession*. That there cannot be any property by which the Holy Spirit may be distinguished from the Son alone or from the Father alone, is evident from this whole discussion.

Accordingly, five properties in all are attributed to the divine persons: *innascibility*, *paternity*, *filiation*, *spiration*, and *procession*.

59
Why these properties are called notions

These five properties can be called notions of the persons, for the reason that the distinction between the persons in God is brought to our notice through them. On the other hand, they cannot be called properties, if the root meaning of *property* is insisted on, so that *property* is taken to mean a characteristic pertaining to one individual alone, for common spiration pertains to the Father and the Son.

But if the word *property* is employed in the sense of an attribute that is proper to some individuals as setting them off from others (in the way that *two-footed*, for example, is proper to man and bird in contradistinction to quadrupeds), there is nothing to prevent

[60] Cf. chap. 49.

even common spiration from being called a property. Since, however, the persons in God are distinguished solely by relations, and distinction among the divine persons is manifested by the notions, the notions must in some sense pertain to relationship.

But only four of the notions are real relations, whereby the divine persons are related to one another. The fifth notion, innascibility, pertains to relation as being the denial of relation (for negations are reduced to the genus of affirmations, and privations are reduced to the genus of habits, as, for example, *not man* is reduced to the genus of man, and *not white* is reduced to the genus of whiteness).[61]

We should note that among the relations whereby the divine persons are related to one another, some have definite names, such as paternity and filiation, which properly signify relationship. But others lack a definite name: those whereby the Father and the Son are related to the Holy Spirit, and the Holy Spirit is related to them. So for these we use names of origin in place of relative names.

We perceive clearly that common spiration and procession signify origin, but not relations that follow origin. This can be brought out in the case of the relations between the Father and the Son. Generation denotes active origin, and is followed by the relation of paternity; and nativity signifies the passive generation of the Son, and is followed by the relation of filiation. In like manner, some relation follows common spiration, and the same is true of procession. But as these relations lack definite names, we use the names of the actions instead of relative names.

---

[61] In connection with these two examples, see the better statement in the *Summa*, Ia, q. 33, a. 4 ad 3: "Negation is reduced to the genus of affirmation, just as *not man* is reduced to the genus of substance, and *not white* to the genus of quality."

60
The number of relations and the number of persons

We must realize that, although the relations subsisting in the Godhead are the divine persons themselves, as was shown above,[62] we are not therefore to conclude that there are five or four persons corresponding to the number of relations. For number follows distinction of some sort. Just as unity is indivisible or undivided, so plurality is divisible or divided. For a plurality of persons requires that relations have power to distinguish by reason of opposition, since formal distinction necessarily entails opposition. If, then, the relations in question are closely examined, paternity and filiation will be seen to have relative opposition to each other; hence they are incompatible in the same *suppositum*. Consequently paternity and filiation in God must be two subsistent persons. Innascibility, on the other hand, although opposed to filiation, is not opposed to paternity. Hence paternity and innascibility can pertain to one and the same person. Similarly, common spiration is not opposed either to paternity or to filiation, nor to innascibility. Thus nothing prevents common spiration from being in both the person of the Father and the person of the Son.

So common spiration is not a subsisting person distinct from the persons of the Father and the Son. But procession has a relation of opposition to common spiration. Therefore, since common spiration pertains to the Father and the Son, procession must be a person distinct from the persons of the Father and the Son.

Accordingly, the reason is clear why God is not called *quiune* (*quinus*) on account of the notions, which are five in number, but is called *triune*, on account of the Trinity of persons. The five

---

[62] Cf. chaps. 54, 55.

notions are not five subsisting things, but the three persons are three subsisting things.

Although several notions or properties may pertain to a single person, only one of them constitutes the person. For a divine person is constituted by the properties, not in the sense that He is constituted by several of them, but in the sense that the relative, subsisting property itself is a person. If several properties were understood as subsisting in themselves apart, they would be several persons, and not one person. Hence we must understand that, of the several properties or notions belonging to a single person, the one that precedes[63] according to the order of nature constitutes the person; the others are understood as inhering in the person already constituted.

Thus it is evident that innascibility cannot be the first notion of the Father, constituting His person, because nothing is constituted by a negation, and also because affirmation naturally precedes negation. Further, common spiration presupposes paternity and filiation in the order of nature, just as the procession of love presupposes the procession of the Word.

Hence common spiration cannot be the first notion of the Father or of the Son either. The first notion of the Father is paternity and the first notion of the Son is filiation, whereas procession alone is the notion of the Holy Spirit.

Accordingly, the notions constituting persons are three in number: paternity, filiation, and procession. And these notions must be strict properties. For that which constitutes a person must pertain to that person alone; individuating principles cannot belong to several individuals. Therefore, the three notions in question are called *personal properties*, in the sense that they constitute

---

[63] The context requires the reading *praecedit* instead of *procedit* (which is found in the Vivès and the Mandonnet editions).

the three persons in the manner described. The remaining notions are called *properties or notions of the persons*, but not *personal properties or notions*, since they do not constitute a person.

61
Dependence of the hypostases on the personal properties

This makes it clear that if we were to remove the personal properties by intellectual abstraction, the *hypostases* could not remain. If a form is removed by intellectual abstraction, the subject of the form remains. Thus if whiteness is removed, the surface remains; if the surface is removed, the substance remains; if the form of the substance is removed, prime matter remains. But if the subject is removed, nothing remains.

In the case of God, the personal properties are the subsisting persons themselves. They do not constitute the persons in the sense that they are added to preexisting *supposita*; for in the Godhead nothing predicated absolutely, but only what is relative, can be distinct. So if the personal properties are removed by intellectual abstraction, no distinct *hypostases* remain. But if non-personal notions are thus removed, distinct *hypostases* do remain.

62
Effect of intellectual removal of personal properties

If the question were to be asked whether, in consequence of the removal of the personal properties by intellectual abstraction, the divine essence would remain, the answer is that in one respect it would remain, but in another it would not. Intellectual abstraction can take place in two ways. The first is by abstracting form from matter. In this abstraction the mind proceeds from the more formal to the more material; the first subject remains until the end, and the ultimate form is removed first. The second way of abstracting is by the abstraction of the universal from the particular, and this proceeds according to an order that is, in a sense, the opposite; the individuating material conditions are first removed, so that what is common may be retained.

In God, of course, there are neither matter and form, nor universal and particular. Nevertheless there is in the Godhead something that is common, and something that is proper and that supposes the common nature. In our human way of thinking, the divine persons are to the divine essence what individual *supposita* are to a common nature. According to the first type of intellectual abstraction, therefore, if we remove the personal properties, which are the subsisting persons themselves, the common nature does not remain. But in the second type of abstraction it does remain.

63
Personal acts and personal properties

We can perceive from this discussion the nature of the order between the personal acts and the personal properties. The personal properties are subsistent persons. But a person subsisting in any nature whatsoever, acts in virtue of his nature when he communicates his nature; for the form of a species is the principle for generating a product that is of like species. Consequently, since personal acts in God have to do with communicating the divine nature, a subsisting person must communicate the common nature in virtue of the nature itself.

Two conclusions follow from this. The first is, that the generative power of the Father is the divine nature itself; for the power of performing any action is the principle in virtue of which a thing acts. The second conclusion is that, according to our way of conceiving, the personal act of generation presupposes both the divine nature and the personal property of the Father, which is the very *hypostasis* of the Father. This is true even though such property, regarded as a relation, follows from the act. Thus, in speaking of the Father, if we attend to the fact that He is a subsistent person, we can say that He generates because He is the Father. But if we are thinking of what pertains to relationship, it seems we should say, contrariwise, that He is the Father because He generates.

64
Generation with respect to the Father and with respect to the Son

However, we should see that the order of active generation (with reference to paternity) is to be taken one way and the order of passive generation or nativity (with reference to filiation) is to be taken another. In the order of nature, active generation presupposes the person of the begetter. But in the same order, passive generation, or nativity, precedes the begotten person, for the begotten person owes his existence to his birth. Thus active generation, according to our way of representing it, presupposes paternity, understood as constituting the person of the Father. Nativity, however, does not presuppose filiation, understood as constituting the person of the Son but, according to our manner of conceiving, precedes it in both respects, that is, both as being constitutive of the person and as being a relation. And whatever pertains to the procession of the Holy Spirit is to be understood in a similar way.

65
Nature of the distinction between notional acts and notional properties

In thus indicating the order between notional acts and notional properties, we do not mean to imply that notional acts differ from personal properties in objective reality: they are distinct only according to our manner of conceiving. Just as God's act of understanding is God Himself understanding, so the Father's act of begetting is the begetting Father, although the modes of signifying are different. Likewise, although one divine person may have several notions, there is no composition in Him. Innascibility cannot cause any composition, since it is a negative property. And the two relations in the person of the Father (paternity and common spiration) are in reality identical as referring to the person of the Father; for, as the paternity is the Father, so common spiration in the Father is the Father, and in the Son is the Son. But these two properties differ according to the terms to which they refer; for by paternity the Father is related to the Son, and by common spiration He is related to the Holy Spirit. Likewise, the Son is related to the Father by filiation and to the Holy Spirit by common spiration.

66

Identity between the relative properties and the divine essence

The relative properties must be the divine essence itself. For the relative properties are precisely the subsistent persons. But a person subsisting in the Godhead cannot be something other than the divine essence; and the divine essence is God Himself, as was shown above.[64] Therefore the relative properties are in all reality identical with the divine essence.

Moreover, whatever is in a being besides its essence, is in it accidentally. But there cannot be any accidents in God, as was pointed out above.[65] Accordingly, the relative properties are not really distinct from the divine essence.

[64] Cf. chap. 10.
[65] Cf. chap. 23.

67

The divine properties are not externally affixed

The view proposed by Gilbert de la Porrée[66] and some of his followers, that the properties under discussion are not in the persons, but are external to them, cannot be defended. Real relations must be in the things that are related. This is evident in the case of creatures, for real relations are in them as accidents in their subjects. But the relations whereby the three persons are distinguished within the Godhead are real relations, as was demonstrated above.[67] Hence they must be in the divine persons, but not, of course, as accidents. Other perfections, too, which in creatures are accidents, cease to be accidents when transferred to God, as was shown above.[68] Such are wisdom, justice, and the like.

Besides, there can be no distinction in God except through the relations; all perfections that are predicated absolutely are common. Therefore, if the relations were external to the persons, no distinction would remain among the persons themselves. And so there are relative properties in the persons; but they are the persons themselves, and also the divine essence itself. In the same way wisdom and goodness are said to be in God, and are God Himself, as well as the divine essence, as was said above.[69]

---

[66] See Gilbert's commentaries, In librum de Trinitate (PL, LXIV, 1292) and In librum de praedicatione trium personarum (PL, LXIV, 1309). Gilbert retracted his error at the Council of Reims in 1148, as St. Bernard relates, In Cantica, serm. LXXX (PL, CLXXXIII, 1170). Cf. Denz., 389, 391.

[67] Cf. chap. 53.

[68] Cf. chap. 23.

[69] Cf. chaps. 10, 22.

Creation from Nothing

68

The effects produced by God

After considering the truths which pertain to the unity of the divine essence and to the Trinity of persons, we turn to a study of the effects produced by the Trinity. The first effect wrought by God in things is existence itself, which all other effects presuppose and on which they are based. Anything that exists in any way must necessarily have its origin from God. In all things that are arranged in orderly fashion, we find universally that what is first and most perfect in any order is the cause of whatever follows in that order. Thus fire, which is hot in the highest degree, is the cause of heat in all other heated bodies. Imperfect objects are always found to have their origin from perfect things. Seeds, for instance, come from animals and plants. But, as we proved above,[70] God is the first and most perfect Being. Therefore He must be the cause of being in all things that have being.

[70] Cf. chaps. 3, 21.

Again, whatever has some perfection by participation is traced back, as to its principle and cause, to what possesses that perfection essentially. Thus molten iron has its incandescence from that which is fire by its essence. We showed above[71] that God is existence itself; hence existence belongs to Him in virtue of His essence, but pertains to all other things by way of participation. The essence of no other thing is its existence, for being that is absolute and *per se* subsistent cannot be more than one, as was brought out above.[72] Therefore God must be the cause of existence of all things that are.

69
Creation from nothing

Thus it is clear that in creating, God does not need preexisting matter from which to fashion things. No agent needs, prior to his action, what he produces by his action; he needs only what he is unable to produce by his action. The builder requires stones and lumber before he can set to work, because he is unable to produce these materials by his action. On the other hand, he does not presuppose a house, but produces it by his activity. But matter must be produced by God's action since, as has just been proved, everything that exists in any way at all has God as the cause of its existence. Therefore the conclusion follows that God does not presuppose matter in His activity.

Besides, act naturally precedes potency, and hence the notion of principle primarily befits act. But any principle that in creating would presuppose some other principle, would verify the concept of principle only in a secondary way. Accordingly, since God is the

---

[71] Cf. chaps. 6, 11.
[72] Cf. chap. 15.

principle of things as the first act, whereas matter is a principle as a being in potency, it is unthinkable that matter should be presupposed before God can act.

Furthermore, the more universal a cause is, the more universal its effect is. Particular causes make use of the effects of universal causes for something determinate; and such determination is related to a universal effect as act to potency. Hence any cause that causes something to be in act, utilizing preexisting material that is in potency to that act, is a particular cause with respect to some more universal cause. But this sort of procedure cannot pertain to God, since He is the first cause, as we showed above.[73] Consequently God does not need matter as a prerequisite to His action. Therefore He has the power to bring things into existence from nothing or, in other words, to create. This is why the Catholic Faith professes that He is the Creator.

70
Creation is possible for God alone

From this it appears, further, that God alone can be Creator. For to create is the prerogative of that cause which does not presuppose another cause that is more universal, as we saw in the preceding chapter. But such causality pertains to God alone. He alone, therefore, is Creator.

Besides, the more remote a potency is from act, the greater must be the power that reduces it to act. But whatever distance may be imagined between potency and act, the distance will ever be still greater if the very potency itself is withdrawn. To create from nothing, then, requires infinite power. But God alone is infinite in

[73] Cf. chap. 68.

power, since He alone is infinite in essence. Consequently God alone can create.

71

Matter is not the cause of diversity in things

The foregoing exposition shows clearly that the cause of diversity in things is not diversity on the part of matter. For, as we have proved,[74] the divine action which brings things into being does not suppose the pre-existence of matter. The cause of diversity in things could not be on the side of matter unless matter were needed prior to the production of things, so that the various forms induced would follow diversity in matter. Therefore the cause of diversity in the things produced by God is not matter.

Again, the plurality or unity of things is dependent on their existence. For, to the extent that anything is a being, it is also one. But forms do not possess existence on account of matter; on the contrary, matter receives existence from form. For act is more excellent than potency; and that which is the reason for a thing's existence must be the more excellent component. Consequently forms are not diverse in order that they may befit various types of matter, but matter is diversified that it may befit various forms.

72

The cause of diversity

If the unity and multiplicity of things are governed by their being, and if the entire being of things depends on God, as has been shown

---

[74] Cf. chap. 69.

to be the case,[75] the cause of plurality in things must be sought in God. How this comes about, must now be examined.

Any active cause must produce its like, so far as this is possible. The things produced by God could not be endowed with a likeness of the divine goodness in the simplicity in which that goodness is found in God. Hence what is one and simple in God had to be represented in the produced things in a variety of dissimilar ways. There had to be diversity in the things produced by God, in order that the divine perfection might in some fashion be imitated in the variety found in things.

Furthermore, whatever is caused is finite, since only God's essence is infinite, as was demonstrated above.[76] The finite is rendered more perfect by the addition of other elements.

Hence it was better to have diversity in created things, and thus to have good objects in greater number, than to have but a single kind of beings produced by God. For the best cause appropriately produces the best effects. Therefore it was fitting for God to produce variety in things.

73
Diversity in things according to degree and order

Diversity among things was rightly established according to a definite order, so that some things might be more excellent than others. For this pertains to the lavishness of the divine goodness, that God should communicate a likeness of His goodness to created things, so far as possible. God is not only good in Himself, but exceeds other beings in goodness, and guides them toward goodness. Consequently, that the likeness which created beings bear to

[75] Cf. chap. 69.
[76] Cf. chap. 18.

God might be heightened, it was necessary for some things to be made better than others, and for some to act upon others, thus leading them toward perfection.

The basic diversity among things consists chiefly in diversity of forms. Formal diversity is achieved by way of contrariety; for genus is divided into various species by contrary differences. But order is necessarily found in contrariety, for among contraries one is always better than the other. Therefore diversity among things had to be established by God according to a definite order, in such a way that some beings might be more excellent than others.

74
Incorporeal substances requisite for the perfection of the universe

A being is noble and perfect in the measure that it approaches likeness to God, who is pure act without any admixture of potency. Therefore beings that are supreme among entities must be more in act and must have less of potency, whereas inferior beings must be more in potency. How this is to be understood, we must now examine.

Since God is eternal and immutable in His being, those things are lowest in the scale of being, as possessing less likeness to God, which are subject to generation and corruption. Such beings exist for a time, and then cease to be. And, since existence follows the form of a thing, beings of this kind exist while they have their form, but cease to exist when deprived of their form. Hence there must be something in them that can retain a form for a time, and can then be deprived of the form. This is what we call matter.

Therefore such beings, which are lowest in degree among things, must be composed of matter and form. But beings that are supreme among created entities approach most closely to likeness with God. They have no potency with regard to existence and non-existence; they have received everlasting existence from God through creation.

Since matter, by the very fact that it is what it is, is a potency for that existence which is imparted through form, those beings which have no potency for existence and non-existence, are not composed of matter and form, but are forms only, subsisting in their being which they have received from God. Such incorporeal substances must be incorruptible. For all corruptible beings have a potency for non-existence; but incorporeal beings have no such potency, as we said. Hence they are incorruptible.

Furthermore, nothing is corrupted unless its form is separated from it, for existence always follows form. Since the substances in question are subsisting forms, they cannot be separated from their forms, and so cannot lose existence. So they are incorruptible.

Between the extremes mentioned, there are certain intermediate beings which have no potency for existence and non-existence, but which have a potency for *ubi*, or *presence in place*. Such are the heavenly bodies, which are not subject to generation and corruption, since contrarieties are not found in them. However, they are changeable according to local presence. Thus in some beings there is found matter as well as motion. For motion is the act of a being in potency. Accordingly, such bodies have matter that is not subject to generation and corruption, but is subject only to change of place.

The Human Soul

The substances mentioned above, which are called immaterial, must also be intellectual. A being is intellectual because it is free from matter. This can be perceived from the way it understands. The intelligible in act and the intellect in act are the same thing.

But it is clear that a thing is intelligible in act because it is separated from matter; we cannot have intellectual knowledge of material things except by abstracting from matter. Accordingly, we must pronounce the same judgment regarding the intellect; that is, whatever is immaterial, is intellectual.

Furthermore, immaterial substances hold the first place and are supreme among beings; for act naturally has precedence over potency. But the intellect is clearly superior to all other beings; for the intellect uses corporeal things as instruments. Therefore immaterial substances must be intellectual.

Moreover, the higher a thing is in the scale of being, the closer it draws to likeness with God. Thus we observe that some things (e.g., those pertaining to the lowest degree, such as lifeless beings) share in the divine likeness with respect to existence only; others, however (such as plants), share in the divine likeness with respect to existence and life; and yet others (such as animals), share in the divine likeness with respect to sense perception. But the highest degree — and that which makes us most like to God — is conferred by the intellect.

Consequently the most excellent creatures are intellectual. Indeed, they are said to be fashioned in God's image for the very reason that among all creatures they approach most closely to likeness with God.

76

Freedom of choice in intellectual substances

This fact shows that such beings have freedom of choice. The intellect does not act or desire without forming a judgment, as lifeless beings do, nor is the judgment of the intellect the product of natural impulse, as in brutes, but results from a true apprehension of the object.

For the intellect perceives the end, the means leading to the end, and the bearing of one on the other. Hence the intellect can be the cause of its own judgment, whereby it desires a good and performs an action for the sake of an end.

But what is a cause unto itself is precisely what we call free. Accordingly, the intellect desires and acts in virtue of a free judgment, which is the same as having freedom of choice. Therefore the highest substances enjoy freedom of choice.

Furthermore, that being is free which is not tied down to any one definite course. But the appetite of an intellectual substance is not under compulsion to pursue any one definite good, for it follows intellectual apprehension, which embraces good universally. Therefore the appetite of an intelligent substance is free, since it tends toward all good in general.

77
Order and degree among intellectual beings

Intellectual substances are superior to other substances in the scale of perfection. They must also differ from each other in degree. They cannot differ from each other by material differentiation, since they lack matter. If plurality is found in them, it must be caused by formal distinction, which establishes diversity of species. In beings that exhibit diversity of species, the degree and order in them must be considered since, just as addition or subtraction of a unit causes variation of species in numbers, so natural entities vary in species by the addition or subtraction of differences. For instance, what is merely alive differs from what is alive and endowed with sense perception; and the latter differs from what is alive, endowed with sense, and rational. So the immaterial substances under discussion must be distinct according to various degrees and orders.

78
Order and degree in intellectual operation

Because the nature of a being's activity is in keeping with its substance, higher intellectual substances must understand more perfectly, since they have intelligible species and powers that are more universal and are more unified. On the other hand, intellectual substances that are less perfect must be weaker in intelligence, and must have species that are more numerous and less universal.

79
Inferiority of man's intellectual nature

Infinite progression is impossible in any series. Among intellectual substances, one must ultimately be found to be supreme, namely, the one which approaches most closely to God. Likewise, one must be found to be the lowest, and this will be the most intimately associated with corporeal matter.

This can be explained in the following way. Understanding is proper to man beyond all the other animals. Evidently, man alone comprehends universals, and the relations between things, and immaterial objects, which are perceptible only to the intelligence. Understanding cannot be an act performed by a bodily organ in the way that vision is exercised by the eye. No faculty endowed with cognitive power can belong to the genus of things that is known through its agency. Thus the pupil of the eye lacks color by its very nature. Colors are recognized to the extent that the species of colors are received into the pupil; but a recipient must be lacking in that which is received. The intellect is capable of knowing all sensible natures. Therefore, if it knew through the medium of a bodily organ, that organ would have to be entirely lacking in sensible nature; but this is impossible.

Moreover, any cognitive faculty exercises its power of knowing in accord with the way the species of the object known is in it, for this is its principle of knowing. But the intellect knows things in an immaterial fashion, even those things that are by nature material; it abstracts a universal form from its individuating material conditions. Therefore the species of the object known cannot exist in the intellect materially; and so it is not received into a bodily organ, seeing that every bodily organ is material.

The same is clear from the fact that a sense is weakened and injured by sensible objects of extreme intensity. Thus the ear is impaired by excessively loud sounds and the eye by excessively bright lights. This occurs because the harmony within the organ is shattered. The intellect, on the contrary, is perfected in proportion to the excellence of intelligible objects; he who understands the higher objects of intelligence is able to understand other objects more perfectly rather than less perfectly. Thus, if man is found to be intelligent, and if man's understanding is not effected through the medium of a bodily organ, we are forced to acknowledge the existence of some incorporeal substance whereby man exercises the act of understanding. For the substance of a being that can perform an action by itself, without the aid of a body, is not dependent on a body. But all powers and forms that are unable to subsist by themselves without a body, cannot exercise any activity without a body. Thus heat does not by itself cause warmth; rather a body causes warmth by the heat that is in it. Accordingly, this incorporeal substance whereby man understands, occupies the lowest place in the genus of intellectual substances, and is the closest to matter.

80
Different kinds of intellect and ways of understanding

Since intellectual being is superior to sentient being (just as intellect is superior to sense) and since lower beings imitate higher beings as best they may (just as bodies subject to generation and corruption imitate in some fashion the circulatory motion of heavenly bodies), it follows that sensible beings resemble, in their own way, intellectual beings. Thus from the resemblance of sense to intellect we can mount to some knowledge of intellectual beings.

In sensible beings a certain factor is found to be the highest; this is act (i.e., form). Another factor is found to be the lowest, for it is pure potency; this is matter. Midway between the two is the composite of matter and form.

We expect to find something similar in the intellectual world. The supreme intellectual being, God, is pure act. Other intellectual substances have something of act and of potency, but in a way that befits intellectual being. And the lowest among intellectual substances, that whereby man understands, has, so to speak, intellectual being only in potency. This is borne out by the fact that man is at first found to be only potentially intelligent, and this potency is gradually reduced to act in the course of time. And this is why the faculty whereby man understands is called the possible intellect.[77]

81
Reception of intelligible forms in the possible intellect

As was stated above, the higher an intellectual substance is in perfection, the more universal are the intelligible forms it possesses. Of all the intellectual substances, consequently, the human intellect, which we have called possible, has forms of the least universality. This is the reason it receives its intelligible forms from sensible things.

This can be made clear from another point of view. A form must have some proportion to the potency which receives it. Therefore, since of all intellectual substances man's possible intellect is found to be the closest to corporeal matter, its intelligible forms must, likewise, be most closely allied to material things.

---

[77] To explain the process of knowledge, scholastic philosophy distinguishes between two faculties of the intellectual soul: the *possible intellect* and the *agent intellect*. The agent intellect or active intellect (*intellectus agens*) illuminates the phantasm, abstracting from it the intelligible species, which are spiritual likenesses of objects, disengaged from all particularizing conditions of matter. See chapter 83 below. According to St. Thomas, "the agent intellect causes the phantasms received from the senses to be actually intelligible through a process of abstraction" (*Summa*, Ia, q. 84, a. 6). The possible (that is, potential) or passive intellect (*intellectus possibilis*) is actuated and informed by the intelligible species resulting from this abstractive operation, and is thereby enabled to elicit the act of understanding.

82
Man's need of sense faculties for understanding

However, we must realize that forms in corporeal things are particular, and have a material existence. But in the intellect they are universal and immaterial. Our manner of understanding brings this out. That is, we apprehend things universally and immaterially. This way of understanding must conform to the intelligible species whereby we understand. Consequently, since it is impossible to pass from one extreme to another without traversing what lies between, forms reaching the intellect from corporeal objects must pass through certain media.

These are the sense faculties, which receive the forms of material things without their matter; what lodges in the eye is the species of the stone, but not its matter. However, the forms of things received into the sense faculties are particular, for we know only particular objects with our sense faculties. Hence man must be endowed with senses as a prerequisite to understanding. A proof of this is the fact that if a man is lacking in one of the senses, he has no knowledge of sensible objects that are apprehended by that sense. Thus a person born blind can have no knowledge of colors.

83
Necessity of the agent intellect

This discussion brings out the truth that knowledge of things in our intellect is not caused by any participation or influence of forms that are intelligible in act and that subsist by themselves, as was taught by the Platonists[78] and certain other philosophers who

---

[78] Cf. Plato, *Phaedo* (100 D); *Timaeus* (28 A; 30 C). See also Aristotle, *Metaph.*, I, 6 (987 b 7); I, 9 (991 b 3).

followed them in this doctrine. No, the intellect acquires such knowledge from sensible objects, through the intermediacy of the senses. However, since the forms of objects in the sense faculties are particular, as we just said, [79] they are intelligible not in act, but only in potency. For the intellect understands nothing but universals. But what is in potency is not reduced to act except by some agent. Hence there must be some agent that causes the species existing in the sense faculties to be intelligible in act. The possible intellect cannot perform this service, for it is in potency with respect to intelligible objects rather than active in rendering them intelligible. Therefore we must assume some other intellect which will cause species that are intelligible in potency to become intelligible in act, just as light causes colors that are potentially visible to be actually visible. This faculty we call the agent intellect, which we would not have to postulate if the forms of things were intelligible in act, as the Platonists held.

To understand, therefore, we have need, first, of the possible intellect which receives intelligible species, and secondly, of the agent intellect which renders things intelligible in act. Once the possible intellect has been perfected by the intelligible species, it is called the habitual intellect (*intellectus in habitu*), for then it possesses intelligible species in such a way that it can use them at will; in other words, it possesses them in a fashion that is midway between pure potency and complete act. But when it has these species in full actuality, it is called the intellect in act. That is, the intellect actually understands a thing when the species of the thing is made the form of the possible intellect. This is why we say that the intellect in act is the object actually understood.

[79] Cf. chap. 82.

84
Incorruptibility of the human soul

A necessary consequence of the foregoing doctrine is that the intellect whereby man understands is incorruptible. Every being acts in a way that is conformable to its existence. The intellect has an activity which it does not share with the body, as we have proved.[80] This shows that it can act by itself. Hence it is a substance[81] subsisting in its own being. But, as was pointed out above, intellectual substances are incorruptible.[82] Accordingly the intellect whereby man understands is incorruptible.

Again, the proper subject of generation and corruption is matter. Hence a thing is immune to corruption to the extent that it is free from matter. Things composed of matter and form are *per se* corruptible; material forms are corruptible indirectly (*per accidens*), though not *per se*. Immaterial forms, which are above material conditions, are wholly incorruptible. The intellect by its very nature is elevated completely beyond matter, as its activity shows: we do not understand anything unless we separate it from matter. Consequently the intellect is by nature incorruptible.

Moreover, corruption cannot occur without contrariety; for nothing is corrupted except by its contrary. This is why the heavenly bodies, which do not admit of contrariety, are incorruptible. But all contrariety is far removed from the nature of the intellect, so much so that things which are contraries in themselves, are not

---

[80] Cf. chap. 79.

[81] On the use of the word *intellect* for the intellectual soul, see the *Summa*, Ia., q. 79, a. 1 ad 1: "The intellectual soul is sometimes called simply *intellect* from its chief power." The same usage occurs in Aristotle, *De anima*, I, 4 (408 b 18) and in St. Augustine, *De Trinitate*, IX, 2 (PL, XLII, 962) and elsewhere.

[82] Cf. chaps. 74, 79.

contraries in the intellect. The intelligible aspect of contraries is one, inasmuch as one thing is understood in terms of another. Thus it is impossible for the intellect to be corruptible.

85
Unity of the possible intellect

An objector may say: the intellect is indeed incorruptible, but there is only one intellect in all men; and so what remains after the corruption of all men is but one. That there is only one intellect for all men, the objector may continue, can be established on many grounds.

The first is on the part of the intelligible species. For if I have one intellect and you have another, there will have to be one intelligible species in me and another in you. Thus there will be one object that I understand and another that you understand.

Hence the intelligible species will be multiplied according to the number of individuals, and so it will not be universal but individual. The conclusion would then seem to follow that it is understood not in act, but only in potency; for individual species are intelligible in potency, not in act.

Moreover, since the intellect, as we have seen, is a substance subsisting in its own being,[83] and since intellectual substances that are numerically many do not belong to one species, as we have also seen,[84] it follows that if I have one intellect and you have another that is numerically different, the two must differ specifically. And so you and I would not belong to the same species.

Further, since all individuals share in one specific nature, there must be something besides specific nature whereby individuals

---

[83] Cf. chap. 84.
[84] Cf. chap. 77.

may be distinguished from one another. Accordingly, if there is one specific intellect in all men, but many intellects that are numerically distinct, something must be found that will make one intellect differ numerically from another. This cannot be anything pertaining to the substance of the intellect, since the intellect is not composed of matter and form.

Consequently any difference that might be admitted on the part of the substance of the intellect would be a formal difference that would cause diversity in the species. The only possibility left is that the intellect of one man cannot differ numerically from the intellect of another man except by reason of the diversity of their bodies. Therefore, when the various bodies corrupt, it seems that only one intellect, and not a plurality of intellects, would remain.

The absurdity of this whole position can easily be perceived. To make this clear, let us proceed as one would proceed against those who deny fundamental principles. That is, let us first establish a truth that simply cannot be denied.

Let us suppose that this man (for example, Socrates or Plato) understands. Our adversary could not deny that the man understands, unless he knew that it ought to be denied. By denying he affirms, for affirmation and denial are intelligent actions. If, then, the man in question understands, that whereby he formally understands must be his form, since nothing acts unless it is in act. Hence that whereby an agent acts, is his act; just as the heat by which a heated body causes warmth, is its act. Therefore the intellect whereby a man understands is the form of this man, and the same is true of another man.

But the same numerical form cannot belong to numerically different individuals, for numerically different individuals do not possess the same existence; and yet everything has existence by reason of its form. Accordingly, the intellect whereby a man understands cannot be but one in all men.

Perceiving the force of this difficulty, some[85] endeavor to find a way of escaping it. They say that the possible intellect, of which there was question above,[86] receives the intelligible species by which it is reduced to act. These intelligible species are, in some way, in the phantasms. Hence the possible intellect is continuous and is joined to us so far as the intelligible species is both in the possible intellect and in the phantasms that are in us. It is thus that we are able to understand through the agency of the possible intellect.

Unfortunately for this solution, it is utterly valueless. In the first place, the intelligible species, as it exists in the phantasms, is a concept only in potency; and as it exists in the possible intellect, it is a concept in act. As existing in the possible intellect, it is not in the phantasms, but rather is abstracted from the phantasms. Hence no union of the possible intellect with us remains. Secondly, even granting that there may be some sort of union, this would not suffice to enable us to understand. The presence of the species of some object in the intellect does not entail the consequence that the object understands itself, but only that it is understood; a stone does not understand, even though a species of it may be in the possible intellect. Hence, from the fact that species of phantasms present in us are in the possible intellect, it does not follow that we thereupon understand. It only follows that we ourselves, or rather the phantasms in us, are understood.

This will appear more clearly if we examine the comparison proposed by Aristotle in Book III of *De anima*, where he says that the intellect is to the phantasm what sight is to color.[87] Manifestly,

---

[85] The Averroists. Cf. Averroes, *In De an.*, III, *comm.* 5 (VI, 164V); St. Thomas, *De unitate intellectus*, III (ed. Keeler, p. 40 f.).

[86] Cf. chap. 81.

[87] *De anima*, III, 7 (431 a 14).

the fact that the species of colors on a wall are in our vision does not cause the wall to see, but to be seen. Likewise, the fact that the species of the phantasms in us come to be in the intellect, does not cause us to understand, but to be understood. Further, if we understand formally through the intellect, the intellectual action of the intellect must be the intellectual action of the man, just as the heating action of fire and of heat are the same. Therefore, if intellect is numerically the same in me and in you, it follows that, with respect to the same intelligible object, my action of understanding must be the same as yours, provided, of course, both of us understand the same thing at the same time. But this is impossible, for different agents cannot perform one and the same numerical operation. Therefore it is impossible for all men to have but a single intellect. Consequently, if the intellect is incorruptible, as has been demonstrated,[88] many intellects, corresponding to the number of men, will survive the destruction of their bodies.

The arguments advanced to support the contrary view are easily answered.

The first argument has many defects. First of all, we concede that the same thing may be understood by all. By the thing understood I mean that which is the object of the intellect. However, the object of the intellect is not the intelligible species, but the quiddity of the thing. The intellectual sciences are all concerned with the natures of things, not with intelligible species (just as the object of sight is color, not the species of color in the eye). Thus, although there may be many intellects belonging to different men, the thing understood by all may be but one (just as a colored object which many look at is but one).

[88] Cf. chap. 84.

Secondly, the consequence does not necessarily follow that, if a thing is individual, it is understood in potency and not in act. This is true only of things that are individuated by matter. Of course, what is understood in act must be immaterial. Accordingly, immaterial substances, even though they may be individuals existing by themselves, are understood in act. The same holds for intelligible species, which are immaterial; although they differ numerically in me and in you, they do not on that account lose their property of being intelligible in act. The intellect that understands its objects by means of them reflects upon itself, thereby understanding its very action of understanding as well as the species whereby it understands. Moreover, we should realize that, even if we admit but one intellect for all men, the difficulty is still the same. There would still remain many intellects, because there are many separate substances endowed with intelligence. And so it would follow, pursuing our adversaries' line of reasoning, that the objects understood would be numerically different, hence individual and not understood in first act. Obviously, therefore, if the objection under discussion had any cogency, it would do away with a plurality of intellects simply as such, and not merely in men. Since this conclusion is false, the argument manifestly does not conclude with necessity.

The second argument is readily answered, if we but consider the difference between an intellectual soul and separate substances. In virtue of its specific nature, the intellectual soul is meant to be united to some body as the latter's form; the body even enters into the definition of the soul. For this reason, souls are numerically differentiated according to the relation they have to different bodies, which is not the case with separate substances.

This also indicates how the third argument is to be answered. In virtue of its specific nature, the intellectual soul does not possess the body as a part of itself, but has only an aptitude for union with the body. Therefore it is numerically differentiated by its capacity for union with different bodies. And this remains the case with souls even after their bodies have been destroyed: they retain a capacity for union with different bodies even when they are not actually united to their respective bodies.

86
The agent intellect is not one in all men

There were also some philosophers who argued that, even granting the diversification of the possible intellect in men, at any rate the agent intellect was but one for all.[89] This view, while less objectionable than the theory discussed in the preceding chapter, can be refuted by similar considerations.

The action of the possible intellect consists in receiving the objects understood and in understanding them. And the action of the agent intellect consists in causing things to be actually understood by abstracting species. But both these functions pertain to one particular man. This man (for example, Socrates or Plato) receives the objects understood, abstracts the species, and understands what is abstracted. Hence the possible intellect as well as the agent intellect must be united to this man as a form. And so both must be numerically multiplied in accord with the number of men concerned.

Moreover, agent and patient must be proportionate to each other. Examples are matter and form, for matter is reduced to act by an agent. This is why an active potency of the same genus corresponds to every passive potency; for act and potency pertain to one genus. But the agent intellect is to the possible intellect

---

[89] Averroes, *In De anima*, III, *comm.* 18 (VI, 169V); *comm.* 19 (VI, 170R); Avicenna, *De anima*, V, 5 (25RB); *Metaph.*, IX, 3 (104RB).

what active potency is to passive potency, as is clear from this discussion.[90] Hence they must both pertain to one genus. Therefore, since the possible intellect has no separate existence apart from us, but is united to us as a form and is multiplied according to the number of men, as we have shown,[91] the agent intellect must likewise be something that is united to us as a form, and must be multiplied according to the number of men.

87

The possible intellect and the agent intellect in the essence of the soul

Since the agent intellect and the possible intellect are united to us as form, we must acknowledge that they pertain to the same essence of the soul. Whatever is formally united to another thing is united to it either in the manner of a substantial form or in the manner of an accidental form. If the possible intellect and the agent intellect were united to man after the fashion of a substantial form, we would have to hold that they share in the one essence of that form which is the soul, since one thing cannot have more than one substantial form. On the other hand, if they are united to man after the fashion of an accidental form, neither of them, evidently, can be an accident of the body. Besides, the fact that their operations are performed without a bodily organ, as we proved above,[92] shows that each of them is an accident of the soul. But there is only one soul in one man. Therefore the agent intellect and the possible intellect must inhere in the one essence of the soul.

Furthermore, every action that is proper to a species proceeds from principles that emanate from the form which confers the

[90] See especially chap. 83.
[91] Cf. chap. 85.
[92] Cf. chap. 79.

species. But the action of understanding is an operation proper to the human species. Therefore the agent intellect and the possible intellect, which are principles of this action, as has been shown,[93] emanate from the human soul, whence man has his species. However, they do not issue from the soul in such a way as to extend to the body, because, as we have said,[94] the operation in question takes place independently of a bodily organ. Since, therefore, action pertains to the same subject as does potency, the possible intellect and the agent intellect inhere in the one essence of the soul.

88

The way these two faculties are united in the same essence of the soul

We have still to consider how this union is possible. Some difficulty may seem to arise in this matter. The possible intellect is in potency with respect to all that is intelligible, whereas the agent intellect causes what is intelligible in potency to be intelligible in act, and so must be related to what is intelligible as act to potency. But the same thing, seemingly, cannot be both in potency and in act with respect to the same object. Thus it would appear that the possible intellect and the agent intellect cannot be united in the same substance of the soul.

This doubt is easily resolved if we examine how the possible intellect is in potency with respect to intelligible objects, and how the agent intellect renders them actually intelligible. The possible intellect is in potency with regard to intelligible objects in the sense that it does not contain within its nature any determinate form of sensible things. In the same way the pupil of the eye is in

---

[93] Cf. chaps. 81, 83.
[94] Cf. chap. 79.

potency with regard to all colors. To the extent, then, that phantasms abstracted from sensible things are likenesses of definite sensible things, they are related to the possible intellect as act to potency. Nevertheless the phantasms are in potency with regard to something that the intellectual soul possesses in act, namely, being as abstracted from material conditions. And in this respect the intellectual soul is related to the phantasms as act to potency.

No contradiction is involved if a thing is in act and potency with regard to the same object according to different points of view. Thus natural bodies act upon each other and are acted upon by each other, for each is in potency with respect to the other. The same intellectual soul, therefore, can be in potency with regard to all intelligible objects and nevertheless, without any contradiction, can be related to them as act, if both a possible intellect and an agent intellect are acknowledged in the soul.

This will be seen more clearly from the way the intellect renders objects actually intelligible. The agent intellect does not render objects actually intelligible in the sense that the latter flow from it into the possible intellect. If this were the case, we would have no need of phantasms and sense in order to understand. No, the agent intellect renders things actually intelligible by abstracting them from phantasms (just as light, in a certain sense, renders colors actual, not as though it contained the colors within itself, but so far as it confers visibility on them). In the same way we are to judge that there is a single intellectual soul that lacks the natures of sensible things but can receive them in an intelligible manner, and that renders phantasms actually intelligible by abstracting intelligible species from them.

The power whereby the soul is able to receive intelligible species is called the possible intellect, and the power whereby it abstracts intelligible species from phantasms is called the agent intellect. The latter is a sort of intelligible light communicated to the intellectual soul, in imitation of what takes place among the higher intellectual substances.

89
Radication of all the faculties in the essence of the soul

Not only the agent intellect and the possible intellect, but also all the other powers that are principles of the soul's operations are united in the essence of the soul. All such powers are somehow rooted in the soul. Some of them, indeed, such as the powers of the vegetative and sensitive parts, are in the soul as in their principle but in the composite as in their subject because their activities pertain to the composite, not to the soul alone; for power and action belong to the same subject. Some of them, on the other hand, are in the soul both as principle and as subject, for their operations pertain to the soul apart from any bodily organ. These are the powers of the intellectual part. But a man cannot have several souls. Accordingly, all the powers must pertain to the same soul.

90
Unicity of the soul

That there cannot be several souls in one body is proved as follows. The soul is evidently the substantial form of any being possessing a soul because a living being is constituted in genus and species by its soul. But the same thing cannot have several substantial forms. A substantial form differs from an accidental form in this, that a substantial form causes a particular thing simply to be, whereas an accidental form is added to a particular being already constituted as such and determines its quality, quantity, or mode of being. Hence, if several substantial forms belong to one and the same thing, either the first of them causes it to be this particular thing or it does not. If it does not, the form is not substantial; if it does, then all the subsequent forms accrue to what is already this particular thing. Therefore none of the subsequent forms will be the substantial form, but only some accidental form.

Clearly, therefore, one and the same thing cannot have several substantial forms; and so one and the same person cannot have several souls.

Furthermore, it is evident that a man is said to be living because he has a vegetative soul; that he is called an animal because he has a sensitive soul; and that he is a man because he has an intellectual soul. Consequently, if there were three souls in man (namely, vegetative, sensitive, and rational), man would be placed in a genus because of one of his souls and in a species because of another. But this is impossible. For thus genus and specific difference would constitute not what is simply one, but what is one *per accidens*, or a sort of conglomeration, such as musical and white; but such is not a being that is simply one. Accordingly, a man can have only one soul.

91
Arguments advanced to show a multiplicity of souls in man

Certain considerations seem opposed to our doctrine. In the first place, specific difference is to genus what form is to matter. Animal is the genus of man and rational is the difference that makes man what he is. Accordingly, since animal is a body animated by a sensitive soul, it seems that a body animated by a sensitive soul is still in potency with respect to the rational soul. Thus the rational soul would be distinct from the sensitive soul.

Moreover, the intellect does not possess a bodily organ. But the sensitive and nutritive powers do possess bodily organs. Hence it seems impossible for the same soul to be both intellectual and sensitive because the same thing cannot both be separated and not separated from another thing.

Further, the rational soul is incorruptible, as we saw above.[95] On the other hand, the vegetative and sensitive souls are corruptible, as they are acts of corruptible organs. Therefore the rational soul is not the same as the vegetative and the sensitive souls, for the same thing cannot be both corruptible and incorruptible.

Besides, in the generation of man the life conferred by the vegetative soul appears before the fetus is observed to be an animal from its sense activity and motion; and this same being is discerned to be an animal through its sense activity and movement before it has an intellect. So if the soul is the same (by which the fetus first lives the life of a plant, then the life of an animal, and thirdly the life of a man), it follows that the vegetative, sensitive, and rational principles come from an outside source or else that the intellectual soul arises from the energy in the semen. Both of these alternatives are inadmissible. On the one hand, since the operations of the vegetative and sensitive soul are not exercised apart from the body, their principles cannot be without a body. On the other hand, the operation of the intellectual soul is exercised without a body; and so, apparently, no bodily energy can be its cause. Therefore the same soul cannot be vegetative, sensitive, and rational.

92
Refutation of the preceding objections

To set aside such quibbles, we should reflect that in material things, one species surpasses another in perfection in the way that, in

---

[95] Cf. chap. 84.

numbers, species are diversified by adding one to another. Whatever perfection is found in lifeless bodies, plants also possess — and more besides. Again, whatever plants have, animals have, too — and something else in addition. And thus we proceed until we come to man, the most perfect of bodily creatures. All that is imperfect is related as matter to what is more perfect. This is clear in the various classes of beings.

The elements constitute the matter of bodies that are composed of similar parts; and again, bodies having similar parts are matter with respect to animals. And this is likewise to be observed in one and the same being. Among natural things, that which is endowed with a higher degree of perfection has, in virtue of its form, whatever perfection is found in lower nature; and in virtue of the same form it has, besides, its own added perfection. Through its soul, the plant is a substance, is corporeal, and besides is an animated body. Through its soul, an animal has all these perfections and, moreover, is sentient. In addition to all this, man is intelligent through his soul. Thus, in any object, if we consider what pertains to the perfection of a lower grade of being, this will be material when compared with what pertains to the perfection of a higher grade. For example, if we observe that an animal has the life of a plant, this life is in some fashion material with respect to what pertains to sensitive life, which is characteristic of an animal.

Genus, of course, is not matter, for then it would not be predicated of the whole. But it is something derived from matter; for the designation attaching to a thing in terms of what is material in it, is its genus. Specific difference is derived from the form of a thing in the same way. This is the reason why living or animated body is the genus of animal, and sensitive is the specific difference that constitutes it. Similarly, animal is the genus of man, and rational is the difference that constitutes him. Therefore, since the form of a higher grade of being comprises within itself all the perfections of a lower grade, there is not, in reality, one form from which genus is derived and another from which specific difference is derived. Rather, genus is derived from a form so far as it has a perfection of lower degree; and specific difference is derived from the same form so far as it has a perfection of higher degree.

Thus, although animal is the genus of man and rational is the specific difference constituting him, there need not be in man a sensitive soul distinct from the intellectual soul, as was urged in the first argument.

This indicates the solution of the second difficulty. As we have pointed out, the form of a higher species comprises within itself all the perfections of lower classes of being.

We must note, however, that the species of a material being is higher in proportion as it is less subject to matter. And so the nobler a form is, the more it must be elevated above matter. Hence the human soul, which is the noblest of all forms of matter, attains to the highest level of elevation, where it enjoys an activity that is independent of the concurrence of corporeal matter. Yet, since the same soul includes the perfection of lower levels, it also has activities in which corporeal matter shares.

However, an activity is exercised by a thing in accordance with the thing's power. Therefore the human soul must have some powers or potentialities that are principles of activities exercised through the body, and these must be actions of certain parts of the body. Such are the powers of the vegetative and sensitive parts.

The soul has also certain powers that are the principles of activities exercised without the body. Such are the powers of the intellectual part, whose actions are not performed by any organs.

For this reason both the possible intellect and the agent intellect are said to be separate; they have no organs as principles of their actions — such as sight and hearing have — but inhere in the soul alone, which is the form of the body. Hence we need not conclude, from the fact that the intellect is said to be separate and lacks a bodily organ (whereas neither of these is true of the senses) that the intellectual soul is distinct from the sensitive soul in man.

This also makes it clear that we are not forced to admit an intellectual soul distinct from the sensitive soul in man on the ground that the sensitive soul is corruptible whereas the intellectual soul is incorruptible, as the third objection set out to prove. Incorruptibility pertains to the intellectual part so far as it is separate.

Therefore, as powers that are separate, in the sense mentioned above, and powers that are not separate, are all rooted in the same essence of the soul, there is nothing to prevent some of the powers of the soul from lapsing when the body perishes, while others remain incorruptible.

The points already made lead to a solution of the fourth objection. All natural movement gradually advances from imperfect to perfect. The same quality is receptive of greater and less; hence alteration, which is movement in quality, being unified and continuous in its progress from potency to act, advances from imperfect to perfect.

But substantial form is not receptive of greater and less, for the substantial nature of each being exists indivisibly. Therefore natural generation does not proceed continuously through many intermediate stages from imperfect to perfect; rather, it is clear that at each level of perfection a new generation and corruption must take place.

Thus in the generation of a man the fetus first lives the life of a plant through the vegetative soul; next, when this form is removed by corruption it acquires, by a sort of new generation, a sensitive soul and lives the life of an animal; finally, when this soul is in turn removed by corruption, the ultimate and complete form is introduced.[96] This is the rational soul, which comprises within itself whatever perfection was found in the previous forms.

93
Production of the rational soul

This ultimate and complete form, the rational soul, is not brought into existence by the power that is in the semen but by a higher cause. For the power that is in the semen is a bodily power. But the rational soul exceeds the whole nature and power of the body, since no body can rise to the heights of the soul's intellectual activity. Nothing can act in a way that surmounts its species, because the agent is nobler than the patient and the maker excels his product. Hence the power possessed by a body cannot produce the rational soul, nor, consequently, can the energy inherent in the semen do so.

Moreover, a thing that has new existence must also have a new becoming; for that which is, must first become, since a thing becomes in order that it may be. Thus things which have being in their own right must have becoming in their own right; such are subsistent beings. But things that do not possess being in their own right do not properly have a becoming; such are accidents and material forms. The rational soul has being in its own right because it has its own operation, as is clear from our previous discussion. Therefore becoming is properly predicated of the rational soul. Since the soul is not composed of matter and form, as was shown above,[97] it cannot be brought into being except by creation. But

---

[96] Needless to say, the theory of the generation of living beings here expressed differs considerably from the teaching of modern biology.

[97] Cf. chaps. 79, 84.

God alone can create, as we said above.[98] Consequently the rational soul is produced by God alone.

We can readily understand why this should be so. In all arts that are hierarchically related to one another, we observe that the highest art induces the ultimate form whereas the lower arts dispose matter for the reception of the ultimate form. The rational soul, evidently, is the ultimate and most perfect form that the matter of beings subject to generation and corruption can achieve. Therefore natural agents, which operate on lower levels, appropriately cause preliminary dispositions and forms, whereas the supreme agent, God, causes the ultimate form, which is the rational soul.

94

The rational soul is not derived from God's substance

However, we are not to imagine that the rational soul is derived from the substance of God, as some have erroneously thought.[99] We demonstrated above that God is simple and indivisible.[100] Therefore He does not join the rational soul to a body as though He had first severed it from His own substance.

Furthermore, we pointed out above that God cannot be the form of any body.[101] But the rational soul is united to the body as the latter's form. Hence it is not derived from the substance of God.

---

[98] Cf. chap. 70.

[99] For example, Varro, according to St. Augustine, *De civitate Dei*, VII, 6 (PL, XLI, 199); Macrobius, *In Somnium Scipionis*, I, 14.

[100] Cf. chap. 9.

[101] Cf. chap. 17.

Besides, we showed above that God is not moved either in Himself or by reason of some other thing that is moved.[102] But the contrary of this takes place in the rational soul, which is moved from ignorance to knowledge, from vice to virtue. Accordingly, the soul is not of the substance of God.

[102] Cf. chaps. 4, 17.

God's Activity in Creating

95
Immediate creation by God

The doctrine established above necessarily leads to the conclusion that things which cannot be brought into existence except by creation, come immediately from God. Thus the heavenly bodies,[103] as is manifest, cannot be produced except by creation. They cannot be said to be made from some preexisting matter, for then they would be capable of generation and corruption and would also be subject to contrariety. But they are not, as their motion proves. For they move in circles; and circular motion has no contrary. Consequently, the heavenly bodies were produced immediately by God.

Similarly the elements, regarded as complete units, do not come from any preexisting matter. Anything that would thus preexist would have some form. Thus some body, other than the elements, would exist prior to them in the order of material cause. But if the matter existing prior to the elements had a distinct form,

---

[103] Cf. chap. 9, note.

one of the elements would have to be prior to the others in the same order, supposing that the preexisting matter had the form of an element. Therefore the very elements must have been produced immediately by God.

It is even more impossible for incorporeal and invisible substances to be created by someone else, for all such substances are immaterial. Matter cannot exist unless it is subject to dimension, whereby it is capable of being marked off, so that many things can be made from the same matter. Hence immaterial substances cannot be made from preexisting matter. Consequently they can be produced only by God through creation. For this reason the Catholic Faith professes that God is the "Creator of Heaven and Earth, and of all things visible," and also "of all things invisible."

96
Voluntariness of God's activity

The truth set forth in the preceding chapter also discloses the fact that God has brought things into existence not through any necessity of His nature but by His will. A single natural agent produces immediately but one effect, whereas a voluntary agent can produce a variety of effects. The reason for this is that every agent acts in virtue of its form. The natural form, whereby a cause operates naturally, is limited to one for each agent. But intellectual forms, whereby an agent operates through his will, are many. Therefore, since many things are immediately produced by God, as we have just shown,[104] God evidently produces things by His will and not under the impulse of natural necessity.

---

[104]Cf. chap. 95.

Besides, in the order of causes, an agent operating through intellect and will is prior to an agent operating by the necessity of its nature. For an agent operating through his will predetermines for himself the end for the sake of which he acts, whereas a natural cause operates on account of an end predetermined for it by another. But, as is clear from all that has gone before, God is the first agent. Hence He acts through His will and not by a necessity of His nature.

Moreover, we showed above that God is infinite in power.[105] Consequently He is not determined to this or that effect but is undetermined with regard to all effects. But what is undetermined regarding various effects is determined to produce one of them by desire or by the determination of the will. Thus a man who is free to walk or not to walk, walks when he wills. Hence effects proceed from God according to the determination of His will. And so He acts, not by a necessity of His nature, but by His will. This is why the Catholic Faith calls the omnipotent God not only *Creator*, but also *Maker*. For making is properly the action of an artificer who operates by his will. And since every voluntary agent acts in virtue of the conception of his intellect, which is called his word, as we indicated above,[106] and since the Word of God is His Son, the Catholic Faith professes that "all things were made" by the Son.

97
Immutability of God in His activity

The fact that God produces things by His will clearly shows that He can produce new things without any change in Himself. The difference between a natural agent and a voluntary agent is this: a

[105] Cf. chap. 19.
[106] Cf. chap. 38.

natural agent acts consistently in the same manner as long as it is in the same condition. Such as it is, thus does it act. But a voluntary agent acts as he wills. Accordingly, it may well be that, without any change in himself, he wishes to act now and not previously. For there is nothing to prevent a person from willing to perform an action later even though he is not doing it now; and this without any change in himself. Thus it can happen, without any change in God, that God, although He is eternal, did not bring things into existence from eternity.

98
Question of the eternity of motion

We might imagine that, although God can produce a new effect by His eternal and immutable will, some sort of motion would have to precede the newly produced effect. For we observe that the will does not delay doing what it wishes to do, unless because of some motive that is operative now but will cease later or because of some motive that is inoperative now but is expected to become operative in the future. In summer a man has the will to clothe himself with a warm garment, which, however, he does not wish to put on at present, but in the future; for now the weather is warm, although it will cease to be warm with the advent of a cold wave later in the year.

Accordingly, if God wished from eternity to produce some effect, but did not produce it from eternity, it seems either that something was expected to happen in the future that had not yet occurred or else that some obstacle had to be removed that was then present. Neither of these alternatives can take place without motion. Thus it seems that a subsequent effect cannot be produced by a preceding will unless some motion previously occurs. And so, if God's will relative to the production of things was eternal, and nevertheless things were not produced from eternity, their production must have been preceded by motion, and consequently by mobile objects. And if the latter were produced by God, but not from eternity, yet other motions and mobile objects must have preceded, and so on, in infinite recession.

The solution to this objection readily comes to mind if we but attend to the difference between a universal and a particular agent. A particular agent has an activity that conforms to a norm and measure prescribed by the universal agent. This is clear even in civil government. The legislator enacts a law which is to serve as a norm and measure. Any particular judge must base his decisions on this law. Again, time is the measure of actions which occur in time. A particular agent is endowed with activity regulated by time, so that he acts for some definite reason now, and not before. But the universal agent, God, instituted this measure, which is time, and He did so in accord with His will. Hence time also is to be numbered among the things produced by God. Therefore, just as the quantity and measure of each object are such as God wishes to assign to it, so the quantity of time is such as God wished to mete out; that is, time and the things existing in time began just when God wished them to begin.

The objection we are dealing with argues from the standpoint of an agent that presupposes time and acts in time, but did not institute time. Hence the question about *why God's eternal will produces an effect now and not earlier* presupposes that time exists; for *now* and *earlier* are segments of time. With regard to the universal production of things, among which time is also to be counted, we should not ask: "Why now and not earlier?" Rather we should ask: "Why did God wish this much time to intervene?" And this depends on the divine will, which is perfectly free to assign this or any other quantity to time. The same may be noted with respect to the dimensional quantity of the world. No one asks why God located the material world in such and such a place rather than higher up or lower down or in some other position; for there is no place outside the world. The fact that God portioned out so much quantity to the world that no part of it would be beyond the place occupied in some other locality, depends on the divine will. However, although there was no time prior to the world and no place outside the world, we speak as if there were. Thus we say that before the world existed there was nothing except God, and that there is no body lying outside the world. But in thus speaking of *before* and *outside*, we have in mind nothing but time and place as they exist in our imagination.

99
Controversy on the eternity of matter

However, even though finished products were not in existence from eternity, we might be inclined to think that matter had to exist from eternity. For everything that has being subsequent to non-being, is changed from non-being to being. Therefore if created things, such as Heaven and Earth and the like, did not exist from eternity, but began to be after they had not been, we must admit that they were changed from non-being to being. But all change and motion have some sort of subject; for motion is the act of a thing existing in potency. However, the subject of the change whereby a thing is brought into existence, is not the thing itself that is produced, because this thing is the *terminus* of the motion, and the *terminus* and subject of motion are not the same. Rather, the subject of the change is that from which the thing is produced, and this is called matter. Accordingly, if things are brought into being after a state of non-being, it seems that matter had to exist prior to them. And if this matter is, in turn, produced subsequent to a period of non-existence, it had to come from some other, preexisting matter. But infinite procession along these lines is impossible. Therefore we must eventually come to eternal matter, which was not produced subsequent to a period of non-existence.

Again, if the world began to exist after it had first not existed, then, before the world actually existed, it was either possible for the world to be or become, or it was not possible. If it was not possible for the world to be or to become, then, by equipollence, it was impossible for the world to be or to become. But if it is impossible for a thing to become, it is necessary for that thing not to become. In that case we must conclude that the world was not made. Since this conclusion is patently false, we are forced to admit that if the world began to be after it had first not been, it was possible for it to be or to become before it actually existed. Accordingly, there was something in potency with regard to the becoming and being of the world. But what is thus in potency to the becoming and existence of something, is the matter of that something, as we see exemplified in the case of wood relative to a bench. Apparently, therefore, matter must have existed always, even if the world did not exist always.

As against this line of reasoning, we showed above that the very matter of the world has no existence except from God.[107] The Catholic Faith does not admit that matter is eternal any more than it admits that the world is eternal. We have no other way of expressing the divine causality in things themselves than by saying that things produced by God began to exist after they had previously not existed. This way of speaking evidently and clearly brings out the truth that they have existence not of themselves, but from the eternal Author.

[107] Cf. chap. 69.

105

The arguments just reviewed do not compel us to postulate the eternity of matter, for the production of things in their totality cannot properly be called change. In no change is the subject of the change produced by the change, for the reason rightly alleged by the objector, namely, that the subject of change and the *terminus* of the change are not identical. Consequently, since the total production of things by God, which is known as creation, extends to all the reality that is found in a thing, production of this kind cannot properly verify the idea of change, even though the things created are brought into existence subsequently to non-existence.

Being that succeeds to non-being does not suffice to constitute real change, unless we suppose that a subject is first in a state of privation and later under its proper form. Hence *this* is found coming after *that* in certain things in which motion or change do not really occur, as when we say that day turns into night. Accordingly, even though the world began to exist after having not existed, this is not necessarily the result of some change. In fact, it is the result of creation which is not a true change, but is rather a certain relation of the created thing, as a being that is dependent on the Creator for its existence and that connotes succession to previous non-existence.

In every change there must be something that remains the same although it undergoes alteration in its manner of being, in the sense that at first it is under one extreme and subsequently under another. In creation this does not take place in objective reality, but only in our imagination. That is, we imagine that one and the same thing previously did not exist, and later existed. And so creation can be called *change* because it has some resemblance to change.

The second objection, too, lacks cogency. Although we can truly say that before the world was, it was possible for the world to be or to become, this possibility need not be taken to mean potentiality. In propositions, that which signifies a certain modality of truth (or in other words, that which is neither necessary nor impossible), is said to be possible. What is possible in this sense does not involve any potentiality, as the Philosopher teaches in Book V of his *Metaphysics*.[108] However, if anyone insists on saying that it was possible for the world to exist according to some potency, we reply that this need not mean a passive potency, but can mean active potency; and so if we say that it was possible for the world to be before it actually was, we should understand this to mean that God could have brought the world into existence before He actually produced it. Hence we are not forced to postulate that matter existed before the world. Thus, the Catholic Faith acknowledges nothing to be coeternal with God, and for this reason professes that He is the "Creator and Maker of all things visible and invisible."

---

[108] Aristotle, *Metaph.*, V, 12 (1019 b 19).

The Purpose of Man

100
Finality of God's creative activity

We showed above that God has brought things into existence, not through any necessity of His nature, but by His intellect and will.[109] Any agent that works in this way, acts for an end: the end is a principle for the operative intellect. Accordingly, everything that is made by God necessarily exists for an end.

Moreover, things were produced by God in a supremely excellent way; for the most perfect Being does everything in the most perfect way. But it is better for a thing to be made for an end than to be made without the intention of achieving an end; for the goodness that is in things which are made comes from their end. Hence things were made by God for an end.

An indication of this is seen in effects produced by nature. None of them is in vain, all are for an end. But it is absurd to say that things produced by nature are in better order than is the very constituting of nature by the first Agent, since the entire order of

---

[109]Cf. chap. 96.

nature is derived from the latter. Clearly, therefore, things produced by God exist for an end.

101
The divine goodness as the ultimate end

The ultimate end of things is necessarily the divine goodness. For the ultimate end of things produced by one who works through his will is that which is chiefly and for its own sake willed by the agent. It is for this that the agent does all that he does. But the first object willed by the divine will is God's goodness, as is clear from a previous discussion.[110] Hence the ultimate end of all things made by God must necessarily be the divine goodness.

Furthermore, the end of the generation of everything that is generated is its form. Once this is achieved, generation ceases. For everything that is generated, whether by art or by nature, is in some way rendered similar to the agent in virtue of its form, since every agent produces an effect that has some resemblance to the agent himself. Thus the house that is realized in matter proceeds from the house existing ideally in the mind of the architect. In the realm of nature, likewise, man begets man. And if anything that is generated or effected by natural processes is not like its generating cause according to species, it is at any rate likened to its efficient causes as imperfect to perfect. The fact that a generated product is not assimilated to its generating cause according to species, is explained by its inability to rise to perfect likeness with its cause; but it does participate in that cause to some extent, however imperfectly. This occurs, for example, in animals and plants that are generated by the power of the sun. Hence in all things that are

[110]Cf. chaps. 32, 33.

made, the end of their generation or production is the form of their maker or generator, in the sense that they are to achieve a likeness of that form. But the form of the first agent, who is God, is nothing else than His goodness. This, then, is the reason why all things were made: that they might be assimilated to the divine goodness.

102
The reason for diversity in things

This enables us to grasp the reason for diversity and distinction in things. Since the divine goodness could not be adequately represented by one creature alone, on account of the distance that separates each creature from God, it had to be represented by many creatures, so that what is lacking to one might be supplied by another. Even in syllogistic conclusions, when the conclusion is not sufficiently demonstrated by one means of proof, the means must be multiplied in order to make the conclusion clear, as happens in dialectic syllogisms.[111] Of course, not even the entire universe of creatures perfectly represents the divine goodness by setting it forth adequately, but represents it only in the measure of perfection possible to creatures.

Moreover, a perfection existing in a universal cause simply and in a unified manner, is found to be multiple and discrete in the effects of that cause. For a perfection has a nobler existence in a cause than in its effects. But the divine goodness is one, and is the simple principle and root of all the goodness found in creatures. Hence creatures must be assimilated to the divine goodness in the way that many and distinct objects are assimilated to what is one and simple. Therefore multiplicity and distinction occur in things

---

[111] A dialectic syllogism is one in which the means of demonstration do not exceed probability, as St. Thomas explains in *Post. Anal.*, I, *lect.* 1.

not by chance or fortune but for an end, just as the production of things is not the result of chance or fortune, but is for an end. For existence, unity, and multiplicity in things all come from the same principle.

The distinction among things is not caused by matter; for things were originally constituted in being by creation, which does not require any matter. Moreover, things which issue purely from the necessity of matter have the appearance of being fortuitous.

Furthermore, multiplicity in things is not explained by the order obtaining among intermediate agents, as though from one simple first being there could proceed directly only one thing that would be far removed from the first being in simplicity, so that multitude could issue from it, and thus, as the distance from the first simple being increased, the more numerous a multitude would be discerned. Some have suggested this explanation.[112] But we have shown[113] that there are many things that could not have come into being except by creation, which is exclusively the work of God, as has been proved.[114] Hence we conclude that many things have been created directly by God Himself. It is likewise evident that, according to the view under criticism, the multiplicity and distinction among things would be fortuitous, as not being intended by the first agent. Actually, however, the multiplicity and distinction existing among things were devised by the divine intellect and were carried out in the real order so that the divine goodness might be mirrored by created things in variety, and that different things might participate in the divine goodness in varying degree. Thus, the very order existing among diverse things

[112] Thus Avicenna, *Metaph.*, IX, 4 (104VA). Cf. *Contra Gent.*, II, 42.
[113] Cf. chap. 95.
[114] Cf. chap. 70.

issues in a certain beauty, which should call to mind the divine wisdom.

103
The divine goodness as the end of action and movement in creatures

The divine goodness is not only the end of the creation of things; it must also be the end of every operation and movement of any creature whatever. The action of every being corresponds to its nature. For example, what is hot, causes heat. But every created thing has, in keeping with its form, some participated likeness to the divine goodness, as we have pointed out.[115] Therefore, too, all actions and movements of every creature are directed to the divine goodness as their end.

Besides, all movements and operations of every being are seen to tend to what is perfect. Perfect signifies what is good, since the perfection of anything is its goodness. Hence every movement and action of anything whatever tends toward good. But all good is a certain imitation of the supreme Good, just as all being is an imitation of the first Being. Therefore the movements and actions of all things tend toward assimilation with the divine goodness.

Moreover, if there are many agents arranged in order, the actions and movements of all the agents must be directed to the good of the first agent as to their ultimate end. For lower agents are moved by the higher agent, and every mover moves in the direction of his own end.

Consequently the actions and movements of lower agents must tend toward the end of the first agent. Thus, in an army the actions of all the subordinate units are directed, in the last instance, to

---

[115] Cf. chap. 102.

victory, which is the end intended by the commander-in-chief. But we showed above that the first mover and agent is God, and that His end is nothing else than His goodness.[116] Therefore all the actions and movements of all creatures exist because of the divine goodness, not, of course, in the sense that they are to cause or increase it, but in the sense that they are to acquire it in their own way by sharing to some extent in a likeness of it.

Created things attain to the divine likeness by their operations in different ways, as they also represent it in different ways conformably to their being. For each of them acts in a manner which corresponds to its being. Therefore, as all creatures in common represent the divine goodness to the extent that they exist, so by their actions they all in common attain to the divine likeness in the conservation of their being and in the communication of their being to others. For every creature endeavors, by its activity, first of all to keep itself in perfect being, so far as this is possible. In such endeavor it tends, in its own way, to an imitation of the divine permanence. Secondly, every creature strives, by its activity, to communicate its own perfect being, in its own fashion, to another; and in this it tends toward an imitation of the divine causality.

The rational creature tends, by its activity, toward the divine likeness in a special way that exceeds the capacities of all other creatures, as it also has a nobler existence as compared with other creatures. The existence of other creatures is finite, since it is hemmed in by matter, and so lacks infinity both in act and in potency. But every rational nature has infinity either in act or in potency, according to the way its intellect contains intelligibles. Thus our intellectual nature, considered in its first state, is in potency to its intelligibles. Since these are infinite, they have a

---

[116]Cf. chaps. 3, 101.

certain potential infinity. Hence the intellect is the species of species, because it has a species that is not determined to one thing alone, as is the case with a stone, but that has a capacity for all species. But the intellectual nature of God is infinite in act, for prior to every consideration it has within itself the perfection of all being, as was shown above.[117] Accordingly, intellectual creatures occupy a middle position between potency and act. By its activity, therefore, the intellectual creature tends toward the divine likeness, not only in the sense that it preserves itself in existence or that it multiplies its existence, in a way, by communicating it; it also has as its end the possession in act of what by nature it possesses in potency. Consequently the end of the intellectual creature, to be achieved by its activity, is the complete actuation of its intellect by all the intelligibles for which it has a potency. In this respect it will become most like to God.

104
The end of the intellectual creature

A thing may be in potency in two ways: either naturally (that is, with respect to perfections that can be reduced to act by a natural agent) or else with respect to perfections that cannot be reduced to act by a natural agent but require some other agent. This is seen to take place even in corporeal beings. The boy grows up to be a man; the spermatozoon develops into an animal. This is within the power of nature. But that lumber becomes a bench or that a blind man receives sight, is not within the power of nature.

The same is the case with our minds. Our intellect has a natural potency with regard to certain intelligible objects, namely, those

[117]Cf. chaps. 18, 21.

that can be reduced to act by the agent intellect. We possess this faculty as an innate principle that enables us to understand in actuality. However, we cannot attain our ultimate end by the actuation of our intellect through the instrumentality of the agent intellect. For the function of the agent intellect consists in render-ing *actually* intelligible the phantasms that of themselves are only *potentially* intelligible. This was explained above.[118] These phan-tasms are derived from the senses. Hence the efficacy of the agent intellect in reducing our intellect to act is restricted to intelligible objects of which we can gain knowledge by way of sense percep-tion. Man's last end cannot consist in such cognition.

The reason is that once the ultimate end has been reached, natural desire ceases. But no matter how much we may advance in this kind of understanding whereby we derive knowledge from the senses, there still remains a natural desire to know other objects. For many things are quite beyond the reach of the senses. We can have but a slight knowledge of such things through information based on sense experience. We may get to know that they exist, but we cannot know what they are, for the natures of immaterial substances belong to a different genus from the natures of sensible things and excel them, we may say, beyond all proportion.

Moreover, as regards objects that fall under sense experience, there are many whose nature we cannot know with any certainty. Some of them, indeed, elude our knowledge altogether; others we can know but vaguely. Hence our natural desire for more perfect knowledge ever remains. But a natural desire cannot be in vain.

Accordingly, we reach our last end when our intellect is actu-alized by some higher agent than an agent connatural to us, that is, by an agent capable of gratifying our natural, inborn craving for

---

[118]Cf. chap. 83.

knowledge. So great is the desire for knowledge within us that, once we apprehend an effect, we wish to know its cause. Moreover, after we have gained some knowledge of the circumstances investing a thing, our desire is not satisfied until we penetrate to its essence. Therefore our natural desire for knowledge cannot come to rest within us until we know the first cause, and that not in any way, but in its very essence. This first cause is God. Consequently the ultimate end of an intellectual creature is the vision of God in His essence.

105
Knowledge of the divine essence by the created intellect

The possibility of such knowledge must be investigated. Manifestly, since our intellect knows nothing except through an intelligible species of the thing known, the species of one thing cannot disclose the essence of another thing. In proportion as the species, whereby the mind knows, is remote from the thing known, the less perfect is the knowledge that our intellect has of that thing's essence. For example, if we should know an ox by the species of an ass, we would have an imperfect knowledge of the essence of the ox, for our concept would be limited to its genus. Our knowledge would be still more defective if we were to know the ox through the medium of a stone, because then we would know it by a more remote genus. And if our knowledge were gained through the species of a thing that did not agree with the ox in any genus, we could not know the essence of the ox at all.

Previous discussion has brought out the fact that no creature is associated with God in genus.[119] Hence the essence of God cannot

---

[119]Cf. chaps. 12, 13.

be known through any created species whatever, whether sensible or intelligible. Accordingly, if God is to be known as He is, in His essence, God Himself must become the form of the intellect knowing Him and must be joined to that intellect, not indeed so as to constitute a single nature with it but in the way an intelligible species is joined to the intelligence. For God, who is His own being, is also His own truth, and truth is the form of the intellect.

Whatever receives a form, must first acquire the disposition which is requisite to the reception of that form. Our intellect is not equipped by its nature with the ultimate disposition looking to that form which is truth; otherwise it would be in possession of truth from the beginning. Consequently, when it does finally attain to truth, it must be elevated by some disposition newly conferred on it. And this we call the light of glory, whereby our intellect is perfected by God, who alone by His very nature has this form properly as His own. In somewhat the same way the disposition which heat has for the form of fire can come from fire alone. This is the light that is spoken of in Psalm 35:10: "In Thy light we shall see light."[120]

106
Fruition of natural desire in the Beatific Vision

Once this end is reached, natural desire must find its full fruition. The divine essence thus united to the intellect of the one who sees God, is the adequate principle for knowing everything, and is the source of all good, so that nothing can remain to be desired. This, too, is the most perfect way of attaining likeness with God: to know God in the way He knows Himself, by His own essence.

[120]Revised Standard Version (RSV): Ps. 36:9.

Of course, we shall never comprehend Him as He comprehends Himself. This does not mean that we shall be unaware of some part of Him, for He has no parts. It means that we shall not know Him as perfectly as He can be known, since the capacity of our intellect for knowing cannot equal His truth and so cannot exhaust His knowability.

God's knowability or truth is infinite, whereas our intellect is finite. But His intellect is infinite, just as His truth is; and so He alone knows Himself to the full extent that He is knowable; just as a person comprehends a demonstrable conclusion if he knows it through demonstration but not if he knows it only in an imperfect way, on merely probable grounds.

This ultimate end of man we call *beatitude*. For a man's happiness or beatitude consists in the vision whereby he sees God in His essence. Of course, man is far below God in the perfection of his beatitude. For God has this beatitude by His very nature, whereas man attains beatitude by being admitted to a share in the divine light, as we said in the previous chapter.

107
Beatitude is essentially in the act of the intellect

We should note that since advance from potency to act is motion, or at least is similar to motion, the process of arriving at beatitude has points of resemblance with natural motion or change. In natural motion we may consider, first, a certain property whereby the mobile object has a proportion to such and such an end, or is inclined in its direction. We observe this, for instance, in the Earth's gravity with respect to whatever is borne downward. No object would move naturally toward a definite end unless it had a proportion to that end. We may consider, secondly, the motion itself toward its end; thirdly, the form or place toward which there is motion; and fourthly, the repose in the form educed or in the place reached.

Similarly, with regard to intellectual movement toward an end, there is, first, the love inclining toward the end; secondly, the desire which is a sort of motion toward the end, and the actions issuing from such desire; thirdly, the form which the intellect receives; and fourthly, the resulting delight, which is nothing else than the repose of the will in the end as reached.

In the same way, the end of natural generation is a form and the end of local motion is a place. However, repose in a form or a place is not the end, but follows upon the attainment of the end; and much less does the end consist in motion or in proportion to the end. Likewise the ultimate end of an intellectual creature is the direct vision of God, but not delight in God. Such delight accompanies attainment of the end and, as it were, perfects it. Much less can desire or love be the ultimate end, because they are present even before the end is reached.

Good and Evil

108
The error of placing happiness in creatures

Clearly, therefore, they are in error who seek happiness in various things outside of God. Some look for happiness in carnal pleasures, which are shared even by brute animals. Others seek happiness in wealth, which is rightly directed to the sustenance of those who have such possessions; this is an end common to every created being.

Others place their happiness in power, which is ordained to the communication of one's own perfection to others; this, too, we said,[121] is common to all beings. Yet others seek happiness in honors or reputation, which are due to a person because of the end he has already reached or because of the noble dispositions which equip him to reach an end. Finally, happiness does not consist in the knowledge of any created things whatever, even though they may be far above man; for man's desire comes to rest in the knowledge of God alone.

[121] Cf. chap. 103.

109

The essential goodness of God; the participated goodness of creatures

All this brings to light the different relationship that God and creatures have to goodness. We may examine this difference from the standpoint of the two kinds of goodness discerned in creatures. Since the good has the nature of perfection and of end, the twofold perfection and end of the creature disclose its twofold goodness. A certain perfection is observed in the creature inasmuch as it persists in its nature. This perfection is the end of its generation or formation. The creature has a further perfection which it reaches by its motion or activity. This perfection is the end of its movement or operation.

In both kinds of perfection the creature falls short of the divine goodness. The form and existence of a thing are its good and perfection when considered from the standpoint of the thing's nature. But a composite substance is neither its own form nor its own existence; and a simple substance, although it is its own form, is not its own existence. God, however, is His own essence and His own existence, as was shown above.[122]

Likewise, all creatures receive their perfect goodness from an end extrinsic to them. For the perfection of goodness consists in attainment of the ultimate end. But the ultimate end of any creature is outside the creature. This end is the divine goodness, which is not ordained to any ulterior end. Consequently God is His own goodness in every way and is essentially good. This cannot be said of simple creatures, because they are not their own existence and also because they are ordained to something external as to their ultimate end. As for composite substances, clearly they are

---

[122]Cf. chaps. 10, 11.

not their own goodness in any way. Hence God alone is His own goodness and He alone is essentially good. All other beings are said to be good according as they participate, to some extent, in Him.

110
God's goodness is incapable of being lost

The foregoing account clearly shows that God cannot in any way be deficient in goodness. For what is essential to a being cannot be lacking. Animality, for instance, cannot be dissociated from man. Hence it is impossible for God not to be good. We can use a more appropriate example to illustrate this: as it is impossible for a man not to be a man, so it is impossible for God not to be perfectly good.

111
Insecurity of the creature's goodness

Let us consider how goodness may be wanting in creatures. In two respects goodness is clearly inseparable from the creature: first, goodness pertains to the creature's very essence; secondly, the creature's goodness is something determinate.

As regards the first point, the goodness which is the form of simple substances is inseparable from them, since they are essentially forms. As regards the second point, such substances cannot lose the good which is existence. For form is not like matter, which is indifferent to existence and non-existence. On the contrary, form goes with existence, even though it is not existence itself.

Therefore simple substances cannot lose the good of nature wherein they subsist, but are immutably established in such good. But composite substances, which are neither their own forms nor their own existence, possess the good of nature in such a way that they can lose it. This is not true, however, of those things whose matter is not in potency to various forms or not in potency to being and non-being. Such is the case with heavenly bodies.

112

Defectibility of the creature's goodness in activity

The goodness of a creature may also be regarded otherwise than as the creature's subsistence in its nature; for the perfection of its goodness is realized in its destiny to its end. And since creatures are to attain their end by their activity, we have still to inquire how creatures may be lacking in goodness from the point of view of their actions, whereby they are destined to attain their end.

In this connection we should first note that a judgment concerning natural operations is equivalent to a judgment concerning the nature which is the principle of these operations. Therefore in beings whose nature cannot suffer defect, no defect in natural operations can develop; but in beings whose nature can admit of defect, a defect in activity can occur.

Thus in incorruptible substances (incorporeal or corporeal) no defect in natural activity can take place. Thus angels forever retain their natural power of exercising their proper activity. Likewise the movements of heavenly bodies never leave their appointed orbits. But in lower bodies many defects in natural activity result from the corruptions and defects incidental to their natures. Thus from a defect in some natural principle come the sterility of plants, monstrosities in the generation of animals, and other such disorders.

113

The twofold principle of activity and the possibility of defect therein

There are certain actions whose principle is not nature but the will. The object of the will is the good, which consists primarily in the end and secondarily in whatever leads to the end. Voluntary action is related to the good as natural action is related to the form by which a thing acts. Consequently, just as a defect in natural activity cannot ensue in things that do not admit of defect in their forms, but can occur only in corruptible things whose forms are defectible, so voluntary actions can be deficient only in beings whose will can deflect from their proper end. Hence, if the will cannot deflect from its proper end, deficiency in voluntary action is clearly impossible.

The will cannot be deficient with regard to the good which is the very nature of the being that wills; for every being seeks in its own way its perfection, which is each one's good. But as regards an external good the will can be deficient, by resting content with a good connatural to it. Therefore if the nature of the being that wills is the ultimate end of its will, no deficiency in voluntary action can arise.

Such is the case with God alone. For His goodness, which is the ultimate end of things, is His very nature. But the nature of other beings endowed with will is not the ultimate end of their will. Hence a defect in voluntary action can occur in them, if their will remains fixed on their own good and does not push on to the supreme good, which is the last end. Therefore in all created intellectual substances a deficiency in voluntary action is possible.

114
The meaning of good and evil in things

A question worthy of consideration arises at this point. As the term *good* signifies "perfect being," so the term *evil* signifies nothing else than "privation of perfect being." In its proper acceptance, privation is predicated of that which is fitted by its nature to be possessed, and to be possessed at a certain time and in a certain manner. Evidently, therefore, a thing is called evil if it lacks a perfection it ought to have. Thus if a man lacks the sense of sight, this is an evil for him. But the same lack is not an evil for a stone, for the stone is not equipped by nature to have the faculty of sight.

115

Impossibility of an evil nature

Evil cannot be a nature. Every nature is either act or potency or a composite of the two. Whatever is act, is a perfection and is good in its very concept. And what is in potency has a natural appetite for the reception of act. But what all beings desire is good. Therefore, too, what is composed of act and potency participates in goodness to the extent that it participates in act. And potency possesses goodness inasmuch as it is ordained to act. An indication of this is the fact that potency is esteemed in proportion to its capacity for act and perfection. Thus, no nature is of itself an evil.

Likewise, every being achieves its fulfillment according as it is realized in act, for act is the perfection of a thing. However, neither of a pair of opposites achieves fulfillment by being mixed with the other, but is rather destroyed or weakened thereby. Therefore evil does not realize its full capacity by sharing in good. But every nature realizes its full capacity by having existence in act; and so, since to be good is the object of every being's natural tendency, a nature achieves fulfillment by participating in good. Accordingly, no nature is an evil.

Moreover, any nature whatever desires the preservation of its being and shuns destruction to the full extent of its power. Consequently, since good is that which all desire, and evil, on the contrary, is that which all shun, we must conclude that for any nature existence is in itself good, and non-existence is evil. To be evil, however, is not good; in fact, not to be evil is included in the notion of good. Therefore no nature is an evil.

116
Good and evil as specific differences and as contraries

We have next to inquire how good and evil may be regarded as contraries, genera of contraries, and differences constituting species of a sort (namely, moral habits). Each member of a pair of contraries is some kind of nature. For non-being can be neither genus nor specific difference, since genus is predicated of a thing according to *what* it is (*in eo quod quid*) and difference according to *what sort* of thing it is (*in eo quod quale quid*).

We must note that, as physical entities receive their species from their form, so moral entities receive their species from the end which is the object of the will and on which all morality depends. In physical entities, moreover, the presence of one form entails the privation of another, as, for instance, the form of fire entails the privation of the form of air. In moral entities, similarly, one end involves the privation of another end. Since the privation of a due perfection is an evil in physical entities, the reception of a form which implies the privation of the form that ought to be possessed, is an evil — not, indeed, because of the form itself — but because of the privation its presence involves. In this sense, to be on fire is an evil for a log of wood.

In the field of morality, likewise, the pursuit of an end that entails the privation of the right end is an evil, not on account of the end itself but because of the privation necessarily implied. In this way two moral actions directed to contrary ends differ as good and evil. Thus the corresponding contrary habits differ in good and evil as by specific differences and as being contrary to each other. This is so not because of the privation from which evil receives its designation, but because of the end which involves the privation.

This is the sense in which some philosophers have understood Aristotle's assertion that good and evil are actually genera of contraries[123] (namely, of moral contraries). But if we closely examine the matter, we shall find that in the sphere of morals, good and evil are differences rather than species. Hence it seems better to say that good and evil are called *genera* according to the opinion of Pythagoras, who reduced everything to good and evil as to supreme genera.[124] This position does, indeed, contain some truth, in the sense that in all contraries one member is perfect, whereas the other is deficient. This is clear in the case of white and black, sweet and bitter, and so on. But invariably, what is perfect pertains to good and what is deficient pertains to evil.

117
Impossibility of essential or supreme evil

Knowing that evil is the privation of a due perfection, we can easily understand how evil corrupts good; this it does to the extent that it is the privation of good. Thus blindness is said to corrupt sight because it is the privation of sight. However, evil does not completely corrupt good, because, as we remarked above,[125] not only form, but also potency to form, is good; and potency is the subject of privation as well as of form. Therefore the subject of evil must be good, not in the sense that it is opposed to evil but in the sense that it is a potency for the reception of evil. This brings out the fact that not every good can be the subject of evil, but only such a good as is in potency with respect to some perfection of which it can be deprived. Hence in beings which are exclusively act or in which act cannot be separated from potency, there can, to this extent, be no evil.

---

[123]*Categories*, XI (14 a 25).
[124]Cf. Aristotle, *Metaph.*, I, 5 (986 a 26).
[125]Cf. chap. 115.

As a result, nothing can be essentially evil since evil must always have as its foundation some subject, distinct from it, that is good. And so there cannot be a being that is supremely evil in the way that there is a being that is supremely good (because it is essentially good).

Further, we see that evil cannot be the object of desire and that it cannot act except in virtue of the good connected with it. For only perfection and end are desirable; and the principle of action is form. However, since a particular perfection or form involves the privation of some other perfection or form, it can happen incidentally that privation or evil may be desired and may be the principle of some action — not precisely because of the evil, but because of the good connected with it. An example of what I mean by *incidentally* is the musician who constructs a house, not in his capacity of musician, but in the capacity of being also a builder.

From this we may also infer that evil cannot be a first principle, for a principle *per accidens* is subsequent to a principle that is such *per se*.

118
Foundation of evil in good as its substratum

Some may feel impelled to lodge a difficulty against this presentation: good cannot be the substratum of evil, for one of a pair of opposites cannot be the substratum of the other, nor do extremes ever exist together in other kinds of opposition. But let such quibblers reflect that other kinds of opposition belong to some definite genus, whereas good and evil are common to all genera. Every being, as such, is good; and every privation, as such, is evil. The substratum of a privation must be a being, hence good. But the subject of a privation need not be white or sweet or endowed with sight, because none of these predicates belongs to being as such. And so black is not in white, nor blindness in the person who sees; but evil is in good, just as blindness is in the sense that is the subject of sight. The reason why the subject of sight, in the case of a blind man, is not called *seeing*, is that seeing is not a predicate common to every being.

119
Two kinds of evil

Since evil is privation and defect, and since defect, as is clear from what we said above,[126] can occur in a thing both as regarded in its nature and as regarded in its relation to an end by its action, we may speak of evil in both senses: that is, by reason of a defect in the thing itself (thus blindness is a certain evil in an animal), and by reason of a defect in a creature's action (thus lameness connotes action with a defect). Evil in an action that is directed to an end in such a way that it is not rightly related to the end, is called fault (*peccatum*) both in voluntary agents and in natural agents. A physician is faulty (*peccat*) in his action, when he does not proceed in such a way as to procure health. Nature, too, is faulty in its activity when it fails to advance a generated being to its proper disposition and form; this is why monsters occur in nature.

120
Three kinds of action, and the evil of sin

We should observe that sometimes action is in the power of the agent. Such are all voluntary actions. By *voluntary action* I mean an action that has its principle in an agent who is conscious of the

---

[126]Cf. chaps. 111, 112.

various factors constituting his action. Sometimes actions are *not* voluntary. In this class are violent actions (whose principle is outside the agent), natural actions, and actions performed in ignorance. These do not proceed from a conscious principle. If a defect occurs in non-voluntary actions that are directed to an end, it is called simply a fault (*peccatum*). But if such a defect occurs in voluntary actions, it is called not only fault, but sin (*culpa*). For in this case the voluntary agent, being master of his own action, deservedly draws blame and punishment on himself. If actions are mixed, that is, are partly voluntary and partly involuntary, the sin is diminished in proportion to the admixture of the voluntary element.

Since natural action follows the nature of a being, a fault in natural activity clearly cannot occur in incorruptible things, for their nature is incapable of change. But the will of an intellectual creature can suffer defect in voluntary action, as has been shown above.[127] Consequently freedom from evil in nature is common to all incorruptible things. But freedom from the evil of sin in virtue of natural necessity — of which rational nature alone is capable — is found to be an exclusive property of God.

121
The evil of punishment

Just as defect in voluntary action constitutes fault and sin, so the withdrawing of some good, in consequence of sin, against the will of him on whom such privation is inflicted, has the character of punishment. Punishment is inflicted as a medicine that is corrective of the sin and also to restore right order violated by the sin.

---

[127]Cf. chap. 113.

Punishment functions as a medicine inasmuch as fear of punishment deters a man from sinning; that is, a person refrains from performing an inordinate action, which would be pleasing to his will, lest he have to suffer what is opposed to his will. Punishment also restores right order. By sinning, a man exceeds the limits of the natural order, indulging his will more than is right. Hence a return to the order of justice is effected by punishment, whereby some good is withdrawn from the sinner's will. As is quite clear, a suitable punishment is not assigned for the sin unless the punishment is more galling to the will than the sin was attractive to it.

122
Punishment variously opposed to the will

Not all punishment is opposed to the will in the same way. Some punishments are opposed to what man actually wills; and this kind of punishment is felt most keenly. Some punishments are opposed not to the actual but to the habitual tendency of the will, as when a person is deprived of something (for instance, his son or his property) without his knowledge. In this case, nothing actually thwarts his will; but the withdrawal of the good would be against his will if he were aware of what was happening. At times a punishment is opposed to the will according to the very nature of that faculty. For the will is naturally turned to what is good. Thus if a person is lacking in a virtue, this need not always be opposed to his actual will, for he may, perhaps, despise this virtue; nor need it be against his habitual will, for he may, perhaps, have a habitual disposition of will toward what is contrary to the virtue. Nevertheless such a privation is opposed to the natural rectitude of the will, whereby man naturally desires virtue.

Consequently, as is evident, the degrees of punishment may be measured by two standards: first, by the quantity of the good of which a man is deprived for his punishment; secondly, by the greater or less opposition it arouses in the will. For withdrawal of a greater good is more opposed to the will than withdrawal of a lesser good.

Divine Providence

123
The universality of Divine Providence

We can see from the foregoing that all things are governed by Divine Providence. Whatever is set in motion toward the end intended by any agent is directed by that agent to the end. Thus all the soldiers in an army are subordinated to the end intended by the commander (which is victory) and are directed by him to that end. We showed above that all things tend by their actions to the divine goodness as their end.[128] Hence all things are directed to this end by God Himself, to whom this end pertains. To be thus directed is the same as to be ruled and governed by Providence. Therefore all things are ruled by Divine Providence.

Moreover, things that are subject to failure and that do not always remain constant, are found to be under the direction of beings that do remain constant. Thus all the movements of lower bodies, being defectible, are regulated in accordance with the undeviating movement of a heavenly body. But all creatures are

[128]Cf. chap. 103.

135

changeable and defectible. As regards intellectual creatures, their very nature is such that deficiency in voluntary action can develop in them. Other creatures have some part in movement, either by way of generation and corruption, or at least according to place. God Himself is the only being in whom no defect can arise. Consequently all creatures are kept in order by Him.

Furthermore, whatever has existence by way of participation is traced back, as to its cause, to that which exists in virtue of its own essence. For example, what is on fire has, in some way or other, fire as the cause that ignited it. Since God alone is good by His very essence and all other things receive their complement of goodness by some sort of participation, all beings must be brought to their complement of goodness by God. This, again, involves rule and government; for things are governed or ruled by being established in the order of good. So all things are governed and ruled by God.

124
God's plan of ruling lower creatures by higher creatures

We can see from this that lower creatures are ruled by God through the agency of higher creatures. Some creatures are said to be higher because they are more perfect in goodness. Creatures receive their order of good from God inasmuch as they are under His rule. Consequently higher creatures have a greater share in the order of divine government than lower creatures. But what has a greater share in any perfection is related to what has a smaller share in that perfection, as act is related to potency, and agent to patient. Therefore higher creatures are related to lower creatures in the order of Divine Providence as agent is related to patient. Accordingly, lower creatures are governed by higher creatures.

Divine goodness has this characteristic, that it communicates a likeness of itself to creatures. This is the sense in which God is said to have made all things for the sake of His goodness, as is clear from a previous chapter.[129] The perfection of divine goodness entails the double truth that God is good in Himself and that He leads other beings to goodness. He communicates goodness to creatures under both aspects: they are good in themselves and some lead others to goodness. In this way God brings some creatures to goodness through other creatures. The latter must be higher creatures, for what receives a likeness of both form and action from some agent is more perfect than what receives a likeness of form but not of action. Thus the moon, which not only glows with light but also illuminates other bodies, receives light from the sun more perfectly than do opaque bodies, which are merely illuminated but do not illuminate. Accordingly, God governs lower creatures by higher creatures.

Likewise, the good of many is better than the good of an individual, and so is more representative of divine goodness, which is the good of the whole universe. If a higher creature, which receives more abundant goodness from God did not cooperate in procuring the good of lower creatures, that abundance of goodness would be confined to one individual. But it becomes common to many by the fact that the more richly endowed creature cooperates in procuring the good of many. Hence the divine goodness requires that God should rule lower creatures by higher creatures.

125

The government of lower intellectual substances by higher ones

Since intellectual creatures excel other creatures, as is clear from what we said earlier,[130] we can readily understand that God governs

---

[129] Cf. chap. 101.
[130] Cf. chap. 75.

all other creatures through the agency of intellectual creatures. Likewise, since some intellectual creatures excel others, God rules the lower through the higher. Accordingly, men — who occupy the lowest place in the order of nature among intellectual substances — are governed by the higher spirits. These are called *angels* (that is, "messengers") because they announce divine messages to men. Among angels, too, the lower are directed by the higher. For they are distributed among various hierarchies or sacred principalities; and each hierarchy is divided into different orders.

126
Rank and order of the angels

Since every action of an intellectual substance, as such, proceeds from the intellect, diversity of operation, of prelature, and of order among intellectual substances follows diversity in their manner of understanding. In proportion to its eminence or dignity, the intellect can contemplate the natures of effects in their higher and more universal cause. Also, as we remarked above, the intelligible species of a higher intellect are more universal.[131]

The first way of understanding suitable to intellectual substances is the knowledge imparted to them of effects, and hence of their own works, in the first cause itself, namely in God; for it is through them that God carries out lower effects. This knowledge is proper to the first hierarchy, which is divided into orders corresponding to the three characteristics discerned in any operative art. The first of these is the end from which the exemplars of the works are derived; the second is the exemplars of the works as existing in the mind of the artificer; the third is the application of

---

[131]Cf. chap. 78.

the work to the effects. Consequently the first order has the privilege of being instructed about the effects of things in the supreme Good itself, regarded as the last end. For this reason angels of the first order are called *seraphim*, as though they were aflame or on fire, with reference to the fire of love; for the object of love is the good. The second order has the function of contemplating God's effects in their intelligible exemplars as they exist in God. Hence angels of this order are called *cherubim*, from the fullness of their knowledge. The third order has the office of meditating, in God Himself, how creatures share in intelligible exemplars as adapted to effects. And so angels of this order are called *thrones*, from the fact that God resides in them.

The second way of understanding is to consider the exemplars of effects as they exist in universal causes. This is suitable to the second hierarchy, which is divided into three orders which correspond to the three characteristics that pertain to universal causes, especially such as operate under the guidance of the intellect.

The first of these characteristics is to plan beforehand what is to be done. Thus, among artificers the highest arts are directive, and are called *architectonic*. From this fact angels belonging to the first order of this hierarchy are known as *dominations*; for direction and planning are functions of a master or *dominus*.

The second characteristic observed in universal causes is the initiating of action for an undertaking, with authority to oversee its execution. Therefore, angels belonging to the second order of this hierarchy are called *principalities* (according to Gregory[132]) or *virtues* (according to Dionysius[133]), understanding *virtues* in the sense that to take the initiative in action is virtuosity in a high degree.

---

[132] St. Gregory the Great, *In evangelia*, II, hom. xxxiv, 7 (PL, LXXVI, 1249).
[133] Pseudo-Dionysius, *De coelesti hierarchia*, VIII, 1 (PG, III, 240).

The third characteristic discerned in universal causes is the removal of obstacles to execution. And so the third order of this hierarchy is that of the *powers*, whose office is to constrain whatever could impede the execution of the divine command; hence, also, the powers are said to hold demons in check.

The third way of understanding is to contemplate the exemplars of effects in the effects themselves. And this is proper to the third hierarchy, which is placed in immediate charge of us, who obtain knowledge of effects from effects themselves. This hierarchy, too, has three orders. The lowest of these is that of the *angels*, who are so called because they announce to men details that pertain to their government; hence they are also called *guardians of men*. Above this order is that of the *archangels*. The office of this order is to announce to men matters that transcend reason, such as the mysteries of Faith.

The highest order of this hierarchy is said by Gregory to be that of the *virtues*,[134] for the reason that they perform deeds beyond the power of nature, in proof of the messages, transcending reason, that they announce to us. Consequently the working of miracles is said to pertain to the virtues.[135] According to Dionysius, however, the highest order of this hierarchy is that of the *principalities*;[136] in his reckoning we are to understand that the princes are they who have charge over individual peoples, while the angels have charge over individual men and the archangels announce to individual men those affairs that pertain to the salvation of all.[137]

Since a lower power acts in virtue of a higher power, a lower order performs actions proper to a higher order by acting in virtue

[134]Gregory, *loc. cit.*

[135]Ibid., 10 (*PL*, LXXVI, 1251).

[136]Pseudo-Dionysius, *op. cit.*, IX, 1 (*PG*, III, 257).

[137]Ibid., 2 (*PG*, III, 257f.).

of that higher power. But the higher orders possess in a more eminent way whatever is proper to the lower orders. Thus all things are in a certain sense common to the various orders. However, they receive their proper names from properties that are characteristic of each order. Nevertheless the lowest order of all retains the common name of angels for itself, for the reason that it acts, as it were, in virtue of all the rest. Furthermore, since the higher naturally influences the lower, and since intellectual action consists in instructing or teaching, the higher angels, in instructing the lower angels, are said to purify, illuminate, and perfect them.

Higher angels purify the lower angels by removing what is wanting to their knowledge. They illuminate them by fortifying the intellects of the lower angels with their own light, thus enabling them to comprehend higher objects. And higher angels perfect lower angels by guiding them to the perfection of higher knowledge. These three operations pertain to the acquisition of knowledge, as Dionysius remarks.[138]

This inequality does not prevent all the angels, even the lowest, from seeing the divine essence. Even though each of the blessed spirits sees God in His essence, some may behold Him more perfectly than others. This should be clear from a previous chapter.[139] However, the more perfectly a cause is known, the more numerous are the effects discerned in it. The divine effects which the higher angels perceive in God more clearly than the other angels, constitute the subject matter in which they instruct the lower angels. But higher angels do not instruct lower angels concerning the divine essence, which they all perceive directly.

---

[138] Ibid., VII, 3 (PG, III, 209).
[139] Cf. chap. 106.

127
Control of lower bodies (but not man's intellect) by higher bodies

Among intellectual substances, therefore, some are divinely governed by others, that is, the lower by the higher. Similarly, lower bodies are controlled, in God's plan, by higher bodies. Hence every movement of lower bodies is caused by the movements of heavenly bodies. Lower bodies acquire forms and species from the influence thus exercised by heavenly bodies, just as the intelligible exemplars of things descend to lower spirits through higher spirits.

However, since an intellectual substance is superior to all bodies in the hierarchy of beings, the order of Providence has suitably disposed matters in such a way that no intellectual substance is ruled by God through a corporeal substance. Accordingly, since the human soul is an intellectual substance, it cannot, so far as it is endowed with intelligence and will, be subject to the movements of heavenly bodies. Heavenly bodies cannot directly act upon or influence either the human intellect or the human will.

Again, no body acts except by movement. Hence whatever is acted upon by a body is moved by it. But the human soul, regarded as intellectual (according as it is the principle of the will) cannot be moved by bodily movement, since the intellect is not the act of any bodily organ. So the human soul cannot be subject, in its intellect or will, to any influence emanating from heavenly bodies.

Furthermore, impressions left in lower bodies from the impact of heavenly bodies are natural. Therefore, if the operations of the intellect and will resulted from the impression made by heavenly bodies, they would proceed from natural instinct. And so man would not differ in his activity from other animals, which are moved to their actions by natural instinct. And thus free will and deliberation and choice and all perfections of this sort, which distinguish man from other animals, would perish.

128
Indirect influence of heavenly bodies on the human intellect

Nevertheless we should not lose sight of the fact that the human intellect is indebted to the sense powers for the origin of its knowledge. This is why intellectual knowledge is thrown into confusion when the soul's faculties of phantasm, imagination, or memory are impaired.

On the other hand, when these powers are in good order, intellectual apprehension grows more efficient. Likewise, a modification in the sensitive appetite tends to bring about a change in the will (which is a rational appetite), as we know from the fact that the object of the will is the good as apprehended. According as we are variously disposed in the matter of concupiscence, anger, fear, and other passions, a thing will at different times appear to us as good or evil.

On the other hand, all the powers of the sensitive part of our soul, whether they are apprehensive or appetitive, are the acts of certain bodily organs. If these undergo modification, the faculties themselves must, indirectly, undergo some change. Therefore, since change in lower bodies is influenced by the movement of the heavens, the operations of the sensitive faculties are also subject to such movement, although only *per accidens*. And thus heavenly movement has some indirect influence on the activity of the human intellect and will, so far as the will may be inclined this way or that by the passions.

Nevertheless, since the will is not subject to the passions in such a way as necessarily to follow their enticement, but on the contrary has it in its power to repress passion by the judgment of reason, the human will is not subject to impressions emanating from heavenly bodies. It retains free judgment either to follow or to resist their attractions, as may seem to it expedient. Only the wise act thus; the masses follow the lead of bodily passions and urgings, for they are wanting in wisdom and virtue.

129
Movement of man's will by God

Everything that is changeable and multiform is traced back, as to its cause, to some first principle that is immobile and is one. Since man's intellect and will are clearly changeable and multiform, they must be reduced to some higher cause that is immobile and uniform. The heavenly bodies are not the cause to which they are reduced, as we have shown;[140] therefore, they must be reduced to yet higher causes.

In this matter the case of the intellect differs from that of the will. The act of the intellect is brought about by the presence of the things understood in the intellect; but the act of the will is accounted for by the inclination of the will toward the things willed. Thus the intellect is adapted by its nature to be perfected by something external that is related to it as act to potency. Hence man can be aided to elicit an act of the intellect by anything external that is more perfect in intelligible being: not only by God but also by an angel or even by a man who is better informed (but differently in each instance). A man is helped to understand by a man when one of them proposes to the other an intelligible object not previously contemplated, but not in such a way that the light of the intellect of one man is perfected by the other because each of these natural lights is in one and the same species.

But the natural light of an angel is by nature of a higher excellence than the natural light of man. So an angel can aid a

[140]Cf. chap. 127.

man to understand, not only on the part of the object proposed to him by the angel, but also on the part of the light that is strengthened by the angel's light. However, man's natural light does not come from an angel, for the nature of the rational soul, which receives existence through creation, is produced by God alone.

God helps man to understand, not only on the part of the object proposed by God to man or by an increase of light, but also by the very fact that man's natural light, which is what makes him intellectual, is from God. Moreover, God Himself is the first truth from which all other truth has its certitude, just as secondary propositions in demonstrative sciences derive their certitude from primary propositions. For this reason nothing can become certain for the intellect except through God's influence, just as conclusions do not achieve certitude in science except in virtue of primary principles.

With regard to the will, its act is a certain impulse flowing from the interior to the exterior, and has much in common with natural tendencies. Accordingly, as natural tendencies are placed in natural things exclusively by the cause of their nature, the act of the will is from God alone, for He alone is the cause of a rational nature endowed with will. Therefore, if God moves man's will, this is evidently not opposed to freedom of choice, just as God's activity in natural things is not contrary to their nature. Both the natural inclination and the voluntary inclination are from God; each of them issues in action according to the condition of the thing to which it pertains. God moves things in a way that is consonant with their nature.

This exposition brings out the fact that heavenly bodies can exert an influence on the human body and on its bodily powers, as they can in the case of other bodies. But they cannot do the same with regard to the intellect, although an intellectual creature can. And God alone can touch the will.

130
Government of the world by God

Second causes do not act except through the power of the first cause; thus instruments operate under the direction of art. Consequently all the agents through which God carries out the order of His government can act only through the power of God Himself. The action of any of them is caused by God, just as the movement of a mobile object is caused by the motion of the mover. In such event the mover and the movement must be simultaneous. Hence God must be inwardly present to any agent as acting therein whenever He moves the agent to act.

Another point: not only the action of secondary agents but their very existence is caused by God, as was shown above.[141] However, we are not to suppose that the existence of things is caused by God in the same way as the existence of a house is caused by its builder. When the builder departs, the house still remains standing. For the builder causes the existence of the house only in the sense that he works for the existence of the house as a house. Such activity is, indeed, the constructing of the house, and thus the builder is directly the cause of the becoming of the house, a process that ceases when he desists from his labors. But God is directly, by Himself, the cause of very existence, and communicates existence to all things just as the sun communicates light to the air and to whatever else is illuminated by the sun. The continuous shining of the sun is required for the preservation of light in the air; similarly God must unceasingly confer existence on things if they are to persevere in existence. Thus all things are related to God as an object made is to its maker, and this not only

---

[141]Cf. chap. 68.

so far as they begin to exist, but so far as they continue to exist. But a maker and the object made must be simultaneous, just as in the case of a mover and the object moved. Hence God is necessarily present to all things to the extent that they have existence. But existence is that which is the most intimately present in all things. Therefore God must be in all things.

Moreover, whoever, through the agency of intermediate causes, carries out the order he has foreseen, must know and arrange the effects of these intermediate causes. Otherwise the effects would occur outside the order he has foreseen. The prearranged plan of a governor is more perfect in proportion as his knowledge and design descend to details. For if any detail escapes the advertence of the governor, the disposition of that detail will elude his foresight. We showed above that all things are necessarily subject to Divine Providence;[142] and Divine Providence must evidently be most perfect, because whatever is predicated of God must befit Him in the highest possible degree. Consequently the ordinations of His Providence must extend to the most minute effects.

131
Immediate disposing of all things by God

In the light of the foregoing, it is clear that, although God's government of things is effected through the agency of secondary causes, as far as the carrying out of His Providence is concerned, yet the plan itself or ordination of Divine Providence extends directly to all details. In arranging all matters from first to last, God does not turn over to others the disposal of the final particulars. Men act thus because of the limitations of their knowledge, which

[142]Cf. chap. 123.

147

cannot at any one time take in many items. This is why higher rulers personally take charge of great concerns, and entrust the management of unimportant affairs to others. But God can take cognizance of a multitude of things simultaneously, as was indicated above.[143] Hence the fact that He attends to the slightest details does not keep Him from organizing the weightiest matters.

132
Objections to God's particular Providence

Some may think that details are not regulated by God. For no one disposes anything in his planning unless he has knowledge thereof. But knowledge of particulars may well seem to be lacking in God, for the reason that particulars are known, not by the intellect, but by the senses. God, who is wholly incorporeal, can have no sense knowledge, but only intellectual knowledge. Consequently details may seem to lie outside the scope of Divine Providence.

Moreover, details are infinite and knowledge of infinity is impossible, since the infinite as such is unknown. Therefore details seemingly escape the divine knowledge and Providence.

Again, many particulars are contingent. But certain knowledge of such objects is out of the question. Accordingly, since God's knowledge must be absolutely certain, it seems that details are not known or regulated by God.

Besides, particulars do not all exist simultaneously, for some things decay only to have others take their place. But there can be no knowledge of non-existent things. Hence, if God has knowledge of details, there must be some things which He begins and ceases to know, and this involves the further consequence that He

---

[143] Cf. chap. 29.

is mutable. Apparently, therefore, He does not know and dispose particulars.

133
Solution of the foregoing objections

These objections are easily answered if we but penetrate to the truth of the matter. God knows Himself perfectly, and therefore He must have knowledge of all that exists in Himself in any manner whatever. Since every essence and power of created being is from Him, and since whatever comes from anyone exists virtually in him, we necessarily conclude that in knowing Himself He knows the essence of created being and whatever is virtually contained in the latter. And thus He knows all particulars that are virtually in Himself and in all His other causes.

The knowledge possessed by the divine intellect is not like our knowledge, as the first objection urged. Our intellect derives its knowledge of things through the species it abstracts, and these are the likenesses of forms and not of matter or of material dispositions, which are principles of individuation. Therefore our intellect cannot know particulars, but only universals. But the divine intellect knows things through its own essence, in which, as in the first principle of being, is virtually contained not only form, but matter. And so God knows not only universals but also particulars.

Likewise God is able to know an infinite number of objects, even though our intellect cannot know the infinite. Indeed, our intellect cannot actually contemplate many things at the same time. Hence, if it knew an infinite number of objects, it would have to review them one after another as it contemplated them, which is contrary to the very notion of infinity. However, our intellect can know infinity virtually and potentially; for example, it can know all the species of numbers or of proportions, seeing that it possesses an adequate principle for knowing all things. But God can know many things simultaneously, as was noted above;[144] and that whereby He knows all things (namely, His essence) is an adequate principle for knowing not only *all that is*, but *all that can be*. Therefore, as our intellect potentially and virtually knows those infinite objects for which it has a principle of cognition, so God actually contemplates all infinities.

Furthermore, although corporeal and temporal particulars do not exist simultaneously, God surely has simultaneous knowledge of them. For He knows them according to His manner of being, which is eternal and without succession. Consequently, as He knows material things in an immaterial way and many things in unity, so in a single glance He beholds objects that do not exist at the same time. And so His knowledge of particulars does not involve the consequence that anything is added to, or subtracted from, His cognition.

This also makes it clear that He has certain knowledge of contingent things. Even before they come into being, He sees them as they actually exist (and not merely as they will be in the future and as virtually present in their causes, in the way we are able to know some future things). Contingent things, regarded as virtually present in their causes with a claim to future existence, are not sufficiently determinate to admit of certain knowledge about them; but, regarded as actually possessing existence, they are determinate, and hence certain knowledge of them is possible. Thus we can know with the certitude of ocular vision that Socrates is sitting while he is seated. With like certitude God knows, in His eternity, all that takes place throughout the whole course of time. For His eternity is in present contact with the whole course of

---

[144]Cf. chap. 29.

time, and even passes beyond time. We may fancy that God knows the flight of time in His eternity, in the way that a person standing on top of a watchtower embraces in a single glance a whole caravan of passing travelers.

134

God's detailed knowledge of contingent futures

To know contingent futures in this way, as being actually in existence (that is, to have certitude about them) is evidently restricted to God alone, of whom eternity is truly and properly predicated. For this reason, certain prediction of future events is accounted a proof of divinity. This accords with Isaiah 41:23: "Show the things that are to come hereafter, and we shall know that ye are gods." Knowledge of future events in their causes is, indeed, possible for others. Such knowledge, however, is not certain, but is rather conjectural, except as regards effects that necessarily flow from their causes. In this way a physician foretells future illnesses and a sailor predicts storms.

135

God's existence in all things by essence, power, and presence

Thus there is no reason why God should not have knowledge of individual effects or why He should not directly regulate them by Himself, even though He may carry them out through intermediate causes. However, in the very execution He is, in some fashion, in immediate touch with all effects, to the extent that all intermediate causes operate in virtue of the first cause, so that in a certain way He Himself appears to act in them all. Thus all the achievements of secondary causes can be attributed to Him, as the effect produced by a tool is ascribed to the artisan: when we say that a smith makes a knife, we are more correct than when we say that a hammer did it. God is also in immediate contact with all effects so far as He is *per se* the cause of their existence and so far as everything is kept in being by Him.

Corresponding to these three immediate modes of influence, God is said to be in everything by essence, power, and presence. He is in everything by His *essence* inasmuch as the existence of each thing is a certain participation in the divine essence; the divine essence is present to every existing thing, to the extent that it has existence, as a cause is present to its proper effect. God is in all things by His *power*, inasmuch as all things operate in virtue of Him. And God is in all things by His *presence*, inasmuch as He directly regulates and disposes all things.

136
The working of miracles proper to God alone

The entire order of secondary causes, as well as their power, comes from God. He Himself, however, produces His effects not out of necessity, but by free will, as was shown above.[145] Clearly, then, He can act outside the order of secondary causes, as when He cures those who are incurable from the standpoint of natural causality or when He does something else of this kind that is not within the sphere of natural causes but is nevertheless consonant with the order of Divine Providence. What God occasionally does in this way, independently of the order of natural causes, is designed by Him for a definite end. When effects are thus wrought by divine power outside the order of secondary causes, they are called miracles; for when we perceive an effect without knowing its cause,

---

[145]Cf. chap. 96.

our wonder is excited (*mirum est*). God is a cause that is completely hidden from us. Therefore, when some effect is wrought by Him outside the order of secondary causes known to us, it is called simply a miracle. But if an effect is produced by some other cause that is unknown to this or that person, it is not a miracle simply as such, but only with regard to him who is ignorant of the cause. Thus an event may appear marvelous to one person without seeming marvelous to another who is acquainted with its cause.

To act in this way, outside the order of secondary causes, is possible for God alone, who is the founder of this order and is not confined to it. All other beings are subject to this order; and so God alone can work miracles, as the Psalmist says: "Who alone doth wonderful things."[146] Therefore, when miracles are apparently worked by some creature, either they are not true miracles but are effects produced by the power of natural agents which may be concealed from us, as happens in the case of miracles wrought by demons with their magical arts; or else, if they are true miracles, someone obtains the power to work them by praying to God. Since such miracles are wrought exclusively by divine power, they are rightly appealed to in proof of the Faith, which has God alone as its author. For a pronouncement issued by a man with a claim to divine authority is never more fittingly attested than by works which God alone can perform.

Although such miracles occur outside the order of secondary causes, we should not simply say that they are against nature. The natural order makes provision for the subjection of the lower to the activity of the higher. Thus effects brought about in lower bodies in consequence of the influence emanating from the heavenly bodies are not said to be simply against nature (although they may

---

[146]Ps. 71:18 (RSV: Ps. 72:18).

at times be against the particular nature of this or that thing, as we observe in the movement of water in the ebb and flow of the tide, which is produced by the action of the moon). In the same way, effects produced in creatures by the action of God may seem to be against some particular order of secondary causes; yet they are in accord with the universal order of nature. Therefore miracles are not contrary to nature.

137
Fortuitous events

Although all events, even the most trifling, are disposed (as we have shown) according to God's plan,[147] there is nothing to prevent some things from happening by chance or accident. An occurrence may be accidental or fortuitous with respect to a lower cause when an effect not intended is brought about, and yet not be accidental or fortuitous with respect to a higher cause, inasmuch as the effect does not take place apart from the latter's intention. For example, a master may send two servants to the same place, but in such a way that neither is aware of the mission of the other. Their meeting is accidental so far as each servant is concerned, but not as regards the master.

So, when certain events occur apart from the intention of secondary causes, they are accidental or fortuitous with respect to those causes; and they may be said without further ado to be fortuitous, because effects are described simply in terms of their proximate causes. But if God's point of view is considered, they are not fortuitous, but foreseen.

---

[147] Cf. chaps. 130, 133.

138
Fate and its nature

This suggests what we ought to think of fate. Many effects are found to occur haphazard if they are regarded from the standpoint of secondary causes. Some thinkers are unwilling to refer such effects to a higher cause that ordains them.[148] In consequence, they must utterly reject fate. On the other hand, others have desired to trace back these seemingly accidental and fortuitous effects to a higher cause that plans them. But, failing to rise above the order of corporeal entities, they attributed such devising to the highest bodies, namely, the heavenly bodies.[149] And so they contended that fate is a force deriving from the position of the stars and that this accounts for happenings of this kind. But we showed above that the intellect and will, which are the true principles of human acts, are not in any proper sense subject to heavenly bodies.[150] Hence we cannot maintain that events which seemingly occur at random and by chance in human affairs are to be referred to heavenly bodies as to the cause that charts them.

There seems to be no place for fate except in human affairs, in which hazard has a part to play. It is only about such events that men are accustomed to inquire in their craving to know the future, and it is also about these that an answer is usually given by fortunetellers. Hence *fate* (*fatum*) is a word formed from the Latin verb *fari* ("to foretell"). To acknowledge fate thus understood is opposed to Faith. Since, however, not only natural things but also

---

[148]Cf. Cicero, *De divinatione*, II, *cap.* 5: *cap.* 10. See also St. Augustine, *De civitate Dei*, V, 9 (*PL*, XLI, 148.)

[149]According to St. Augustine, this was a view common among astrologers. See *De civitate Dei*, V, 7 (*PL*, XLI, 147).

[150]Cf. chap. 127.

human affairs are under Divine Providence, those events that seem to happen at random in men's lives must be referred to the ordination of Divine Providence. Thus, those who hold that all things are subject to Divine Providence must admit the existence of fate. Fate in this sense is related to Divine Providence as a real effect of the latter. For it is an explanation of Divine Providence as applied to things and is in agreement with the definition given by Boethius, who says that fate is a "disposition" (i.e., an unchangeable ordination) "inherent in changeable things."[151]

Yet, since we ought not to have even words in common with infidels, so far as possible, lest an occasion for going astray be taken by those who do not understand, it is more prudent for the faithful to abstain from the word *fate*, because *fate* is more properly and generally used in the first sense. Therefore Augustine says that if anyone believes in the existence of fate in the second sense, he may keep to his opinion but should correct his language.[152]

139
Contingency of some effects

The order of Divine Providence as carried out in things is certain. This is why Boethius could say that fate is "an unchangeable disposition inherent in changeable things."[153] But we may not conclude from this that all things happen of necessity. For effects are said to be necessary or contingent according to the condition of proximate causes. Evidently, if the first cause is necessary and the second cause is contingent, a contingent effect will follow. Thus in the case of lower bodies, the first cause of generation is the

---

[151] *De consolatione philosophiae*, IV, *pros.* 6 (PL, LXIII, 815).

[152] *De civitate Dei*, V, 1 (PL, XLI, 141).

[153] *De consolatione philosophiae*, IV, *pros.* 6 (PL, LXIII, 815).

movement of a heavenly body. Although this movement takes place necessarily, generation and corruption in those lower bodies occur contingently, because the lower causes are contingent and can fail. As we demonstrated above, God carries out the order of His Providence through the intermediacy of lower causes.[154] Thus, some of the effects of Divine Providence will be contingent, in keeping with the condition of the lower causes.

140
Divine Providence compatible with contingency

The contingency of effects or of causes cannot upset the certainty of Divine Providence. Three things seem to guarantee the certainty of Providence: the infallibility of divine foreknowledge, the efficaciousness of the divine will, and the wisdom of the divine management, which discovers adequate ways of procuring an effect. None of these factors is opposed to the contingency of things.

God's infallible knowledge embraces even contingent futures, inasmuch as God beholds in His eternity future events as actually existing. But we dealt with this question above.[155] Moreover, God's will, since it is the universal cause of things, decides not only that something will come to pass but that it will come about in this or that manner. The efficaciousness of the divine will demands not only that what God wishes will happen, but that it will happen in the way He wishes. But He wills that some things should happen necessarily and that other things should happen contingently; both are required for the perfection of the universe. That events may occur in both ways, He applies necessary causes to some things and contingent causes to others. In this manner, with some things

---

[154]Cf. chaps. 124, 125, 127, 130.
[155]Cf. chap. 133.

happening necessarily and other things happening contingently, the divine will is efficaciously carried out.

Furthermore, it is clear that the certainty of Providence is safeguarded by the wisdom of the divine dispensation, without prejudice to the contingency of things. Even the providence exercised by man can enable him so to bolster up a cause which can fail to produce an effect that, in some cases, the effect will inevitably follow. We find that a physician acts thus in exercising his healing art, as also does the vine-dresser who employs the proper remedy against barrenness in his vines. Much more, then, does the wisdom of the divine economy bring it about that, although contingent causes left to themselves can fail to produce an effect, the effect will inevitably follow when certain supplementary measures are employed; nor does this do away with the contingency of the effect. Evidently, therefore, contingency in things does not exclude the certainty of Divine Providence.

141
Providence and evil

The same process of reasoning enables us to perceive that, without prejudice to Divine Providence, evil can arise in the world because of defects in secondary causes. Thus in causes that follow one another in order, we see that evil finds its way into an effect owing to some fault in a secondary cause, although this fault is by no means the product of the first cause. For example, the evil of lameness is caused by a curvature in the leg, not by the motive power of the soul. Whatever movement there is in the progress of a lame man, is attributed to the motive power as to its cause; but the unevenness of the progress is caused by the curvature of the leg, not by the motive power. Similarly the evil that arises in things, so far as it has existence or species or a certain nature, is referred to God as to its cause, for there can be no evil unless it resides in something good, as is clear from what we said above.[156] But with regard to the defect that disfigures it, the evil is referred to a lower, defectible cause. Accordingly, although God is the universal cause of all things, He is not the cause of evil as evil. But whatever good is bound up with the evil, has God as its cause.

142
God's goodness and the permission of evil

God's permission of evil in the things governed by Him is not inconsistent with the divine goodness. For, in the first place, the function of Providence is not to destroy but to save the nature of the beings governed. The perfection of the universe requires the existence of some beings that are not subject to evil and of other beings that can suffer the defect of evil in keeping with their nature. If evil were completely eliminated from things, they would not be governed by Divine Providence in accord with their nature; and this would be a greater defect than the particular defects eradicated.

Secondly, the good of one cannot be realized without the suffering of evil by another. For instance, we find that the generation of one being does not take place without the corruption of another being, and that the nourishment of a lion is impossible without the destruction of some other animal, and that the patient endurance of the just involves persecution by the unjust. If evil were completely excluded from things, much good would be rendered impossible. Consequently it is the concern of Divine Providence, not to safeguard all beings from evil, but to see to it that the evil which arises is ordained to some good.

[156]Cf. chap. 117.

Thirdly, good is rendered more estimable when compared with particular evils. For example, the brilliance of white is brought out more clearly when set off by the dinginess of black. And so, by permitting the existence of evil in the world, the divine goodness is more emphatically asserted in the good, just as is the divine wisdom when it forces evil to promote good.

Sin, Grace, and Eternity

143
God's special Providence over man by grace

Accordingly, Divine Providence governs individual beings in keeping with their nature. Since rational creatures, because of the gift of free will, enjoy dominion over their actions in a way impossible to other creatures, a special Providence must be exercised over them in two respects: first, with regard to the aids God gives to rational creatures in their activity; secondly, with regard to the recompense allotted for their works. God gives to irrational creatures only those aids by which they are naturally moved to act. But to rational creatures are issued instructions and commands regulating their lives. A precept is not fittingly given except to a being that is master of his actions, although in an analogous sense God is said to give commands to irrational creatures also, as is intimated in Ps. 148:6: "He hath made a decree, and it shall not pass away." But this sort of decree is nothing else than the dispensation of Divine Providence moving natural things to their proper actions.

The deeds of rational creatures are imputed to them in blame or in praise, because they have dominion over their acts. The actions of men are ascribed to them not only by a man who is placed over them, but also by God. Thus any praiseworthy or blameworthy action that a man performs is imputed to him by the person to whose rule he is subject. Since good actions merit a reward and sin calls for punishment, as was said above,[157] rational creatures are punished for the evil they do and are rewarded for the good they do, according to the measure of justice fixed by Divine Providence. But there is no place for reward or punishment in dealing with irrational creatures, just as there is none for praise or blame.

Since the last end of rational creatures exceeds the capacity of their nature and since whatever conduces to the end must be proportionate to the end according to the right order of Providence, rational creatures are given divine aids that are not merely proportionate to nature but that transcend the capacity of nature. God infuses into man, over and above the natural faculty of reason, the light of grace whereby he is internally perfected for the exercise of virtue, both as regards knowledge, inasmuch as man's mind is elevated by this light to the knowledge of truths surpassing reason, and as regards action and affection, inasmuch as man's affective power is raised by this light above all created things to the love of God, to hope in Him, and to the performance of acts that such love imposes.

These gifts or aids supernaturally given to man are called *graces* for two reasons. First, because they are given by God *gratis*. Nothing is discoverable in man that would constitute a right to aids of this sort, for they exceed the capacity of nature. Secondly, they are called *graces* because in a very special way, man is made *gratus* (or "pleasing to God") by such gifts. Since God's love is the cause of goodness in things and is not called forth by any preexisting

---

[157]Cf. chaps. 103, 121.

goodness, as our love is, a special intensity of divine love must be discerned in those whom He showers with such extraordinary effects of His goodness. Therefore God is said chiefly and simply to love those whom He endows with these effects of His love by which they are enabled to reach their last end, which is He Himself, the fountainhead of all goodness.

144
Remission of sin by the gifts of grace

Sins arise when actions deflect from the right course leading to the end. Since man is conducted to his end not only by natural aids, but by the aids of grace, the sins men commit must be counteracted not by natural aids alone, but also by the helps which grace confers. Contraries exclude each other; therefore, as the aids of grace are taken from man by sin, so sins are forgiven by the gifts of grace. Otherwise man's malice in committing sin would be more powerful in banishing divine grace than the divine goodness is in expelling sin by the gifts of grace.

Furthermore, God's Providence over things is in harmony with their mode of being. Changeable things are so constituted that contraries can succeed each other in them. Examples of this are generation and corruption in corporeal matter, and white and black in a colored object. Man is changeable in will as long as he lives his earthly life. Hence man receives from God the gifts of grace in such a way that he is able to forfeit them by sin; and the sins man commits are such that they can be remitted by the gifts of grace.

Besides, in supernatural acts, possible and impossible are regarded from the standpoint of divine power, not from the standpoint of natural power. The fact that a blind man can be made to see or that a dead man can rise, is owing not to natural power but to divine power. But the gifts of grace are supernatural. Therefore a person's capacity to receive them depends on divine power. To say that once a person has sinned he cannot receive the gifts of grace, is derogatory to the power of God. Of course, grace cannot coexist with sin; for by grace man is rightly ordered to his end, from which he is turned away by sin. But the contention that sin is irremissible impugns the power of God.

145
No sin unforgivable

The suggestion might be put forward that sins are unforgivable, not through any lack of power on God's part, but because divine justice has decided that anyone who falls from grace shall never more be restored to it.

But such a position is clearly erroneous. There is no provision in the order of divine justice to the effect that, while a person is on the road, he should have assigned to him what belongs to the end of the journey. But unyielding adherence to good or to evil pertains to the end of life's course; immobility and cessation from activity are the *terminus* of movement. On the other hand, the whole of our present life is a time of wayfaring, as is shown by man's changeableness both in body and in soul. Accordingly, divine justice does not determine that after sinning a man must remain immovably in the state of sin.

Moreover, divine benefits do not expose man to danger, particularly in affairs of supreme moment. But it would be dangerous for man, while leading a life subject to change, to accept grace if, after receiving grace, he could sin but could not again be restored to grace.

This is so especially in view of the fact that sins preceding grace are remitted by the infusion of grace; and at times such sins are more grievous than those man commits after receiving grace. Therefore we may not hold that man's sins are unforgivable either before or after they are committed.

146
Remission of sin by God alone

God alone can forgive sin. For only the one against whom an offense is directed can forgive the offense. Sin is imputed to man as an offense not only by another man, but also by God, as we said above.[158] However, we are now considering sin as imputed to man by God. Accordingly, God alone can forgive sin.

Again, since by sin man is deflected from his last end, sins cannot be forgiven unless man is again rightly ordered to his end. This is accomplished through the gifts of grace which come from God alone, since they transcend the power of nature. Therefore only God can remit sin.

Further, sin is imputed to man as an offense because it is voluntary. But only God can effect a change in the will. Consequently He alone can truly forgive sins.

147
Some articles of Faith on the effects of divine government

This, then, is the second of God's effects, namely, the government of things, and especially of rational creatures, to whom God gives grace and whose sins He forgives. This effect is touched on in the Creed. When we profess that the Holy Spirit is God, we imply that all things are ordained to the end of divine goodness, since it

---

[158]Cf. chap. 143.

belongs to God to order His subjects to their end. And the words of the Creed which express our belief that the Holy Spirit is "the giver of life," suggest that God moves all things. For, as the movement flowing from the soul to the body is the life of the body, so the movement whereby the universe is moved by God is, so to speak, a certain life of the universe.

Further, since the entire process of divine government is derived from the divine goodness, which is appropriated to the Holy Spirit who proceeds as love, the effects of Divine Providence are fittingly thought of in connection with the person of the Holy Spirit.

As regards the effect of supernatural knowledge which God produces in men through faith, the Creed proclaims: "I believe in one holy Catholic Church"; for the Church is the congregation of the faithful. Concerning the grace which God communicates to men, the Creed states: "I believe in . . . the Communion of Saints." And with respect to the remission of sin it says: "I believe in . . . the forgiveness of sins."

148
All creation is for man

All things are directed to the divine goodness as to their end, as we have shown.[159] Among things ordained to this end, some are closer to the end than others and so participate in the divine goodness more abundantly. Therefore lesser creatures, which have a smaller share in the divine goodness, are in some way subordinated to higher beings as to their ends. In any hierarchy of ends, beings that are closer to the ultimate end are also ends with respect

---

[159]Cf. chap. 101.

to beings that are more remote. For instance, a dose of medicine is administered to procure a purge; the purge is designed to promote slimness; and slimness is desirable for health. Thus slimness is, in a sense, the purpose of the purging, as the purging is the purpose of the medicine. And such subordination is reasonable. As in the order of efficient causes, the power of the first agent reaches the ultimate effects through intermediate causes, so in the order of ends, whatever is farther removed from the end attains to the ultimate end through the intermediacy of beings that are closer to the end.

Thus, in our example, the medicine has no relation to health except through purging. Similarly, in the order of the universe, lower beings realize their last end chiefly by their subordination to higher beings.

The same conclusion is manifest if we turn our attention to the order of things in itself. Things that come into being by a natural process, act as they are equipped by nature to act. As we observe, however, imperfect beings serve the needs of more noble beings: plants draw their nutriment from the earth; animals feed on plants; and these in turn serve man's use. We conclude, then, that lifeless beings exist for living beings, plants for animals, and the latter for men. And since, as we have seen,[160] intellectual nature is superior to material nature, the whole of material nature is subordinate to intellectual nature. But among intellectual natures, that which has the closest ties with the body is the rational soul, which is the form of man. In a certain sense, therefore, we may say that the whole of corporeal nature exists for man, inasmuch as he is a rational animal. And so the consummation of the whole of corporeal nature depends, to some extent, on man's consummation.

[160]Cf. chaps. 74, 127.

149
The ultimate end of man

Man's consummation consists in the attainment of his last end, which is perfect beatitude or happiness; and this consists in the vision of God, as was demonstrated above.[161] The Beatific Vision entails immutability in the intellect and will. As regards the intellect, its questing ceases when at last it comes to the first cause, in which all truth can be known. The will's variability ceases, too; for, when it reaches its last end, in which is contained the fullness of all goodness, it finds nothing further to be desired. The will is subject to change because it craves what it does not possess. Clearly, therefore, the final consummation of man consists in perfect repose or unchangeableness as regards both intellect and will.

150
Consummation of man in eternity

We showed in an earlier chapter that the idea of eternity involves immutability.[162] As motion causes time, in which priority and posteriority are discerned, so the cessation of motion puts a stop to priority and posteriority; and so nothing remains but eternity, which is simultaneously whole. Therefore in his final consummation man attains eternal life, not only in the sense that he lives an immortal life in his soul — for this is a property of the rational soul by its very nature, as was shown above[163] — but also in the sense that he is brought to the perfection of immobility.

---

[161]Cf. chap. 104.
[162]Cf. chap. 8.
[163]Cf. chap. 84.

Death and Bodily Resurrection

151
Reunion with the body is requisite for the soul's perfect happiness

We should note that the disquiet of the will cannot be wholly overcome unless natural desire is completely satisfied. Elements that are by nature destined for union, naturally desire to be united to each other; for any being seeks what is suited to it by nature. Since, therefore, the natural condition of the human soul is to be united to the body, as was pointed out above,[164] it has a natural desire for union with the body. Hence the will cannot be perfectly at rest until the soul is again joined to the body. When this takes place, man rises from the dead.

Besides, final perfection requires possession of a being's original perfection. But the first perfection of anything requires that it be perfect in its nature, and final perfection consists in attainment of the last end. In order, therefore, that the human soul may be brought to complete perfection with regard to its end, it must be perfect in its nature. This is impossible unless the soul is united to

_____

[164]Cf. chaps. 82, 90, 92.

the body. For by nature the soul is a part of man as his form. But no part is perfect in its nature unless it exists in its whole. Therefore man's final happiness requires the soul to be again united to the body.

Moreover, the accidental and all that is contrary to nature cannot be everlasting. But a state wherein the soul is separated from the body is surely *per accidens* and contrary to nature, if naturally and *per se* the soul has a longing for union with the body. Therefore the soul will not be forever separated from the body. So, since the soul's substance is incorruptible, as was shown above,[165] we conclude that the soul is to be reunited to the body.

152
Separation of body from soul is both natural and contrary to nature

We may have a suspicion that separation of the soul from the body is not *per accidens* but is in accord with nature. For man's body is made up of contrary elements. Everything of this sort is naturally corruptible. Therefore the human body is naturally corruptible. But when the body corrupts, the soul must survive as a separate entity if the soul is immortal, as in fact it is.[166] Apparently, then, separation of the soul from the body is in accord with nature.

In view of these considerations, we must take up the question of how this separation is according to nature, and how it is opposed to nature. We showed above that the rational soul exceeds the capacity of all corporeal matter in a measure impossible to other forms.[167] This is demonstrated by its intellectual activity, which it exercises without the body. To the end that corporeal matter might

[165] Cf. chap. 84.
[166] Cf. chap. 84.
[167] Cf. chaps. 74, 79.

be fittingly adapted to the soul, there had to be added to the body some disposition that would make it suitable matter for such a form. And in the same way that this form itself receives existence from God alone through creation, that disposition, transcending as it does corporeal nature, was conferred on the human body by God alone for the purpose of preserving the body itself in a state of incorruption so that it might match the soul's perpetual existence. This disposition remained in man's body as long as man's soul cleaved to God.

But when man's soul turned from God by sin, the human body deservedly lost that supernatural disposition whereby it was unrebelliously subservient to the soul. And hence man incurred the necessity of dying.

Accordingly, if we regard the nature of the body, death is natural. But if we regard the nature of the soul and the disposition with which the human body was supernaturally endowed in the beginning for the sake of the soul, death is *per accidens* and contrary to nature, inasmuch as union with the body is natural for the soul.

153
The soul's resumption of the same body

Since the soul is united to the body as its form, and since each form has the right matter corresponding to it, the body to which the soul will be reunited must be of the same nature and species as was the body laid down by the soul at death. At the resurrection the soul will not resume a celestial or ethereal body, or the body of some animal, as certain people fancifully prattle.[168] No, it will resume a

---

[168]Origen, *Peri archon*, III, 6 (PG, XI, 337); cf. St. Gregory the Great, *Moralia*, XIV, 56 (PL, LXXV, 1077).

human body made up of flesh and bones, and equipped with the same organs it now possesses.

Furthermore, just as the same specific form ought to have the same specific matter, so the same numerical form ought to have the same numerical matter. The soul of an ox cannot be the soul of a horse's body, nor can the soul of this ox be the soul of any other ox. Therefore, since the rational soul that survives remains numerically the same, at the resurrection it must be reunited to numerically the same body.

154
Miraculous nature of the resurrection

When substances corrupt, the survival of the species (but not the restoration of the individual) is effected by the action of nature. The cloud from which rain is produced and the cloud which is again formed by evaporation from the fallen rain water, are not numerically the same. Accordingly, since the human body substantially dissolves in death, it cannot be restored to numerical identity by the action of nature. But the concept of resurrection requires such identity, as we have just shown. Consequently, the resurrection of man will not be brought about by the action of nature (as some philosophers have held in their theory that, when all bodies return to the position formerly occupied after untold cycles of years, then also men will return to life in the same numerical identity).[169] No, the restoration of all who rise will be effected solely by divine power.

Moreover, it is clear that senses once destroyed and anything possessed as a result of generation cannot be restored by the

---

[169]Thus Empedocles, in H. Diels, *Die Fragmente der Vorsokratiker*, no. 126 (I, 270); cf. Hippolytus, *Philosophumena* (Pseudo-Origen, *Contra Haereses*), I, 3 (PG, XVI, 3028).

activity of nature, for the simple reason that the same numerical being cannot be generated several times. If any such perfection is restored to anyone (for example, an eye that has been torn out or a hand that has been cut off), it will be through divine power which operates beyond the order of nature, as we said above.[170] Thus, since all the senses and members of man corrupt in death, a dead man cannot be brought back to life except by divine action.

The fact that, as we hold, the resurrection will be effected by divine power, enables us to perceive readily how the same numerical body will be revived. Since all things, even the very least, are included under Divine Providence, as we showed above,[171] the matter composing this human body of ours, whatever form it may take after man's death, evidently does not elude the power or the knowledge of God. Such matter remains numerically the same, in the sense that it exists under quantitative dimensions, by reason of which it can be said to be this particular matter and is the principle of individuation. If then, this matter remains the same, and if the human body is again fashioned from it by divine power, and if also the rational soul which remains the same in its incorruptibility is united to the same body, the result is that identically the same man is restored to life.

Numerical identity cannot be impeded, as some object, by the consideration that the humanity is not numerically the same as before. In the view of some philosophers, humanity, which is said to be the form of the whole, is nothing else than the form of a part, namely, the soul, and they admit that humanity is the form of the body also, in the sense that it confers species on the whole.[172] If

---

[170] Cf. chap. 136.

[171] Cf. chaps. 123, 130.

[172] Averroes, *In Metaph.*, VII, comm. 21; comm. 34 (VIII, 80V; 87R). Cf. St. Thomas, *In Metaph. Aristotelis*, VII, lect. 9 (ed. Cathala, no. 1467).

this is true, evidently the humanity remains numerically the same, since the rational soul remains numerically the same.

Humanity, however, is that which is signified by the definition of man, as the essence of anything whatever is that which is signified by its definition. But the definition of man signifies not form alone but also matter, since matter must be comprised in the definition of material things. Hence we shall do better to say, with others, that both soul and body are included in the notion of humanity,[173] although otherwise than in the definition of man. The notion of humanity embraces only the essential principles of man, prescinding from all other factors. For, since humanity is understood to be that whereby man is man, whatever cannot truly be said to constitute man as man, is evidently cut off from the notion of humanity. But when we speak of man, who has humanity, the fact that he has humanity does not exclude the possession of other attributes (for instance, whiteness, and the like). The term *man* signifies man's essential principles, but not to the exclusion of other factors, even though these other factors are not actually, but only potentially, contained in the notion of man. Hence *man* signifies as a whole (*per modum totius*) whereas *humanity* signifies as a part (*per modum partis*) and is not predicated of man. In Socrates, then, or in Plato, this determinate matter and this particular form are included. Just as the notion of man implies composition of matter and form, so if Socrates were to be defined, the notion of him would imply that he is composed of this flesh and these bones and this soul. Consequently, since humanity is not some third form in addition to soul and body, but is composed of both, we see clearly that, if the same body is restored and if the same soul remains, the humanity will be numerically the same.

[173]Cf. Avicenna, *Metaph.* V, 5 (89VA). See St. Thomas, *loc. cit.* (ed. Cathala, no. 1469).

The numerical identity in question is not frustrated on the ground that the corporeity recovered is not numerically the same, for the reason that it corrupts when the body corrupts. If by corporeity is meant the substantial form by which a thing is classified in the genus of corporeal substance, such corporeity is nothing else than the soul, seeing that there is but one substantial form for each thing. In virtue of this particular soul, this animal is not only *animal*, but is *animated body*, and *body*, and also *this thing existing in the genus of substance*. Otherwise the soul would come to a body already existing in act, and so would be an accidental form. The subject of a substantial form is something existing only in potency, not in act. When it receives the substantial form it is not said to be generated merely in this or that respect, as is the case with accidental forms, but is said to be generated simply, as simply receiving existence. And therefore the corporeity that is received remains numerically the same, since the same rational soul continues to exist.

If, however, the word *corporeity* is taken to mean a form designating body (*corpus*), which is placed in the genus of quantity, such a form is accidental, since it signifies nothing else than three-dimensional existence. Even though the same numerical form, thus understood, is not recovered, the identity of the subject is not thereby impeded, for unity of the essential principles suffices for this. The same reasoning holds for all the accidents, the diversity among which does not destroy numerical identity. Therefore, since union is a kind of relation (and therefore an accident), its numerical diversity does not prevent the numerical identity of the subject; nor, for that matter, does numerical diversity among the powers of the sensitive and vegetative soul, if they are supposed to have corrupted. For the natural powers existing in the human composite are in the genus of accident; and what we call *sensible* is derived, not from the senses according as sense is the specific

175

difference constituting animal, but from the very substance of the sensitive soul, which in man is essentially identical with the rational soul.

155
Resurrection to new life

Although men will rise as the same individuals, they will not have the same kind of life as before. *Now* their life is corruptible; *then* it will be incorruptible. If nature aims at perpetual existence in the generation of man, much more so does God in the restoration of man. Nature's tendency toward never-ending existence comes from an impulse implanted by God. The perpetual existence of the species is not in question in the restoration of risen man, for this could be procured by repeated generation. Therefore what is intended is the perpetual existence of the individual. Accordingly, risen men will live forever.

Besides, if men once risen were to die, the souls separated from their bodies would not remain forever deprived of the body, for this would be against the nature of the soul, as we said above.[174] Therefore they would have to rise again; and the same thing would happen if they were to die again after the second resurrection. Thus death and life would revolve around each man in cycles of infinite succession, which seems futile. Surely a halt is better called at the initial stage, so that men might rise to immortal life at the first resurrection.

However, the conquest of mortality will not induce any diversity either in species or in number. The idea of mortality contains nothing that could make it a specific difference of man, since it

---

[174]Cf. chap. 151.

signifies no more than a passion. It is used to serve as a specific difference of man in the sense that the nature of man is designated by calling him mortal, to bring out the fact that he is composed of contrary elements, just as his proper form is designated by the predicate *rational;* material things cannot be defined without including matter. However, mortality is not overcome by taking away man's proper matter. For the soul will not resume a celestial or ethereal body, as was mentioned above;[175] it will resume a human body made up of contrary elements. Incorruptibility will come as an effect of divine power, whereby the soul will gain dominion over the body to the point that the body cannot corrupt. For a thing continues in being as long as form has dominion over matter.

156

Cessation of nutrition and reproduction after the resurrection

When an end is removed, the means leading to that end must also be removed. Therefore, after mortality is done away with in those who have risen, the means serving the condition of mortal life must cease to have any function. Such are food and drink, which are necessary for the sustenance of mortal life, during which what is dissolved by natural heat has to be restored by food. Consequently there will be no consumption of food or drink after the resurrection.

Nor will there be any need of clothing. Clothes are necessary for man so that the body may not suffer harm from heat or cold, which beset him from outside. Likewise, exercise of the reproductive functions, which is designed for the generation of animals, must cease. Generation serves the ends of mortal life, so that what

---

[175]Cf. chap. 153.

cannot be preserved in the individual may be preserved at least in the species. Since the same individual men will continue in eternal existence, generation will have no place among them; nor, consequently, will the exercise of reproductive power.

Again, since semen is the superfluous part of nourishment, cessation of the use of food necessarily entails cessation of the exercise of the reproductive functions. On the other hand, we cannot maintain with propriety that the use of food, drink, and the reproductive powers will remain solely for the sake of pleasure. Nothing inordinate will occur in that final state because then all things will receive their perfect consummation, each in its own way. But deordination is opposed to perfection. Also, since the restoration of man through resurrection will be effected directly by God, no deordination will be able to find its way into that state; whatever is from God is well ordered.[176] But desire for the use of food and the exercise of the reproductive powers for pleasure alone, would be inordinate; indeed, even during our present life people regard such conduct as vicious. Among the risen, consequently, the use of food, drink, and the reproductive functions for mere pleasure, can have no place.

157
Resurrection of all the bodily members

Although risen men will not occupy themselves with such activities, they will not lack the organs requisite for such functions. Without these organs the risen body would not be complete. But it is fitting that nature should be completely restored at the renovation of risen man, for such renovation will be accomplished

---

[176]Cf. Rom. 13:1: "Let every soul be subject to higher powers; for there is no power but from God; and those that are, are ordained of God."

directly by God, whose works are perfect. Therefore all the members of the body will have their place in the risen, for the preservation of nature in its entirety rather than for the exercise of their normal functions.

Moreover, as we shall bring out later, men will receive punishment or reward in that future state for the acts they perform now.[177] This being the case, it is no more than right that men should keep the organs with which they served the reign of sin or of justice during the present life, so that they may be punished or rewarded in the members they employed for sin or for merit.

158
Absence of defects in the resurrection

In like manner, it is fitting that all natural defects be corrected in the risen body. Any defect of this sort is prejudicial to the integrity of nature. So if human nature is to be completely renewed by God at the resurrection, such defects must be rectified. Besides, these defects arose from a deficiency in the natural power which is the principle of human generation. But in the resurrection there will be no active causality other than the divine, which does not admit of deficiency. Therefore such defects as are found in men naturally begotten, will have no place in men restored by the resurrection.

159
Resurrection restricted to what is necessary for true human nature

These remarks about the integrity of risen men should be understood as referring to whatever pertains to the true state of human

---

[177]Cf. chaps. 172, 173.

nature. What is not required for the reality of human nature will not be resumed by risen man. Thus, if all the accretion of matter from the food that has been changed into flesh and blood were to be resumed, the size of risen man would exceed all bounds. The proper condition of any nature is regulated by its species and form. Accordingly, all the parts that are consonant with the human species and form will be integrally present in risen man (i.e., not only organic parts, but other parts of like nature, such as flesh and sinews, which enter into the composition of the various organs). Of course, not all the matter that was ever contained in those parts during man's natural life will again be taken up, but only so much as will be enough to constitute the species of the parts in integrity.

Even though not all the material elements ever possessed by man will arise, we cannot say on this account that man will not be the same individual or that he will not be complete. During the course of the present life, man evidently remains numerically the same from birth to death. Nevertheless the material composition of his parts does not remain the same, but undergoes gradual flux and reflux, in somewhat the way that the same fire is kept up although some logs are consumed and others are fed to the blaze. Man is whole when his species and the quantity due to his species are preserved intact.

160
God's action in supplying what is lacking in the body

For the same reason that God, in restoring the risen body, does not reclaim all the material elements once possessed by man's body, He will supply whatever is wanting to the proper amount of matter. Nature itself has such power. In infancy we do not as yet possess our full quantity; but by assimilating food and drink we receive enough matter from outside sources to round out our perfect quantity. Nor on this account does a man cease to be the same individual he was before. Surely, then, divine power can do the same thing much more easily, so that those who do not have sufficient quantity may be supplied from outside matter with whatever was lacking to them in this life as regards integrity of natural members or suitable size. Thus, although some may lack certain of their members during this life or may not attain to perfect size, the amount of quantity possessed at the moment of death makes no difference; at the resurrection they will receive, through God's power, the due complement of members and quantity.

161
Solution of possible objections

This enables us to answer the objections that some raise against the resurrection. For instance, they say that a cannibal may have eaten human flesh, and later, thus nourished, may beget a son, who eats the same kind of food. If what is eaten is changed into the substance of the eater's flesh, it seems impossible for both to rise in their full integrity, for the flesh of one has been changed into the flesh of the other. The difficulty apparently grows if semen is the product of surplus food, as the philosophers teach;[178] for the semen whereby the son is begotten would then be derived from the flesh of another person. And so it seems impossible for a boy begotten from such seed to rise, if the men (whose flesh the father and the son himself devoured) rise intact.

But this state of affairs is not incompatible with a general resurrection. As was noted above, not all the material elements ever present in any man need be resumed when he rises;[179] only

[178] Aristotle, *De generatione animalium*, I, 18 (726 a 26).
[179] Cf. chap. 159.

so much matter is required as suffices to keep up the amount of quantity he ought to have. We also pointed out that if anyone is lacking in the matter required for perfect quantity, divine power will supply what is needed.[180]

We should note, moreover, that the material elements existing in man's body are found to pertain to true human nature in various degrees. First and foremost, what is received from one's parents is brought to perfection within the reality of the human species, as its purest element, by the parents' formative causality. Secondly, what is contributed by food is necessary for the proper quantity of the body's members. And lastly, since the introduction of a foreign substance always weakens a thing's energy, growth must eventually cease and the body must become old and decay, just as wine eventually becomes watery if water is mixed in with it.

Further, certain superfluities are engendered in man's body from food. Some of these are required for special purposes (for instance, semen for reproduction and hair for covering and adornment). But other superfluities serve no useful end and these are expelled through perspiration and other eliminating processes, or else are retained in the body, not without inconvenience to nature.

At the general resurrection all this will be adjusted in accord with Divine Providence. If the same matter existed in different men, it will rise in that one in whom it fulfilled the higher function. If it existed in two men in exactly the same way, it will rise in him who had it first; in the other, the lack will be made up by divine power. And so we can see that the flesh of a man that was devoured by another will rise not in the cannibal but in him to whom it belonged originally. But as regards the nutritive fluid present in it, it will rise in the son begotten of semen formed from

---

[180]Cf. chap. 160.

that flesh.[181] The rest of it will rise in the first man in this series, and God will supply what is wanting to each of the three.

162
The resurrection of the dead as an article of Faith

That we may give expression to our faith in the Resurrection, we are instructed to say in the Apostles' Creed: "I believe . . . in the resurrection of the body." The word *body* was inserted not without reason: even in the age of the Apostles there were some who denied the resurrection of the body[182] and admitted no more than a spiritual resurrection, whereby a man rises from the death of sin. Therefore the Apostle, in 2 Timothy 2:18, has occasion to refer to certain individuals: "Who have erred from the truth, saying that the resurrection is past already, and have subverted the Faith of some." To abolish this error, so that belief in the future resurrection may be professed, the Creed of the Fathers[183] proclaims: "I look for the resurrection of the dead."

163
Nature of risen man's activity

We go on to consider the nature of the activity exercised by risen men. Each living being must have some activity that mainly

---

[181] See St. Thomas, *Summa,* Ia, q. 119, a. 1 ad 3: "The nutritive fluid is that which has not yet completely received the specific nature, but is on the way to it: for example, the blood, and the like." Also, cf. ibid., a. 2: "Nutritive power is said to serve generative power, because what was transformed by the nutritive power is received as semen by the generative power."

[182] Cf. Matt. 22:23; Acts 23:8, regarding the Sadducees.

[183] That is, the Nicene Creed.

engrosses its attention; and its life is said to consist in this occupation. Thus those who cultivate pleasure more than anything else are said to lead a voluptuous life; those who give their time to contemplation are said to lead a contemplative life; and those who devote their energies to civil government, are said to lead a political life. We have shown that risen men will have no occasion to use food or the reproductive functions,[184] although all bodily activity seems to tend in the direction of such use. But even if the exercise of bodily functions ceases, there remain spiritual activities, in which man's ultimate end consists, as we have said;[185] and the risen are in a position to achieve this end once they are freed from their former condition of corruption and changeableness. Of course, man's last end consists not in spiritual acts of any sort whatever, but in the vision of God according to His essence, as was stated above.[186] And God is eternal; hence the intellect must be in contact with eternity. Accordingly, just as those who give their time to pleasure are said to lead a voluptuous life, so those who enjoy the vision of God possess eternal life, as is indicated in John 17:3: "This is eternal life: that they may know Thee, the only true God, and Jesus Christ whom Thou hast sent."

[184]Cf. chap. 156.
[185]Cf. chaps. 107, 149.
[186]Cf. chap. 107.

Glorified Body and Beatific Vision

164
The vision of God in His essence

The created intellect will see God in His essence and not in any mere likeness. In the latter kind of vision, the object understood may be at a distance from the present intellect (as a stone is present to the eye by its likeness, but is absent in substance). But, as was seen above,[187] God's very essence is in some mysterious way united to the created intellect, so that God may be seen just as He is.

Thus, when we arrive at our last end, what was formerly *believed* about God will be *seen*, and what was *hoped for* as absent will be closely *embraced* as present. This is called *comprehension*, according to the expression used by the Apostle in Philippians 3:12: "I follow after, if I may by any means apprehend."[188] This is not to be understood in the sense that comprehension implies all-inclusive knowledge, but in the sense that it denotes the presence and a certain clasping of what is said to be comprehended.

---

[187]Cf. chap. 105.

[188]Vulgate: "*si quomodo comprehendam.*"

165
Supreme perfection and happiness in the vision of God

Moreover, delight is engendered by apprehension of a suitable good: sight rejoices in beautiful colors and taste in sweet savors. But this delight of the senses can be prevented if the organ is indisposed: light that delights healthy eyes annoys sore eyes. However, since the intellect does not understand by employing a bodily organ, as we saw above,[189] no sorrow mars the delight that consists in the contemplation of truth. Of course, sadness can indirectly attend the mind's contemplation, when the object of truth is apprehended as harmful. Thus knowledge of truth may delight the intellect even while the object known may sadden the will, not precisely because the object is known but because its action is pernicious. God, however, by the fact that He exists, is truth. So the intellect that sees God must rejoice in the vision of Him.

Besides, God is goodness itself, which is the cause of love. So God's goodness must be loved by all who apprehend it. Although a thing that is good may not awaken love or even be hated, this is because it is apprehended as harmful rather than good. Thus, in the vision of God, who is goodness and truth itself, there must be love or joyous fruition, no less than comprehension. This accords with Isaiah 66:14: "You shall see and your heart shall rejoice."

166
Confirmation in good in the Beatific Vision

This enables us to understand that the soul which sees God — and the same is true of any other spiritual creature — has its will firmly

---

[189]Cf. chap. 79.

fixed in Him, so that it can never turn to what is opposed to Him. For, since the object of the will is the good, the will cannot incline to anything whatever unless it exhibits some aspect of good. Any particular good may be wanting in some perfection, which the knower is then free to seek in another quarter. Therefore the will of him who beholds some particular good need not rest content with its possession but may search farther afield beyond its orbit. But God, who is universal good and very goodness itself, is not lacking in any good that may be sought elsewhere, as was shown above.[190] And so those who enjoy the vision of God's essence cannot turn their will from Him, but must rather desire all things in subordination to Him.

Something similar occurs in the process of understanding. Our mind, when in doubt, turns this way and that until it reaches a first principle; then the intellect must come to a halt. Since the end has the same function in the field of desire that a principle has in the matter of understanding, the will can veer in opposite directions until it comes to the knowledge or fruition of the last end, in which it must rest. The nature of perfect happiness would be contradicted if man, after achieving it, could turn to what is opposed to it. For then fear of losing happiness would not be wholly excluded and so desire would not be completely satisfied. Hence Revelation 3:12 says of the blessed person that "he shall go out no more."

167
Complete subjection of the body to the soul

The body is for the soul, as matter is for form and a tool for the craftsman. Thus, at the resurrection when eternal life is attained,

---

[190]Cf. chap. 21.

God will join to the soul a body such as befits the beatitude of the soul; for whatever exists for the sake of an end, must be duly disposed according to the demands of the end. A soul that has attained the highest intellectual activity cannot properly have a body that would in any way impede or burden it. But the human body, by reason of its corruptibility, does obstruct and slow down the soul, so that the soul can neither devote itself to uninterrupted contemplation nor reach the heights of contemplation.

This is why men are able to grasp divine truths more readily when they rise above the bodily senses. And so prophetic revelations are made to men when asleep or when they are lost in mental ecstasy, as we read in Numbers 12:6: "If there be among you a prophet of the Lord, I will appear to him in a vision or I will speak to him in a dream." Therefore the bodies of risen saints will not be corruptible and will not burden down the soul, as they do now. On the contrary, they will be incorruptible and will be wholly obedient to the soul, so as not to resist it in any way whatever.

168
Qualities of the glorified body

This doctrine gives us an insight into the condition of the bodies of the blessed. The soul is both the form and the motive force of the body. In its function as form, the soul is the principle of the body, not only as regards the body's substantial being but also as regards its proper accidents, which arise in the subject from the union of form with matter. The more dominant the form is, the less can any outside cause interfere with the impression made by the form on matter. We see this verified in the case of fire, whose form, generally accounted the noblest of all elementary forms, confers on fire the power of not being easily diverted from its natural disposition by the influence emanating from any cause.

Since the blessed soul, owing to its union with the first principle of all things, will be raised to the pinnacle of nobility and power, it will communicate substantial existence in the most perfect degree to the body that has been joined to it by divine action. And thus, holding the body completely under its sway, the soul will render the body *subtile* and *spiritual*. The soul will also bestow on the body a most noble quality, namely, the radiant beauty of *clarity*. Further, because of the influence emanating from the soul, the body's stability will not be subject to alteration by any cause, which means that the body will be *impassible*. Lastly, since the body will be wholly submissive to the soul (as a tool is to him who plies it), it will be endowed with *agility*. Hence the properties of the bodies belonging to the blessed will be these four: subtility, clarity, impassibility, and agility.

This is the sense of the Apostle's words in 1 Corinthians 15:42-44: In death the body "is sown in corruption; it shall rise in incorruption." This refers to impassibility. "It is sown in dishonor; it shall rise in glory." This refers to clarity. "It is sown in weakness; it shall rise in power." Hence, it will have agility. "It is sown a natural body; it shall rise a spiritual body." In other words, it will be endowed with subtility.

169
Renovation of man and of material nature

It is manifest that all things existing for some definite end are disposed in an order required by the end. Therefore, if that to which other things are related as means can vary from perfect to imperfect, the means subordinated to it must be subject to parallel variation, so as to serve the end in either state. Food and clothing, for instance, are prepared otherwise for a child than for a grown man. We have already called attention to the fact that material creation is subordinated to rational nature as to its end.[191] Consequently, when man is admitted to his final perfection after the resurrection, material creation must take on a new condition. This is why we are told that the world is to undergo renovation when man rises, as is taught in Revelation 21:1: "I saw a new Heaven and a new Earth," and in Isaiah 65:17: "For behold, I create new heavens and a new Earth."

170
Renovation restricted to certain classes of creatures

However, we should remember that the different kinds of material creatures are subordinated to man in different ways. Plants and animals serve man by aiding him in his weakness, in the sense that they supply him with food, clothing, transportation, and like conveniences, whereby human feebleness is strengthened. But in the final state that comes after the resurrection, all such defects will be eliminated from man. Men will no longer need food to eat, since they will be incorruptible, as we have pointed out.[192] Nor will men need garments to cover their nakedness, because they will be clothed with the radiance of glory. Nor will they require animals to carry them, as they will be endowed with agility. Nor will they need medicines to keep them in health, since they will be impassible. In that state of final consummation, therefore, as we should expect, there will be no material creatures of this kind, namely, plants and animals and other like mixed bodies.

But the four elements — fire, air, water, and earth — are for man not only as regards the utility of bodily life, but also as regards the composition of his body. The human body is made up of these

[191]Cf. chap. 148.
[192]Cf. chap. 168.

elements. And so the elements have an essential ordination to the human body. Hence, when man is glorified in body and soul, the elements have to remain also, although they will be changed to a better condition of existence.

As for the heavenly bodies, their substance is not used to support man's corruptible life and does not enter into the substance of the human frame. However, they serve man in the sense that by their beauty and enormous size they show forth the excellence of their Creator. For this reason man is often exhorted in Sacred Scripture to contemplate the heavenly bodies, so as to be moved by them to sentiments of reverence toward God. This is exemplified in Isaiah 40:26: "Lift up your eyes on high and see who hath created these things." And although, in the state of consummated perfection, man is not brought to the knowledge of God by a consideration of sensible creatures (since he sees God as He is in Himself), still it is pleasing and enjoyable for one who knows the cause to observe how the likeness of the cause shines forth in the effect. Thus a consideration of the divine goodness as mirrored in bodies — and particularly in the heavenly bodies, which appear to have a preeminence over other bodies — gives joy to the saints. Moreover, the heavenly bodies have some sort of essential relationship with the human body under the aspect of efficient causality, just as the elements have under the aspect of material causality: man generates man, and the sun, too, has some part in this operation. This, then, is another reason why the heavenly bodies should remain in existence.

The doctrine here advocated follows not only from the relationship which various bodies have with man, but also from an examination of the natures of the material creatures we have been discussing. No object wanting in an intrinsic principle of incorruptibility ought to remain in the state that is characterized by incorruption. The heavenly bodies are incorruptible in whole and in part. The elements are incorruptible as wholes, but not as parts. Man is incorruptible in part — namely, in his rational soul — but not as a whole because the composite is dissolved by death. Animals and plants and all mixed bodies are incorruptible neither in whole nor in part. In the final state of incorruption, therefore, men, the elements, and the heavenly bodies will fittingly remain, but not other animals or plants or mixed bodies.

We can argue reasonably to the same conclusion from the nature of the universe. Since man is a part of the material universe, the material universe should remain when man is brought to his final consummation; a part would seem to lack its proper perfection if it were to exist without the whole. On the other hand, the material universe cannot remain in existence without its essential parts. But the essential parts of the universe are the heavenly bodies and the elements, for the entire world machine is made up of them. Other bodies do not, apparently, pertain to the integrity of the material universe, but contribute rather to its adornment and beauty. They befit its changeable state in the sense that, with a heavenly body acting as efficient cause and with the elements as material causes, animals and plants and minerals are brought into being. But in the state of final consummation another kind of adornment will be given to the elements, in keeping with their condition of incorruption. In that state, accordingly, there will remain men, elements, and heavenly bodies, but not animals or plants or minerals.

171
Cessation of motion in the heavenly bodies

Since the heavenly bodies are in constant motion, so far as we can judge, it may seem that if their substance remains, they will keep on moving also in the state of consummation. And, indeed, if motion were possessed by heavenly bodies for the same reason as that for which it is possessed by elements, such an assertion would be logical. Motion is found in heavy or light elements to promote the perfection they are to attain: by their natural motion they tend to the place that suits them, where they are in a better condition. Hence in the ultimate state of consummation each element and each part thereof will be in its own proper place.

But this cannot be maintained of the motion of heavenly bodies, for a heavenly body does not come to rest in any place it may occupy; as it travels naturally to any particular place, it no less naturally departs thence. Therefore heavenly bodies suffer no loss if they are deprived of motion because motion is not found in them for their own perfection. Also, it would be ridiculous to contend that a heavenly body is moved in circles by its nature as an active principle, in the way that a light body is impelled upward by its nature. For, as is evident, nature tends invariably in the direction of unity; and therefore that which by its very concept opposes unity cannot be the ultimate goal of nature. But motion is opposed to unity, in the sense that what moves varies in its mode of being by the very fact that it is in motion. Therefore nature does not produce motion just for the sake of motion, but in causing motion has in view the *terminus* to be reached by motion.

For instance, a body that is naturally light seeks an elevated place in its ascent; and so of other bodies. Consequently, since the circular motion of a heavenly body does not tend to a definite position, we cannot say that the active principle of a heavenly body's circular motion is nature, in the sense that nature is the principle of the motion of heavy and light bodies. Accordingly, there is no reason why heavenly bodies should not come to rest, without any change in their nature, even though fire, if its nature is to remain constant, cannot cease from its restlessness as long as it exists outside its proper sphere. Nevertheless we say that the motion of a heavenly body is natural; but it is natural not by reason of an active principle of motion in it, but by reason of the mobile body itself that has an aptitude for such motion. We conclude, therefore, that motion is communicated to a heavenly body by some intellect.

However, since an intellect does not impart movement except in view of some end, we must discover the end of the motion of heavenly bodies. The motion itself cannot be this end. For motion is the way leading to perfection and so does not verify the concept of end but rather pertains to that which is tending toward an end. Likewise we cannot maintain that a succession of locations is the term of the movement of a heavenly body, as though a heavenly body moved for the purpose of actually occupying every position for which it has a potency; this would entail endless wandering, and what is endless contradicts the notion of end.

We ought to think of the end of the heaven's motion somewhat as follows. Any body set in motion by an intellect is evidently an instrument of the latter. But the end of an instrument's motion is a form conceived by the principal agent, a form that is reduced to act by the motion of the instrument. The form conceived by the divine intellect, to be realized by the motion of the heavens, is the perfection of things as achieved by way of generation and corruption. But the ultimate end of generation and corruption is the noblest of all forms, the human soul; and the soul's ultimate end is eternal life, as we said above.[193] Accordingly, the ultimate end of the movement of the heavens is the multiplication of men, who are to be brought into being for eternal life.

Such a multitude cannot be infinite; the intention to be realized by any intellect comes to rest in something definite. So, once

[193] Cf. chaps. 150, 163.

the number of men who are to be brought into being for eternal life is filled out and they are actually established in the possession of eternal life, the movement of the heavens will cease, just as the motion of any instrument ceases after a project has been carried through to completion. And when the movement of the heavens ceases, all movement in lower bodies will cease by way of consequence, excepting only the movement that will be in men as flowing from their souls. And thus the entire material universe will have a different arrangement and form, in accordance with the truth proclaimed in 1 Corinthians 7:31: "The fashion of this world passeth away."

Heaven, Hell, and Purgatory

172
Man's reward or misery according to his works

This leads to our next point. If there is a definite way of reaching a fixed end, they who travel along a road leading in the opposite direction or who turn aside from the right road, will never reach the goal. A sick man is not cured by using the wrong medicines, forbidden by the doctor, except, perhaps, quite by accident.

There is such a definite way of arriving at happiness (namely, the practice of virtue). Nothing will reach its end unless it performs well the operations proper to it. A plant will not bear fruit if the procedure natural to it is not followed. A runner will not win a trophy or a soldier a citation, unless each of them carries out his proper functions. To say that a man discharges his proper office is equivalent to saying that he acts virtuously; for the virtue of any being is that which makes its possessor good and also makes his work good, as is stated in the second book of Aristotle's *Ethics*.[194] Accordingly, since the ultimate end of man is eternal life, of which

---

[194] Aristotle, *Nicomachean Ethics*, II, 6 (1106 a 15).

we spoke previously,[195] not all attain it, but only those who act as virtue requires.

Besides, as we said above, not natural things alone, but also human affairs are contained under Divine Providence, and this not only in general but in particular.[196] But He who has care of individual men has disposal of the rewards to be assigned for virtue and of the punishments to be inflicted for sin. For, as we stated above,[197] punishment has a medicinal value with regard to sin and restores right order when it is violated by sin; and the reward of virtue is happiness, to be granted to man by God's goodness. Therefore God will not grant happiness to those who act against virtue, but will assign as punishment the opposite of happiness (namely, extreme wretchedness).

173
Reward and misery postponed to the next world

In this matter we should note that contrary causes beget contrary effects. Thus action that proceeds from malice is contrary to action that proceeds from virtue. Accordingly, wretchedness, in which evil action issues, is the opposite of happiness, which virtuous action merits. Furthermore, contraries pertain to the same genus. Therefore, since final happiness, which is reached by virtuous action, is a good that belongs not to this life but to the next life (as is clear from an earlier discussion[198]), final wretchedness, also, to which vice leads, must be an evil belonging to the next world.

[195]Cf. chap. 150.
[196]Cf. chaps. 123, 133, 143.
[197]Cf. chap. 121.
[198]Cf. chap. 150.

Besides, all goods and ills of this life are found to serve some purpose. External goods, and also bodily goods, are organically connected with virtue, which is the way leading directly to beatitude, for those who use such goods well. But for those who use these goods ill, they are instruments of vice, which ends up in misery. Similarly the ills opposed to such goods (such as sickness, poverty, and the like) are an occasion of progress in virtue for some but aggravate the viciousness of others, according as men react differently to such conditions. But what is ordained to something else cannot be the final end, because it is not the ultimate in reward or punishment. Therefore neither ultimate happiness nor ultimate misery consists in the goods or ills of this life.

174
Wretchedness flowing from the punishment of loss

Since the wretchedness to which vice leads is opposed to the happiness to which virtue leads, whatever pertains to wretchedness must be understood as being the opposite of all we have said about happiness. We pointed out above that man's ultimate happiness, as regards his intellect, consists in the unobstructed vision of God.[199] And as regards man's affective life, happiness consists in the immovable repose of his will in the first Good. Therefore man's extreme unhappiness will consist in the fact that his intellect is completely shut off from the divine light, and that his affections are stubbornly turned against God's goodness. And this is the chief suffering of the damned. It is known as the punishment of loss.

However, as should be clear from what we said on a previous occasion,[200] evil cannot wholly exclude good, since every evil has

[199]Cf. chaps. 104, 106.
[200]Cf. chap. 117.

199

its basis in some good. Consequently, although suffering is opposed to happiness, which will be free from all evil, it must be rooted in a good of nature. The good of an intellectual nature consists in the contemplation of truth by the intellect and in the inclination to good on the part of the will.

But all truth and all goodness are derived from the first and supreme good, which is God. Therefore the intellect of a man situated in the extreme misery of Hell must have some knowledge of God and some love of God, but only so far as He is the principle of natural perfections. This is natural love. But the soul in Hell cannot know and love God as He is in Himself, nor so far as He is the principle of virtue or of grace and the other goods through which intellectual nature is brought to perfection by Him; for this is the perfection of virtue and glory.

Nevertheless men buried in the misery of Hell are not deprived of free choice, even though their will is immovably attached to evil. In the same way the blessed retain the power of free choice, although their will is fixed on the Good. Freedom of choice, properly speaking, has to do with election. But election is concerned with the means leading to an end. The last end is naturally desired by every being. Hence all men, by the very fact that they are intellectual, naturally desire happiness as their last end, and they do so with such immovable fixity of purpose that no one can wish to be unhappy. But this is not incompatible with free will, which extends only to means leading to the end. The fact that one man places his happiness in this particular good while another places it in that good, is not characteristic of either of these men so far as he is a man, since in such estimates and desires men exhibit great differences. This variety is explained by each man's condition. By this I mean each man's acquired passions and habits; and so if a man's condition were to undergo change, some other good would appeal to him as most desirable.

This appears most clearly in men who are led by passion to crave some good as the best. When the passion, whether of anger or lust, dies down, they no longer have the same estimate of that good as they had before.

Habits are more permanent, and so men persevere more obstinately in seeking goods to which habit impels them. Yet, so long as habit is capable of change, man's desire and his judgment as to what constitutes the last end are subject to change. This possibility is open to men only during the present life, in which their state is changeable. After this life the soul is not subject to alteration. No change can affect it except indirectly, in consequence of some change undergone by the body.

However, when the body is resumed, the soul will not be governed by changes occurring in the body.[201] Rather, the contrary will take place. During our present life the soul is infused into a body that has been generated of seed, and therefore, as we should expect, is affected by changes experienced in the body. But in the next world the body will be united to a preexisting soul, and so will be completely governed by the latter's conditions. Accordingly, the soul will remain perpetually in whatever last end it is found to have set for itself at the time of death, desiring that state as the most suitable, whether it is good or evil. This is the meaning of Ecclesiastes 11:3: "If the tree fall to the south or to the north, in what place soever it shall fall, there shall it be." After this life, therefore, those who are found good at the instant of death will have their wills forever fixed in good. But those who are found evil at that moment will be forever obstinate in evil.

---

[201] The editions appear to give a defective reading here. In translating this sentence, I understand *anima* to be the antecedent of *ipsa*, and read *mutationem* for *mutatio.*—*Trans.*

175
Forgiveness of sin in the next world

This enables us to perceive that mortal sins are not forgiven in the next world but venial sins are forgiven there. Mortal sins are committed by turning away from our last end, in which man is irrevocably settled after death, as we have just said. Venial sins, however, do not regard our last end, but rather the road leading to that end.

If the will of evil men is obstinately fettered to evil after death, they forever continue to desire what they previously desired, in the conviction that this is the best. Therefore they are not sorry they have sinned; for no one is sorry he has achieved what he judges to be the best.

But we should understand that those who are condemned to final misery cannot have after death what they craved as the best. Libertines in Hell will have no opportunity to gratify their passions; the wrathful and the envious will have no victims to offend or obstruct; and so of all the vices in turn.

But the condemned will be aware that men who have lived a virtuous life in conformity with the precepts of virtue obtain what they desired as best. Therefore the wicked regret the sins they have committed, not because sin displeases them, for even in Hell they would rather commit those same sins, if they had the chance, than possess God; but because they cannot have what they have chosen, and can have only what they have detested.

Hence their will must remain forever obstinate in evil, and at the same time they will grieve most agonizingly for the sins they have committed and the glory they have lost. This anguish is called remorse of conscience and in Scripture is it is referred to metaphorically as a worm, as we read in Isaiah 66:24: "Their worm shall not die."

176
Properties of the bodies of the damned

As we said above in speaking of the saints, the beatitude of the soul will in some manner flow over to the body.[202] In the same way the suffering of lost souls will flow over to their bodies.

Yet we must observe that suffering does not exclude the good of nature from the body, any more than it does from the soul. Therefore the bodies of the damned will be complete in their kind, although they will not have those qualities that go with the glory of the blessed.

That is, they will not be subtile and impassible; instead, they will remain in their grossness and capacity for suffering, and, indeed, these defects will be heightened in them. Nor will they be agile, but will be so sluggish as scarcely to be maneuverable by the soul. Lastly, they will not be radiant but will be ugly in their swarthiness, so that the blackness of the soul may be mirrored in the body, as is intimated in Isaiah 13:8: "Their countenances shall be as faces burnt."

177
Suffering compatible with incorruptibility in the bodies of the damned

Although the bodies of the damned will be capable of suffering, they will not be subject to corruption. This is a fact we have to admit, even though it may seem to disagree with present experience, according to which heightened suffering tends to deteriorate substance. In spite of this, there are two reasons why suffering that lasts forever will not corrupt the bodies undergoing it.

[202]Cf. chap. 168.

First, when the movement of the heavens ceases, as we said above,[203] all transformation of nature must come to a stop. Nothing will be capable of alteration in its nature; only the soul will be able to admit some alteration.

In speaking of an *alteration of nature,* I mean, for instance, a change from hot to cold in a thing or any other such variation in the line of natural qualities. And by *alteration of the soul* I mean the modification that takes place when a thing receives a quality, not according to the quality's natural mode of being, but according to its own spiritual mode of being. For example, the pupil of the eye receives the form of a color — not that it may be colored itself, but that it may perceive color.

In this way the bodies of the damned will suffer from fire or from some other material agent, not that they may be transformed into the likeness or quality of fire, but that they may experience the effects characteristic of its qualities.

Furthermore, this experience will be painful, because the effects produced by the action of fire are opposed to the harmony in which the pleasure of sense consists. Yet the action of Hellfire will not cause corruption, because spiritual reception of forms does not modify bodily nature, except, it may be, indirectly.

The second reason is drawn from a consideration of the soul, in whose perpetual duration the body will be forced, by divine power, to share. The condemned person's soul, so far as it is the form and nature of such a body, will confer perpetual existence on the latter. But because of its imperfection, the soul will not be able to bestow on the body immunity from suffering. Consequently the bodies of the damned will suffer forever, but will not undergo dissolution.

---

[203] Cf. chap. 171.

178
Punishment of the damned prior to the resurrection

This discussion makes it clear that both happiness and wretchedness are experienced chiefly in the soul. They affect the body secondarily and by a certain derivation. Hence the happiness or misery of the soul will not depend on the well-being or suffering of the body; rather, the reverse is true. Souls remain in existence after death and prior to the resumption of the body, some adorned with the merit of beatitude, others disfigured by deserved wretchedness. Therefore we can see that even before the resurrection the souls of some men enjoy the happiness of Heaven, as the Apostle indicates in 2 Corinthians 5:1: "For we know, if our earthly house of this habitation is dissolved, that we have a building of God, a house not made with hands, eternal in Heaven." A little below, in verse 8, he adds: "But we are confident and have a good will to be absent rather from the body and to be present with the Lord." But the souls of some will live in torment, as is intimated in Luke 16:22: "The rich man also died, and he was buried in Hell."

179
Spiritual and corporal punishment of the damned

We should realize that the happiness enjoyed by the souls of the saints will consist exclusively in spiritual goods. On the other hand, the punishment inflicted on the souls of the damned, even before the resurrection, will not consist solely in spiritual evils, as some have thought;[204] lost souls will also undergo corporal punishment.

---

[204]Thus Origen, *Peri archon*, II, 10 (PG, XI, 236); Theophylact, *In evangelium Marci*, cap. IX, *vers.* 42-49 (PG, CXXIII, 593); Avicenna, *Metaph.*, IX, 7 (106VB).

The reason for this difference is as follows. When the souls of the saints were united to their bodies here in this world, they observed right order, not subjecting themselves to material things but serving God alone. And so their whole happiness consists in the enjoyment of Him, not in any material goods. But the souls of the wicked, in violation of the order of nature, set their affections on material things, scorning divine and spiritual goods. In consequence, they are punished not only by being deprived of spiritual goods, but by being subjected to the tyranny of material things. Accordingly, if Sacred Scripture is found to promise a reward of material goods to the souls of the saints, such passages are to be interpreted in a mystical sense; for spiritual things are often described in Scripture in terms of their likeness to material things. But texts that portend the corporal punishments of the souls of the damned, specifying that they will be tormented by the fires of Hell, are to be understood literally.

180
The soul and corporeal fire

The assertion that a soul separated from its body can be tortured by corporeal fire should not seem nonsensical when we reflect that it is not contrary to the nature of a spiritual substance to be confined to a body. This happens in the ordinary course of nature, as we see in the union of the soul with the body. The same effect is sometimes produced by the arts of black magic, by which a spirit is imprisoned in images or amulets or other such objects.

The power of God can undoubtedly bring it about that spiritual substances, which are raised above the material world by their nature, may nevertheless be tied down to certain bodies, such as Hellfire; not in the sense that they animate the body in question, but in the sense that they are in some way fettered to it. And this very fact, brought home to the consciousness of a spiritual sub-stance, namely, that it is thus subjected to the dominion of a lowly creature, is grievous to it.

Inasmuch as this awareness is distressing to the spiritual sub-stance, the contention that the soul "burns by the very fact that it perceives itself to be in fire,"[205] is substantiated. Thus understood, the fire is plainly spiritual, for what directly causes the distress is the fire apprehended as imprisoning. But inasmuch as the fire in which the spirit is incarcerated is corporeal fire, the further state-ment made by Gregory is borne out, namely, that "the soul is in agony not only because it perceives, but also because it experi-ences, the fire."[206]

Furthermore, since this fire has the power of imprisoning the spiritual substance, not of its own nature, but by the might of God, the view is fittingly expressed by some that the fire acts on the soul as an instrument of God's vindictive justice.[207] This does not mean that the fire acts on the spiritual substance as it acts on bodies, by heating, parching, and consuming; its action is restrictive, as we said.

And since that which directly afflicts the spiritual substance is the awareness that the fire incarcerates it for its punishment, we can reasonably suppose that the suffering does not cease even if, by God's dispensation, the spiritual substance should happen for a time to be released from the fire. In the same way a criminal who has been sentenced to perpetual irons feels no diminution of his unremitting pain even though the chains should be struck off for an hour.

---

[205] St. Gregory the Great, *Dialogi*, IV, 29 (*PL*, LXXVII, 368).

[206] Ibid.

[207] Cf. St. Augustine, *De civitate Dei*, XXI, 10 (*PL*, XLI, 725); Julian of Toledo, *Prognosticon*, II, 17 (*PL*, XCVI, 482).

181
Punishments of Purgatory for unexpiated mortal sins

Although some souls may be admitted to eternal beatitude as soon as they are released from their bodies, others may be held back from this happiness for a time. For it sometimes happens that during their lives people have not done full penance for the sins they have committed, but for which they have been sorry in the end. Since the order of divine justice demands that punishment be undergone for sins, we must hold that souls pay after this life the penalty they have not paid while on Earth.

This does not mean that they are banished to the ultimate misery of the damned. For by their repentance they have been brought back to the state of charity, whereby they cleave to God as their last end, so that thereby they have merited eternal life. Hence we conclude that there are certain purgatorial punishments after this life, by which the debt of penalty not previously paid is discharged.

182
Punishment in Purgatory for venial sins

It also happens that some men depart this life free from mortal sin but nevertheless stained with venial sin. The commission of such sins does not, indeed, turn them from their last end; but by committing them they have erred with regard to the means leading to the end, out of undue attachment to those means. In the case of some perfect men sins of this kind are expiated by the fervor of their love. But in others these sins must be atoned for by punishment of some sort; no one is admitted to the possession of eternal life unless he is free from all sin and imperfection. Therefore we must acknowledge the existence of purgatorial punishment after this life.

Such punishments derive their cleansing power from the condition of those who suffer them. For the souls in Purgatory are adorned with charity, by which their wills are conformed to the divine will; it is owing to this charity that the punishments they suffer avail them for cleansing.

This is why punishment has no cleansing force in those who lack charity, such as the damned. The defilement of their sin remains forever, and so their punishment endures forever.

183
Eternal punishment for momentary sin is compatible with divine justice

The suffering of eternal punishment is in no way opposed to divine justice. Even in the laws men make, punishment need not correspond to the offense in point of time. For the crime of adultery or murder, either of which may be committed in a brief span of time, human law may prescribe lifelong exile or even death, by both of which the criminal is banned forever from the society of the state. Exile, it is true, does not last forever, but this is purely accidental, owing to the fact that man's life is not everlasting; but the intention of the judge, we may assume, is to sentence the criminal to perpetual punishment, so far as he can. In the same way it is not unjust for God to inflict eternal punishment for a sin committed in a moment of time.

We should also take into consideration the fact that eternal punishment is inflicted on a sinner who does not repent of his sin, and so he continues in his sin up to his death. And since he is in sin for eternity, he is reasonably punished by God for all eternity. Furthermore, any sin committed against God has a certain infinity when regarded from the side of God, against whom it is committed. For, clearly, the greater the person who is offended, the more grievous is the offense. He who strikes a soldier is held more gravely accountable than if he struck a peasant; and his offense is much more serious if he strikes a prince or a king. Accordingly, since God is infinitely great, an offense committed against Him is in a certain respect infinite; and so a punishment that is in a certain respect infinite is duly attached to it. Such a punishment cannot be infinite in intensity, for nothing created can be infinite in this way. Consequently a punishment that is infinite in duration is rightly inflicted for mortal sin.

Moreover, while a person is still capable of correction, temporal punishment is imposed for his emendation or cleansing. But if a sinner is incorrigible, so that his will is obstinately fixed in sin, as we said above is the case with the damned,[208] his punishment ought never to come to an end.

184
The eternal lot of other spiritual substances is similar to that of souls

In his intellectual nature man resembles the angels, who are capable of sin, as also man is. We spoke of this above.[209] Hence all that has been set forth about the punishment or glory of souls should be understood also of the glory of good angels and the punishment of bad angels. Men and angels exhibit only one point of difference in this regard: the wills of human souls receive confirmation in good or obstinacy in evil when they are separated from their bodies, as was said above;[210] whereas angels were immediately made blessed or eternally wretched as soon as, with full deliberation of will, they fixed upon God or some created good as their end. The variability found in human souls can be accounted

[208] Cf. chap. 174.
[209] Cf. chap. 113.
[210] Cf. chaps. 166, 174.

for not only by the liberty of their wills but also by the modifications their bodies undergo; but in the angels such variability comes from the freedom of will alone. And so angels achieve immutability at the very first choice they make; but human souls are not rendered immutable until they leave their bodies.

To express the reward of the good, we say in the Creed: "I believe . . . in life everlasting." This life is to be understood as eternal not because of its duration alone, but much more because it is the fruition of eternity. Since in this connection there are proposed for our belief many other truths that concern the punishments of the damned and the final state of the world, the Creed of the Fathers[211] sums up the whole doctrine in this proposition: "I look for . . . the life of the world to come." This phrase ("the world to come") takes in all these points.

---

[211] The Nicene Creed.

The Humanity of Christ

The Second Treatise on Faith

Prologue

As was remarked in the beginning of this work, the Christian Faith revolves about two main doctrines: the divinity of the Trinity and the humanity of Christ.[212] In the foregoing treatise on the Divine Trinity,[213] we reviewed the truths that pertain to divinity and its effects. We now turn to a consideration of matters pertaining to the humanity of Christ.

Since, however, as the Apostle remarks in 1 Timothy 1:15, "Christ Jesus came into this world to save sinners," we shall do well to inquire first how the human race fell into sin, so that we may understand more clearly how men are freed from their sins through Christ's humanity.

[212] Cf. chap. 2.
[213] Chaps. 2-184.

Adam, Eve, and Original Sin

186
The commands given to Adam and his perfection in the pristine state

We saw above that man was originally constituted by God in such a condition that his body was completely subject to his soul.[214] Further, among the faculties of the soul, the lower powers were subject to reason without any rebelliousness; and man's reason itself was subject to God. In consequence of the perfect subjection of the body to the soul, no passion could arise in the body that would in any way conflict with the soul's dominion over the body. Therefore neither death nor illness had any place in man. And from the subjection of the lower powers to reason there resulted in man complete peace of mind, for the human reason was troubled by no inordinate passions. Finally, owing to the submission of man's will to God, man referred all things to God as to his last end, and in this his justice and innocence consisted.

Of these three subordinations, the last was the cause of the other two. Surely man's freedom from dissolution or from any

[214]Cf. chap. 152.

suffering that would be a threat to his life did not come from the nature of his body, as we see if we regard its component parts; for the body was made up of contrary elements. Similarly, the fact that man's sense faculties were subservient to reason without any rebelliousness did not come from the nature of the soul, since the sense powers naturally tend toward objects that cause pleasure in the senses, even when, as often happens, delights of this sort are at odds with right reason.

This harmony came from a higher power, the power of God. It was God who, in the first instance, united to the body the rational soul that so immeasurably surpasses the body and the bodily faculties, such as the sense powers. Likewise it was God who gave to the rational soul the power to control the body itself in a manner that exceeded the natural condition of the body, and also to govern the sense faculties so that they would function in a way befitting a rational soul.

In order, therefore, that reason might firmly hold the lower faculties under its sway, reason itself had to be firmly kept under the dominion of God, from whom it received this power so greatly surpassing the condition of nature.

Accordingly, man was so constituted that, unless his reason was subservient to God, his body could not be made subject to the beck of the soul, nor could his sense powers be brought under the rule of reason. Hence in that state life was in a certain way immortal and impassible; that is, in that state man could neither die nor suffer, so long as he did not sin. Nevertheless he retained the power to sin, since his will was not yet confirmed in good by the attainment of the last end. In the event that this happened, man could suffer and die.

It is precisely in this respect that the impassibility and immortality possessed by the first man differ from the impassibility and immortality to be enjoyed after the resurrection by the saints, who will never be subject to suffering and death, since their wills will be wholly fixed upon God, as we said above.[215] There is another difference: after the resurrection men will have no use for food or the reproductive functions. But the first man was so constituted that he had to sustain his life with food and he had a mandate to perform the work of generation; for the human race was to be multiplied from this one parent. Hence he received two commands, in keeping with his condition. The first is that mentioned in Genesis 2:16: "Of every tree of Paradise thou shalt eat." The other is reported in Genesis 1:28: "Increase and multiply and fill the Earth."

187
The state of Original Justice

This wonderfully ordered state of man is called *Original Justice*. By it, man himself was subject to God on high and all lower creatures were subordinate to man, as is indicated in Genesis 1:26: "Let him have dominion over the fishes of the sea and the fowls of the air." And among the component parts of man, the lower were subservient to the higher without any conflict. This state was granted to man, not as to a private individual, but as to the first principle of human nature, so that through him it was to be handed down to his descendants together with human nature.

Moreover, since every one ought to have a habitation befitting his condition, man thus harmoniously constituted was placed in a most temperate and delightful region, so that all inconvenience, not only of internal annoyance but also of external surroundings, might be far removed from him.

---

[215] Cf. chap. 166.

188
The tree of knowledge of good and evil

This state enjoyed by man depended on the submission of the human will to God. That man might be accustomed from the very beginning to follow God's will, God laid certain precepts on him. Man was permitted to eat of all the trees in Paradise, with one exception: he was forbidden under pain of death to eat of the tree of knowledge of good and evil.

Eating of the fruit of this tree was prohibited not because it was evil in itself, but so that at least in this slight matter man might have some precept to observe for the sole reason that it was so commanded by God. Hence eating of the fruit of this tree was evil because it was forbidden. The tree was called the *tree of knowledge of good and evil* not because it had the power to cause knowledge, but because of the sequel: by eating of it man learned by experience the difference between the good of obedience and the evil of disobedience.

189
Seduction of Eve by the Devil

The Devil, who had already fallen into sin, saw that man was so equipped that he could arrive at everlasting happiness, from which the Devil himself had been cast out. Yet, as he knew, man could still sin.

So he sought to lead man astray from the straight path of justice by attacking him on his weaker side; that is, he tempted the woman, in whom the gift of light or wisdom shone with a lesser brilliance. The more easily to induce her to break the command, he lyingly drove from her mind the fear of death and he promised her what man naturally desires (the overcoming of ignorance).

"Your eyes shall be opened,"[216] he said and in adding: "You shall be as gods," he held out to her the excellence of greatness. He further promised perfect knowledge, with the words: "knowing good and evil." On the part of his intellect man naturally shuns ignorance and desires knowledge; and on the part of his will, which is naturally free, he desires high station and perfection, so that he may be subject to no one, or at any rate to as few as possible.

190
The woman's sin

The woman craved both the promised exaltation and the perfection of knowledge. Added to this were the beauty and sweetness of the fruit, which drew her to eat of it. And so, scorning the fear of death, she violated God's command and ate of the forbidden tree.

Her sin has many aspects. First, there is a sin of pride, whereby she inordinately desired her own excellence. Second is a sin of curiosity, whereby she coveted knowledge beyond the limits fixed for her. Third is a sin of gluttony, whereby the sweetness of the fruit enticed her to eat. Fourth is a sin of infidelity, growing out of a false estimate of God, so that she believed the words of the Devil who gave the lie to God. Fifth is a sin of disobedience, consisting in a transgression of God's command.

191
The man's sin

The sin came to the man through the woman's blandishments. He, however, as the Apostle says in 1 Timothy 2:14, "was not seduced,"

[216]Gen. 3:5.

221

as the woman was. That is, he did not believe the words the Devil spoke against God. The thought could not cross his mind that God would utter a lying threat or that He would forbid the use of a thing for no good purpose. Yet he was drawn by the Devil's promise to an undue desire of excellence and knowledge. As a result, his will fell away from the right pursuit of justice and, consenting to his wife's importunities, he followed her in transgressing the divine command and ate of the fruit of the forbidden tree.

192
Effect of the sin in the rebellion of the lower faculties against reason

The harmonious integrity of the original state depended entirely on the submission of man's will to God. Consequently, as soon as the human will threw off the yoke of subjection to God, the perfect subjection of the lower powers to reason and of the body to the soul likewise disintegrated. As a result, man experienced in his lower, sensitive appetite the inordinate stirrings of concupiscence, anger, and all the other passions. These movements no longer followed the order set by reason but rather resisted reason, frequently darkening the mind and, so to speak, throwing it into confusion. This is that rebellion of the flesh against the spirit which Scripture mentions.[217] For, since the sensitive appetite, like all the other sense powers, operates through a bodily instrument, whereas reason functions without any bodily organ, what pertains to the sensitive appetite is rightly ascribed to the flesh, and what pertains to reason is attributed to the spirit. This is why substances that are without bodies are commonly called *spiritual substances*.

---

[217] Cf. Rom. 7:23: "But I see another law in my members fighting against the law of my mind and captivating me in the law of sin that is in my members."

193
The punishment as regards the necessity of dying

A further consequence was that the defect which consists in corruption was experienced in the body, and so man incurred the necessity of dying; his soul was no longer able to sustain the body forever by conferring life on it. Thus man became subject to suffering and death, not only in the sense that he was capable of suffering and dying as before, but in the sense that he was now under the necessity of suffering and dying.

194
Evils affecting the intellect and will

Many other defects began to appear in man. Inordinate stirrings of passion quickly followed one another in the lower appetites and at the same time the light of wisdom, which supernaturally illuminated man as long as his will was submissive to God, grew dim in his intellect. The result of this was that man turned his love to sensible objects. Immersed in these, he wandered far from God and fell into repeated sins.

Further, he gave his fidelity to unclean spirits he thought would help him to live a life of sensual pleasure and to acquire material goods. In this way, idolatry and other sins arose in the human race. The more man yielded to their baneful influence, the farther he left behind the knowledge and desire of spiritual and divine goods.

195
Transmission of these evils to posterity

The blessing of Original Justice was conferred by God on the human race in the person of its first parent in such a way that it was to be transmitted to his posterity through him. But when a cause is removed, the effect cannot follow. Therefore, when the first man stripped himself of this good by his sin, all his descendants were likewise deprived of it. And so for all time — that is, ever since the sin of the first parent — all men come into the world bereft of Original Justice and burdened with the defects that attend its loss.

This is in no way against the order of justice, as though God were punishing the sons for the crime of their first father. For the punishment in question is no more than the withdrawing of goods that were supernaturally granted by God to the first man for transmission, through him, to others. These others had no right to such goods, except so far as the gifts were to be passed on to them through their first parent. In the same way, a king may reward a soldier with the grant of an estate which is to be handed on by him to his heirs. If the soldier then commits a crime against the king, and so is adjudged to forfeit the estate, it cannot afterwards pass to his heirs. In this case the sons are justly dispossessed in consequence of their father's crime.

196
Privation of Original Justice as sin in Adam's descendants

But there remains a more pressing question: whether the privation of Original Justice can have the nature of sin in those who descend from the first parent. The notion of sin seems to require, as we said above, that the evil known as culpable should be in the power of him to whom it is imputed as fault.[218] No one is blamed for that which is beyond his power to do or not to do. But it is not in the

[218]Cf. chap. 120.

power of the person begotten to be born with Original Justice or without it. Hence we might be inclined to judge that such a privation cannot have the character of sin.

This question is easily solved if we but distinguish between person and nature. As there are many members in one person, so there are many persons in one human nature. Thus, by sharing in the same species, many men may be thought of as one man, as Porphyry remarks.[219] In this connection we should note that in the sin of one man different sins are committed by different members. Nor does the notion of sin require that the various sins be voluntary by the wills of the members whereby they are committed, for it is enough that they be voluntary by the will of that which is most excellent in man, that is, his intellectual part. For the hand cannot but strike and the foot cannot help walking, when the will so commands.

In this way, then, the privation of Original Justice is a sin of nature, in the sense that it has its origin in the inordinate will of the first principle in human nature, namely, of the first parent. Thus it is voluntary with respect to nature, that is, by the will of the first principle of nature. And so it is transmitted to all who receive human nature from him, for they are all, as it were, his members.

This is why it is called Original Sin, for it is transferred from the first parent to his descendants by their origin from him. Other sins (that is, actual sins) pertain immediately to the person who commits them; this sin directly touches nature. The first parent infected nature by his sin, and nature thus contaminated thereupon

---

[219] *Isagoge: De specie*, in H. Busse, *Commentaria in Aristotelem Graeca* (Berlin, 1887), IV.1, 6, 21. Cf. Boethius, *Commentaria in Porphyrium*, III (*PL*, LXIV, 111).

infects the persons of the children who receive their nature from the first parent.

197
Not all sins are transmitted to posterity

It does not follow, however, that all other sins, either of the first parent or of other parents, are handed down to posterity. For only the first sin of the first parent extirpated in its entirety the gift that had been supernaturally granted to human nature in the person of the first father. This is the reason why sin is said to have corrupted or infected nature.

Subsequent sins do not encounter anything of this sort that they can uproot from the whole of human nature. Such sins do, indeed, take away from man (or at least tarnish) some particular good, namely, a personal good; but they do not corrupt nature except so far as nature pertains to this or that person. Since man begets his like not in person but only in nature, the sin that defiles the person is not handed down from a parent to his descendants. Only the first sin that defiled nature as such is thus transmitted.

Christ's Incarnation

198
Insufficiency of Adam's merit to restore nature

Although the sin of the first parent infected the whole of human nature, neither his repentance nor any merit of his was able to restore nature in its entirety. Adam's repentance or any other merit of his was clearly the act of an individual person. But no act of any individual can affect the entire nature of the species. Causes that can affect a whole species are equivocal causes, not univocal. The sun is a cause of generation in the whole human species, but a man is only the cause of the generation of a particular man. Hence the individual merit of Adam (or of any other mere man) could not suffice to re-establish the whole of nature. True, all nature was defiled by a single act of the first man; but this effect followed only indirectly in the sense that, once the state of innocence had been devastated in him, it could not be conveyed through him to others.

Even if Adam were to recover grace through penance, he could not return to his pristine innocence, in view of which God had granted the gift of Original Justice. Moreover, the state of Original Justice was manifestly a very special gift of grace. Grace, however, is not acquired by merits, but is given *gratis* by God. Therefore the

Original Justice which the first man had from the beginning was not the result of his merit but was a gift of God. Much less, after his sin, could Adam merit it by his repentance or by the performance of any other work.

199

The restoration of human nature by Christ

Nevertheless in the plan of Divine Providence it was decreed that human nature, which had been ravaged in the manner described, should be restored. It could not be admitted to perfect beatitude unless it were freed of its defilement.

Beatitude, being a perfect good, tolerates no defect, especially the defect of sin; for sin is, in its own way, opposed to virtue, which is the path leading to beatitude, as was established above.[220] And so, since man was made for beatitude — seeing that beatitude is his ultimate end — one might conclude that God's work in creating so noble a being was doomed to frustration. But this the Psalmist holds to be inadmissible, for he says in Psalm 88:48: "Hast Thou made all the children of men in vain?"[221] Accordingly, it was fitting that human nature should be restored.

Furthermore, divine goodness exceeds the creature's capacity for good. As long as man leads a mortal life in this world, we know that his condition is such that he is neither immovably confirmed in good nor immovably obstinate in evil.[222]

Hence the very condition of human nature implies that it is capable of being cleansed from the contamination of sin. Surely the divine goodness would hardly allow this capacity to remain

[220]Cf. chap. 172.
[221]RSV: Ps. 89:47.
[222]Cf. chaps. 144, 145.

forever unrealized; but this would have been so had God not provided a remedy devised for man's restoration.

200
Restoration of man by God through the Incarnation

We indicated above that the reparation of human nature could not be effected either by Adam or by any other purely human being.[223] For no individual man ever occupied a position of preeminence over the whole of nature; nor can any mere man be the cause of grace.

The same reasoning shows that not even an angel could be the author of man's restoration. An angel cannot be the cause of grace, just as he cannot be man's recompense with regard to the ultimate perfection of beatitude to which man was to be recalled. In this matter of beatitude angels and men are on a footing of equality. Nothing remains, therefore, but that such restoration could be effected by God alone.

But if God had decided to restore man solely by an act of His will and power, the order of divine justice would not have been observed. Justice demands satisfaction for sin.

But God cannot render satisfaction, just as He cannot merit. Such a service pertains to one who is subject to another. Thus God was not in a position to satisfy for the sin of the whole of human nature; and a mere man was unable to do so, as we have just shown. Hence divine Wisdom judged it fitting that God should become man, so that thus one and the same person would be able both to restore man and to offer satisfaction. This is the reason for the

[223] Cf. chap. 198.

divine Incarnation assigned by the Apostle in 1 Timothy 1:15: "Christ Jesus came into this world to save sinners."

201
Other reasons for the Incarnation

There are also other reasons for the divine Incarnation. Man had withdrawn from spiritual things and had delivered himself up wholly to material things, from which he was unable by his own efforts to make his way back to God.

Therefore divine Wisdom, who had made man, took to Himself a bodily nature and visited man immersed in things of the body, so that by the mysteries of His bodily life He might recall man to spiritual life.

Furthermore, the human race had need that God should become man to show forth the dignity of human nature, so that man might not be subjugated either by devils or by things of the body.

At the same time, by willing to become man, God clearly displayed the immensity of His love for men, so that henceforth men might serve God, no longer out of fear of death, which the first man had scorned, but out of the love of charity.

Moreover, the Incarnation holds up to man an ideal of that blessed union whereby the created intellect is joined, in an act of understanding, to the uncreated Spirit. Since the time when God became united to man by taking a human nature to Himself, it is no longer incredible that a creature's intellect should be capable of union with God by beholding the divine essence.

Lastly, the Incarnation puts the finishing touch to the whole vast work envisaged by God. For man, who was the last to be created, returns by a sort of circulatory movement to his first beginning, being united by the work of the Incarnation to the very principle of all things.

202
The error of Photinus concerning the Incarnation

This mystery of the divine Incarnation, Photinus[224] set aside, so far as he was able. Following Ebion,[225] Cerinthus,[226] and Paul of Samosata,[227] he asserted that our Lord Jesus Christ was no more than a man and that He did not exist before the Virgin Mary, but earned the glory of divinity by the merit of a blessed life and by patiently enduring death; and thus He was called God not on account of His nature but by the grace of adoption. In this event no union of God with man would have been effected; only a man would be deified by grace. Elevation of this sort is not peculiar to Christ, but is common to all the saints, although some may be considered more highly endowed with such grace than others.

This error contradicts the authority of Sacred Scripture. In John 1:1 we read: "In the beginning was the Word." Shortly afterward the Evangelist adds: "And the Word was made flesh."[228] Hence the Word that in the beginning was with God assumed flesh. But Scripture does not say that a man who lacked previous existence was deified by the grace of adoption. Likewise, in John 6:38 the Lord says: "I came down from Heaven not to do my own

---

[224]Cf. St. Augustine, *De haeresibus*, 45 (*PL*, XLII, 34); Vigilius Tapsensis, *Contra Arianos dialogus*, I, 4 (*PL*, LXII, 182).

[225]Cf. St. Augustine, *De haeresibus*, 10 (*PL*, XLII, 27). The Ebionites, an ancient Judaeo-Christian sect deriving their name from a Hebrew word meaning "poor," lived mostly in the region around the Dead Sea and in Syria. They claimed to be followers of the original Christian community in Jerusalem, who are called "the poor" in Romans 15:26 and Galatians 2:10. Their Faith was not completely uniform, but denial of Christ's divinity was characteristic of all of them.

[226]Cf. St. Augustine, ibid., 8 (*PL*, XLII, 27).

[227]Cf. St. Augustine, ibid., 44 (*PL*, XLII, 34).

[228]John 1:14.

will, but the will of Him that sent me." According to the error of Photinus, Christ could not come down from Heaven, but could only go up to Heaven. Against him is the Apostle, who says in Ephesians 4:9: "That He ascended, what is it but because He also descended first into the lower parts of the Earth?" This enables us to understand clearly that the Ascension would have no place in Christ unless His descent from Heaven had preceded.

203
Error of Nestorius about the Incarnation

Nestorius[229] wished to avoid this contradiction. In part he disagreed with the error of Photinus. For Nestorius held that Christ was the Son of God not only by the grace of adoption but by the divine nature in which He existed coeternal with the Father. In part, however, he sided with Photinus, because he taught that the Son of God was united to man by mere habitation in him, but not in such a way that there was only one person who was both God and man. And so that man who, according to Photinus, is called God through grace alone, is called *the son of God* by Nestorius, not because he is truly God but because the Son of God dwells in him through the inhabitation effected by grace.

This error is also opposed to Scripture. For the union of God with man is called by the Apostle an "emptying"; in Philippians 2:6-7 he says of the Son of God: "Who, being in the form of God, thought it not robbery to be equal with God, but emptied Himself, taking the form of a servant." But there is no emptying of God when He dwells in a rational creature by grace. Otherwise the

---

[229] Cf. St. John Damascene, *De fide orthodoxa*, III, 3 (PG, XCIV, 993); Theodore of Mopsuestia, *Fragmentum de Incarnatione*, VII (PG, LXVI, 976); Second Council of Constantinople, can. 4, 5 (Denz., 216, 217).

Father and the Holy Spirit would be emptied out also, since they too dwell in the rational creature by grace. Thus in John 14:23 our Lord says of Himself and the Father: "We will come to him and will make our abode with him." And in 1 Corinthians 3:16 the Apostle says of the Holy Spirit: "The Spirit of God dwelleth in you."

Moreover, the man in question could hardly use words signifying divinity unless He were personally God. He would have been guilty of supreme presumption in saying, as He does in John 10:30, "I and the Father are one," and also in 8:58, "Before Abraham was made, I am." For the pronoun *I* indicates the person of the speaker, but He who uttered these words was a man. Hence the person of God and this man are one and the same.

To preclude such errors, both the Apostles' Creed and the Creed of the Nicene Fathers, after mentioning the person of the Son, add that He was conceived of the Holy Spirit, was born, suffered, died, and rose. Surely what pertains to the man would not be predicated of the Son of God unless the person of the Son of God and of the man were the same. What is proper to one person is, by that very fact, not said of another person; for example, what is proper to Paul is, for that precise reason, not predicated of Peter.

204
The error of Arius about the Incarnation

In their eagerness to proclaim the unity of God and man in Christ, some heretics went to the opposite extreme and taught that not only was there one person, but also a single nature in God and man. This error arose from Arius.[230] To defend his position that those

---

[230]Cf. St. Athanasius, *Contra Apollinarium*, I, 15; II, 3 (PG, XXVI, 1121, 1136); St. Augustine, *De haeresibus*, 49 (PL, XLII, 39); and Council of Nicaea (Denz., 54).

scriptural passages where Christ is shown as inferior to the Father, must refer to the Son of God Himself (in His assuming nature), Arius taught that in Christ there is no other soul than the Word of God who replaced the soul in Christ's body. So when Christ says in John 14:28, "The Father is greater than I" or when He prays or is sad, such matters refer to the nature of the Son of God. If this were so, the union of God's Son with man would be effected not only in the person, but also in the nature. For, as we know, the unity of human nature comes from union of soul and body.

The falsity of this position, so far as regards the assertion that the Son is less than the Father, was brought out above when we showed that the Son is equal to the Father.[231] And with respect to the theory that the Word of God took the place of the soul in Christ, the absurdity of this error can be shown by reverting to a point previously set forth. For, as we demonstrated above, the soul is united to the body as the latter's form.[232] But God cannot be the form of a body, as we also demonstrated above.[233] Arius could not counter by maintaining that this is to be understood of God the Father on high, since the same can be proved even of the angels (namely, that they cannot, of their very nature, be united to a body in the manner of a form, seeing that by nature they are separated from bodies). Much less, then, can the Son of God, by whom the angels were made (as even Arius admits[234]) be the form of a body.

Besides, even if the Son of God were a creature, as Arius falsely teaches, He nevertheless excels all created spirits in beatitude,

---

[231] Cf. chap. 41.

[232] Cf. chap. 90.

[233] Cf. chap. 17.

[234] Cf. the fragment of the *Thalia* preserved by St. Athanasius, *Contra Arianos*, I, 5 (PG, XXVI, 21); *Epistola ad Alexandrum*, in St. Athanasius, *De synodis*, 17 (PG, XXVI, 709).

according to the heresiarch himself.[235] But the beatitude of the angels is so great that they can suffer no sadness. Their happiness would not be true and complete if anything were wanting to their desires, since the notion of beatitude requires it to be the ultimate and perfect good wholly satisfying all desire. Much less can the Son of God be subject to sadness or fear in His divine nature. Yet we read that He was sad: "He began to fear and to be heavy" and "to be sad."[236] And He Himself gave witness of His sorrow, saying, "My soul is sorrowful even unto death."[237] Sadness, assuredly, pertains not to the body but to some substance capable of apprehension. So, besides the Word and the body, there must have been in Christ another substance that could suffer sadness. This we call the soul.

Further, if Christ assumed what is ours in order to cleanse us of sin, and if our greater need was to be cleansed in soul, from which sin arises and which is the subject of sin, we must conclude that He assumed not a body without a soul, but a body together with its soul, for the soul was the more important part for Him to assume.

205
The error of Apollinaris in regard to the Incarnation

These points also refute the error of Apollinaris,[238] who at first followed Arius in refusing to admit any soul in Christ other than the Word of God. However, he did not follow Arius in teaching

---

[235] *Thalia*, in St. Athanasius, *Contra Arianos*, I, 5 (PG, XXVI, 21); also, another fragment of the same work in St. Athanasius, *De synodis*, 15 (PG, XXVI, 707).

[236] Mark 14:33; Matt. 26:37.

[237] Mark 14:34.

[238] Cf. St. Athanasius, *Contra Apollinarium*, I, 2 (PG, XXVI, 1096); St. Augustine, *De haeresibus*, 55 (PL, XLII, 40); St. Leo the Great, *serm.* XXIV (*In nativitate Domini*, IV), 5 (PL, LIV, 207).

that the Son of God was a creature; for many things are said of Christ which cannot be ascribed to the body and are inadmissible in the Creator, such as sadness, fear, and the like. He was, then, finally driven to grant the existence in Christ of some soul which gave sense life to the body and could be the subject of such passions. Yet this soul was without reason and intellect and the Word Himself took the place of intellect and reason in the man Christ.

This theory is false on many grounds. First, the very concept of nature is incompatible with the opinion that a non-rational soul is the form of man, whose body nevertheless must have some form. But nothing monstrous or unnatural can be thought of in connection with Christ's Incarnation. Secondly, this hypothesis would be inconsistent with the purpose of the Incarnation, namely, the reparation of human nature. Above all, human nature needs to be restored in the intellectual sphere, for that which can have part in sin is precisely the rational soul. Hence it chiefly befitted God's Son to assume man's intellectual nature. Besides, Christ is said to have marveled.[239] But surprise cannot be experienced without a rational soul, and of course is wholly inadmissible in God. Therefore, as the sorrow Christ experienced forces us to admit that He had a sensitive soul, so the wonderment He expressed compels us to acknowledge the existence of a rational soul in Him.

206
The error of Eutyches regarding union in nature

To some extent, Eutyches also embraced the error of these heresiarchs.[240] He taught that there was one nature common to both

---

[239] Cf., e.g., Matt. 8:10: "And Jesus hearing this, marveled, saying . . . : I have not found so great faith in Israel."

[240] Cf. St. Leo the Great, *epist.* XXVIII, *Ad Flavianum*, 6 (PL, LIV, 777);

God and man after the Incarnation. However, he did not hold that Christ was lacking in soul or in intellect or in anything pertaining to the integrity of nature.

The erroneousness of this theory is plainly apparent. The divine nature is perfect in itself and is incapable of change. But a nature that is perfect in itself cannot combine with another nature to form a single nature unless it is changed into that other nature (as food is changed into the eater) or unless the other nature is changed into it (as wood is changed into fire) or unless both natures are transformed into a third nature (as elements are when they combine to form a mixed body). The divine immutability excludes all these alternatives. For neither that which is changed into another thing, nor that into which another thing can be changed, is immutable. Since, therefore, the divine nature is perfect in itself, it can in no way combine with some other nature to form a single nature.

Moreover, as we see if we reflect on the order of things, the addition of a greater perfection causes variation in the species of a nature. Thus a thing (such as a plant) that not only exists but lives, differs in species from a thing that merely exists.

And that which exists and lives and feels (such as an animal), differs in species from the plant, which merely exists and lives. Likewise a being that exists, lives, feels, and understands (namely, a man), differs in species from the brute animal, which merely exists, lives, and feels. So if the single nature which the Eutychean theory ascribes to Christ has the perfection of divinity in addition to all these other perfections, that nature necessarily differs in species from human nature in the way that human nature differs

Boethius, *De persona et duabus naturis*, 5-7 (PL, LXIV, 1347-52); St. John Damascene, *De fide orthodoxa*, III, 3 (PG, XCIV, 993); Council of Chalcedon (Denz., 148).

specifically from the nature of a brute animal. On this supposition, therefore, Christ would not be a man of the same species as other men, a conclusion shown to be false by Christ's descent from men according to the flesh. This is brought out by Matthew in his Gospel, which begins with the words: "The book of the generation of Jesus Christ, the son of David, the son of Abraham."[241]

207
Refutation of the Manichaean error about the nature of Christ's body

Photinus emptied the mystery of the Incarnation of all meaning by denying Christ's divine nature. Manichaeus did the same by denying Christ's human nature.[242] He held that the whole of material creation was the work of the Devil and that the Son of the good God could not becomingly take to Himself a creature of the Devil. Therefore he taught that Christ did not have real flesh but only phantom flesh. Consequently he asserted that everything narrated in the Gospel as pertaining to the human nature of Christ was done in appearance only and not in very truth.

This theory plainly gives the lie to Sacred Scripture, which relates that Christ was born of the Virgin, that He was circumcised, that He was hungry, that He ate, and that He had other experiences common to the nature of human flesh. Hence in recording such things of Christ, what is written in the Gospels would be false.

Besides, Christ says of Himself: "For this was I born, and for this came I into the world, that I should give testimony to the truth."[243] If He had displayed in Himself what really did not exist, He would

---

[241] Matt. 1:1.
[242] Cf. St. Augustine, *De haeresibus*, 46 (*PL*, XLII, 37).
[243] John 18:37.

have been a witness not of truth but rather of error; especially since He foretold that He would suffer that which He could not suffer without a body (namely, that he would be betrayed into the hands of men, that he would be spat upon, scourged, and crucified). Accordingly, to say that Christ did not have true flesh and that He suffered such indignities not in truth but only in appearance, is to accuse Him of lying.

Furthermore, to banish true conviction from men's minds is the act of a liar. Christ did expel a certain notion from the minds of His disciples. After His resurrection He appeared to the disciples, who thought that He was a spirit or a specter. To banish suspicion of this kind from their hearts, He said to them: "Handle and see: for a spirit hath not flesh and bones, as you see me to have."[244] On another occasion, when He was walking on the sea to the consternation of His disciples who thought He was an apparition, our Lord said: "It is I, fear ye not."[245] If the opinion entertained by the disciples about a spectral body is true, we have to concede that Christ was deceitful. But Christ is the Truth, as He testified of Himself.[246] Therefore the Manichaean theory is false.

208
The reality of Christ's earthly body, against Valentinus

Valentinus[247] admitted that Christ had a real body. However, he insisted that our Lord did not take flesh from the Blessed Virgin,

---

[244]Luke 24:39 (RSV: Luke 24:38).

[245]Matt. 14:27.

[246]John 14:6.

[247]Cf. St. Irenaeus, *Adversus haereses*, I, 7; 11 (PG, VII, 513, 561); Tertullian, *Adversus Valentinianos*, 27 (PL, II, 581); St. Augustine, *De haeresibus*, 11 (PL, XLII, 28).

but rather brought down with Him a body formed of celestial matter. This body passed through the Virgin without receiving anything from her, much as water passes through a canal.

This hypothesis, too, contradicts the truth of Scripture. In Romans 1:3 the Apostle says that God's Son "was made to Him of the seed of David, according to the flesh." And St. Paul writes in Galatians 4:4: "God sent His Son, made of a woman." Matthew likewise relates: "And Jacob begot Joseph, the husband of Mary, of whom was born Jesus, who is called Christ."[248] Later, Matthew refers to her as Christ's mother: "When His mother Mary was espoused to Joseph."[249]

None of this would be true if Christ had not received His flesh from the Virgin. Accordingly, the doctrine that Christ brought with Him a celestial body is false.

It is true that in 1 Corinthians 15:47 the Apostle states that "the second man" Christ [as contrasted with Adam, "the first man"] was "from Heaven, heavenly." But this is to be understood in the sense that He came down from Heaven in His divinity, not according to the substance of His body.

Moreover, there would be no reason why the Son of God, bringing His body from Heaven, should have entered the Virgin's womb, if He were to receive nothing from her. Such a procedure would seem to be a kind of deceit if, coming forth from His mother's womb, He were to intimate that He had received from her a body which in fact He had not received. Since, therefore, all falsehood is foreign to Christ, we must acknowledge without reservation that He came forth from the Virgin's womb in such a way that He really took His flesh from her.

[248] Matt. 1:16.
[249] Matt. 1:18.

209
The teaching of Faith about the Incarnation

We can gather together the various points established in the foregoing chapters and assert that, according to the true teaching of the Catholic Faith, Christ had a *real body* of the same nature as ours, a *true rational soul*, and, together with these, *perfect deity*. These three substances are united in one person, but do not combine to form one nature.

In undertaking to explain this truth, some theologians have taken the wrong path. Persuaded that every perfection accruing to a being subsequent to its complete existence is joined to it accidentally (as a garment is joined to a man), certain theologians taught that humanity was joined to divinity in the person of the Son by an accidental union, in such a way that the assumed nature would be related to the person of God's Son as clothing is related to a man.[250]

To bolster up this view, they brought forward what the Apostle says of Christ in Philippians 2:7, that He was "in habit found as a man." Likewise, they reflected that from the union of soul and body an individual possessed of rational nature is formed and that such an individual is called a *person*. If, therefore, the soul was united to the body in Christ, they were unable to see how they could escape the conclusion that a person would be constituted by such a union. In this event there would be two persons in Christ: the person who assumes and the person who is assumed. On the other hand, there are not two persons in a man who is clothed, because clothing does not possess what is required for the notion of a person. If, however, the clothes were a person, there would be

---

[250]Cf. Peter Lombard, *Sent.*, III, *dist.* 6, c. 4 (Quaracchi, II, 578f.).

two persons in a clothed man. To avoid this conclusion, therefore, some proposed that Christ's soul was never united to His body, but that the person of God's Son assumed soul and body separately.

This view, while trying to escape one absurdity, falls into a greater, for it entails the necessary consequence that Christ would not be true man. Surely true human nature requires the union of soul and body: a man is a being made up of both. A further consequence is that Christ would not be true flesh, and that none of His members would be a true member. For if the soul is taken away, there is no eye or hand or flesh and bone, except in an equivocal sense, as when these parts of the body are depicted in paint or fashioned in stone. Further, it would follow that Christ did not really die. Death is the privation of life. Obviously the divinity could not be deprived of life by death; and the body could not be alive if a soul were not united to it. A final consequence would be that Christ's body could not experience sensation; for the body has no sensation except through the soul united to it.

This theory falls back into the heresy of Nestorius, which it set out to overthrow. The error of Nestorius consisted in holding that the Word of God was united to Christ the man by the indwelling of grace, so that the Word of God would reside in that man as in His temple. It makes no difference, with regard to the doctrine proposed, whether we say that the Word is in the man as in a temple or whether we say that human nature is joined to the Word as a garment to the person wearing it, except that the second opinion is the worse, inasmuch as it cannot admit that Christ was true man. Accordingly, this view is condemned,[251] and deservedly so. Moreover, the man who is clothed cannot be the person of the clothes or garment, nor can he in any way be said to be in the

[251] By Alexander III, in *Epist. ad Willelmum*, "Cum Christus" (Denz., 393).

species of clothing. If, therefore, the Son of God took human nature to Himself, He cannot in any sense be called the person of the human nature, nor can He be said to pertain to the same species as the rest of men. Yet the Apostle says of Him that He was "made in the likeness of men."[252] Clearly, therefore, this theory is to be utterly rejected.

210
Exclusion of two supposita in Christ

Other theologians, wishing to avoid these absurdities, proposed that in Christ the soul was indeed united to the body and that this union constituted a certain man who, they maintained, was assumed by the Son of God in unity of person.[253] By reason of this assumption they said that the man in question was the Son of God and that the Son of God was that man. Further, since this assumption had unity of person as its *terminus*, they admitted that in Christ there was one person of God and man. But since this man who, they maintain, is composed of soul and body, is a certain *suppositum* or *hypostasis* of human nature, they place two *supposita* and two *hypostases* in Christ: one of human nature, created and temporal; the other of divine nature, uncreated and eternal.

As far as words go, this view appears to recede from the error of Nestorius. But if we examine it a little more closely, we find that it slips into the heresy identified with Nestorius.

For a person, clearly, is nothing else than an individual substance possessed of rational nature. But human nature is rational. Therefore by the very fact that a *hypostasis* or *suppositum* of human

---

[252] Phil. 2:7.
[253] Cf. Peter Lombard, *Sent.*, III, *dist.* 6, c. 2 (Quaracchi, II, 574).

nature, temporal and created, is admitted in Christ, a person that is temporal and created is also admitted in Him. This is precisely what the name of *suppositum* or *hypostasis* signifies (namely, an individual substance). Accordingly, if these people understand what they are saying, they must place two persons in Christ when they place two *supposita* or two *hypostases* in Him.

Another consideration is the following. Things that differ as *supposita* exist in such a way that what is proper to one cannot belong to another. Therefore, if the Son of God is not the same *suppositum* as the Son of man, it follows that what belongs to the Son of man cannot be attributed to the Son of God, and vice versa. Hence we could not say that God was crucified or born of the Virgin: which is characteristic of the Nestorian infamy.

If anyone should undertake to protest, in reply to this, that what pertains to the man in question is ascribed to the Son of God, and conversely, because of the unity of person, even though the *supposita* may be different, his answer simply cannot stand. Evidently the eternal *suppositum* of the Son of God is nothing else than His very person. Hence whatever is said of the Son of God by reason of His person would also be said of Him by reason of His *suppositum*. But what pertains to the man is not said of Him by reason of His *suppositum*, for the Son of God is represented as differing from the Son of man in *suppositum*. Therefore what is proper to the Son of man (such as his birth from the Virgin, his death, and the like) cannot be said of the Son of God by reason of the person.

Furthermore, if the name of God is predicated of a temporal *suppositum*, this will be something recent and new. But any being that is recently and newly called God, is not God unless he has been made God.

What is made God, however, is God not by nature, but only by adoption. Consequently the man in question would be God, not in fact and by nature, but merely by adoption: which, again, pertains to the error of Nestorius.

211
One suppositum and one person in Christ

Accordingly, we must say that in Christ there is not only one person of God and man, but also that there is but one *suppositum* and one *hypostasis*. There is not, however, only one nature, but two natures.

To see that this is so, we have but to reflect that the names *person*, *hypostasis*, and *suppositum* signify a whole of a certain kind. We cannot say that a hand or flesh or any of the other parts is a person or a *hypostasis* or a *suppositum*, but the whole, which is this man, is such. But terms that are common to individuals in the line of substance and accident (such as *individual* and *singular*) can be applied both to a whole and to its parts. Parts have something in common with accidents, in the sense that they do not exist by themselves but inhere in other things, although in a different way. We can say that the hand of Socrates or Plato is a certain kind of individual or singular thing, even though it is not a *hypostasis* or a *suppositum* or a person.

Furthermore, we should note that sometimes a union of various ingredients, considered just in itself, constitutes an integral whole, although in another being it does not constitute an integral whole because the addition of some other component is needed. Thus in a stone the combination of the four elements constitutes an integral whole; and so the object composed of the elements can, in the stone, be called a *suppositum* or *hypostasis*, which is this stone. It cannot, of course, be called a person, because it is not a *hypostasis* endowed with rational nature. But the combination of elements in an animal constitutes not an integral whole, but only a part (namely, the body). Something else must be added to make up the complete animal, and this is the soul. Hence the combination of elements in an animal does not constitute a *suppositum* or *hypostasis*; rather, this whole animal is the *hypostasis* or *suppositum*. Nevertheless the combination of elements is not, on this account, any less effectual in an animal than in a stone, but is rather more so, because it is ordained to the formation of a nobler being.

In all men save one the union of soul and body constitutes a *hypostasis* and *suppositum*, because in their case the *hypostasis* or *suppositum* is nothing else but these two components. But in our Lord Jesus Christ, besides soul and body, a third substance enters in, namely, the Godhead. In Him, therefore, the composite of body and soul is not a separate *suppositum* or *hypostasis*, nor is it a person. The *suppositum*, *hypostasis*, or person is that which is made up of three substances (namely, the body, the soul, and the divinity). In Christ, accordingly, just as there is but one person, so there is but one *suppositum* and one *hypostasis*. But the way His soul is joined to His body differs from the way His divinity is united to both. His soul comes to the body as its self-existing form, so that one nature, which is called human nature, is composed of these two. But the Godhead does not come to the soul and body as a form or as a part: this is against the very concept of divine perfection. Therefore the divinity and the soul and the body do not constitute one nature: but the divine nature, complete in itself and existing in its purity, took to itself, in a way that is incomprehensible and indescribable, the human nature composed of soul and body.

This called for an exercise of God's infinite power. For we know from experience that the greater an agent's power, the more effectively he avails himself of the instrument he uses to carry out an undertaking. Therefore, as the divine power, because of its infinity, is infinite and incomprehensible, the way Christ united human nature to Himself, as a sort of organ to effect man's salvation, is beyond human expression and surpasses every other union of God with creatures.

We pointed out above that *person*, *hypostasis*, and *suppositum* signify an integral whole. So if the divine nature in Christ had the function of a part (like the soul in the composition of a man) and were not something whole, then the one person of Christ would not be accounted for by the divine nature alone but would be a certain composite of three elements, just as in man the person, *hypostasis*, and *suppositum* is a composite of soul and body. However, since the divine nature is an integral whole that took human nature to itself by a mysterious, ineffable union, the person is accounted for by the divine nature, as is the *hypostasis* and *suppositum*. Yet the soul and body are drawn to the personality of the divine person, so that He is the person of the Son of God and is also the person, *hypostasis*, and *suppositum* of the Son of man.

Some sort of example of this can be found in creatures. Thus subject and accident are not united in such a way that some third thing is formed from them. In a union of this kind, the subject does not have the function of a part, but is an integral whole, which is a person, *hypostasis*, and *suppositum*. But the accident is drawn to the personality of the subject, so that the person of the man and of the color of whiteness is one and the same, and the *hypostasis* or *suppositum* is likewise the same. In a somewhat similar fashion the person, *hypostasis*, and *suppositum* of the Son of God is the person, *hypostasis*, and *suppositum* of the human nature in Christ. Influenced by comparisons of this sort, some theologians went so far as to say that the human nature in Christ deteriorates into an accident and is accidentally united to the Son of God;[254] they were unable to discriminate between literal truth and analogy.

---

[254] Peter Lombard, *Sent.*, III, *dist.* 6, c. 4 (Quaracchi, II, 578f.).

In any case, the foregoing exposition makes it clear that there is no other person in Christ but the eternal person, who is the person of the Son of God. Nor is there any other *hypostasis* or *suppositum*. Hence when we say, *this man,* pointing to Christ, we mean the eternal *suppositum*. Nevertheless the name *man* is not for that reason predicated equivocally of Christ and of other men. Equivocation does not follow diversity of supposition, but follows diversity of signification. The name of man, as attributed to Peter and to Christ, signifies the same thing, namely, human nature. But it does not have the same supposition; for in the one case it stands for the eternal *suppositum* of the Son of God, in the other case it stands for a created *suppositum*.

Since, however, we can predicate of a *suppositum* of any nature all that is proper to that nature to which the *suppositum* pertains, and since in Christ the *suppositum* of the human nature is the same as the *suppositum* of the divine nature, it is evident that everything belonging to the divine nature and everything belonging to the human nature can be predicated indifferently of this *suppositum* which pertains to both natures. This is true both when the name we use signifies the divine nature or person, and when it signifies the human nature. We can say, for example, that the Son of God is eternal, and that the Son of God was born of the Virgin. Likewise we can say that this man is God, that He created the stars, and that he was born, died, and was buried.

What is predicated of a *suppositum* is predicated of it according to some form or matter. Thus Socrates is white according to the whiteness of his skin and is rational according to his soul. But, as we pointed out in the beginning of this chapter, in Christ there are two natures and one *suppositum*. Therefore, if reference is made to the *suppositum*, human and divine attributes are to be predicated indifferently of Christ. Yet we must heed the sense in which each attribute is predicated; that is, divine attributes are predicated of

Christ according to His divine nature, and human attributes are predicated of Him according to His human nature.

212
Unity and multiplicity in Christ

Since there are in Christ one person and two natures, we have to examine the relationship between them to determine what is to be spoken of as one, and what is to be spoken of as multiple in Him.

Whatever is multiplied in accord with the diversity of Christ's natures, must be acknowledged to be plural in Him. In this connection we must consider, first of all, that nature is received by generation or birth. Consequently, as there are two natures in Christ, there must also be two generations or births: one that is eternal, whereby He received divine nature from His Father, and one that occurred in time, whereby He received human nature from His mother. Likewise, whatever is rightly attributed to God and man as pertaining to nature, must be predicated of Christ in the plural. To God are ascribed intellect and will and their perfections, such as knowledge or wisdom, and charity, and justice. These are also attributed to man as pertaining to human nature; for will and intellect are faculties of the soul, and their perfections are wisdom, justice, and the like. Therefore we must acknowledge two intellects in Christ, one human and one divine, and likewise two wills, as well as a double knowledge and charity (namely, the created and the uncreated).

But whatever belongs to the *suppositum* or *hypostasis* must be declared to be one in Christ. Hence if existence is taken in the sense that one *suppositum* has one existence, we are forced, it appears, to assert that there is but one existence in Christ. Of course, as is evident, when a whole is divided, each separate part has its own proper existence; but according as parts are considered in a whole, they do not have their own existence for they all exist with the existence of the whole. Therefore, if we look upon Christ as an integral *suppositum* having two natures, His existence will be but one, just as the *suppositum,* too, is one.

Since actions belong to *supposita,* some have thought that, as there is but one *suppositum* in Christ, so there is only one kind of action in Him.[255] But they did not rightly weigh the matter. For many actions are discerned in any individual, if there are many principles of activity in him. Thus in man the action of understanding differs from the action of sense perception because of the difference between sense and intellect. Likewise in fire the action of heating differs from the action of soaring upward, because of the difference between heat and lightness. Nature is related to action as its principle. Therefore it is not true that Christ has only one kind of activity because of the one *suppositum.* Rather, there are two kinds of action in Him, because of the two natures, just as, conversely, there is in the Holy Trinity but one activity of the three persons because of the one nature.

Nevertheless the activity of Christ's humanity has some part in the activity proper to His divine power. For of all the factors that come together in a *suppositum,* that which is the most eminent is served by the rest in an instrumental capacity, just as all the lesser faculties of man are instruments of his intellect. Thus in Christ the human nature is held to be, as it were, the organ of His divine nature. But it is clear that an instrument acts in virtue of the principal agent. This is why, in the action of an instrument, we are

---

[255]Thus Macarius, patriarch of Antioch; Cyrus, patriarch of Alexandria; Sergius, patriarch of Constantinople; and others. See the Third Council of Constantinople, *Actio* 13, especially *Actio* 18 (Mansi, XI, 554f., 638f.; Denz., 291f.). Cf. Leo II, *Epist. IV, Ad episcopos Hispaniae; Epist.* VI, *Ad Ervigium regem Hispaniae* (PL, XCVI, 414, 419); St. John Damascene, *De fide orthodoxa,* III, 15 (PG, XCIV, 1045).

able to discern not only the power of the instrument but also that of the principal agent. A chest is made by the action of an axe, but only so far as the axe is directed by the carpenter. In like manner the activity of the human nature in Christ received a certain efficacy from the divine nature, over and above its human power. When Christ touched a leper, the action belonged to His human nature; but the fact that the touch cured the man of his leprosy is owing to the power of the divine nature. In this way all the human actions and sufferings of Christ were efficacious for our salvation in virtue of His divinity. For this reason Dionysius calls the human activity of Christ *theandric*,[256] that is, "divine-human," because actions of this sort proceeded from His human nature in such a way that the power of the divinity was operative in them.

A doubt is raised by some theologians concerning sonship, whether there is only one filiation in Christ because of the oneness of the *suppositum*,[257] or two filiations because of the duality of His nativity.[258] It may seem that there are two filiations; for when a cause is multiplied, the effect is multiplied, and the cause of sonship is nativity. Since, therefore, there are two nativities of Christ, the consequence may seem to follow that there are also two filiations.

This view is not rejected by the fact that filiation is a personal relation (that is, that it constitutes a person). In the case of Christ, this is true of the divine filiation; the human filiation does not constitute a person, but comes to a person already constituted as

[256] *De divinis nominibus*, II, 6 (*PG*, III, 644).

[257] St. Bonaventure, III *Sent.*, d. 8, a. 2, q. 2 (Quaracchi, III, 194); St. Albert the Great, III *Sent.*, d. 8, a. 1 (ed. A. Borgnet, XXVIII, 163).

[258] This is the teaching of Robert Kilwardby, *Comment. in Sent.*, *lib.* III (Cod. 131, fol. 109r-v of Merton College, Oxford); cited by E. Longpré, O.F.M., "De B. Virginis maternitate et relatione ad Christum," *Antonianum*, VII (1932), 295. Cf. Peter Abelard, *Sic et non*, 75 (*PL*, CLXXVIII, 1448).

such. In the same way there is no reason why one man should not be related to his father and mother by a single filiation; he is born of both parents by the same nativity. Wherever the cause of a relation is the same, the relation is in reality but one, even though it may have many respects. There is nothing to prevent a thing from having a reference to another thing, even though no relation is really in it. Thus the knowable is referred to knowledge, although no relation exists in it. So, too, there is no reason why a single real relation should not have a number of respects. Just as a relation depends on its cause for its existence as a certain thing, so it also depends on its cause for the fact that it is one or multiple. Therefore, since Christ does not proceed from His Father and His mother by the same nativity, there may seem to be in Him two real filiations because of the two nativities.

But there is one reason why several real filiations cannot be attributed to Christ. Not everything that is generated by another can be called a son; only a complete *suppositum* can be called a son. Not a man's hand or foot, but the whole individual, Peter or John, is called son. Hence the proper subject of filiation is the *suppositum* itself. But we have shown earlier that the only *suppositum* in Christ is the uncreated *suppositum*,[259] which cannot receive any real relation beginning in time. As we intimated above, every relation of God to creatures is purely mental.[260] Consequently the filiation whereby the eternal *suppositum* of the Son is related to His virgin mother cannot be a real relation, but must be a purely mental relation.

However, this does not prevent Christ from being really and truly the Son of His virgin mother, because He was truly born of her. In the same way God is really and truly the Lord of His

[259] Cf. chap. 211.
[260] Cf. chaps. 54, 99.

creatures, because He possesses real power to coerce them; yet the relation of dominion is attributed to God only by a mental operation. Of course, if there were several *supposita* in Christ, as some theologians have taught,[261] there would be nothing to keep us from admitting two filiations in Christ, for in that case the created *suppositum* would be subject to temporal sonship.

213
Perfection of grace and wisdom in Christ

As was mentioned in the preceding chapter, the humanity of Christ is related to His divinity as a sort of organ belonging to it. The disposition and quality of organs are gauged chiefly by the purpose, though also by the dignity, of the person using them. Consequently we are to esteem the quality of the human nature assumed by the Word of God in accord with these norms. The purpose the Word of God had in assuming human nature was the salvation and reparation of human nature. Therefore Christ had to be of such excellence in His human nature that He could fittingly be the author of man's salvation. But the salvation of man consists in the enjoyment of God, whereby man is beatified; and so Christ must have had in His human nature a perfect enjoyment of God. For the principle in any genus must be perfect. But fruition of God has a twofold aspect: it requires satisfaction of the will and of the intellect. The will must adhere unreservedly to God by love; the intellect must know God perfectly.

Perfect attachment of the will to God is brought about by love and by grace, whereby man is justified, according to Romans 3:24: "Being justified freely by His grace." For man is made just by union

---

[261] Cf. Peter Lombard, *Sent.*, III, d. 6, c. 2 (Quaracchi, II, 574.)

with God through love. Perfect knowledge of God is effected by the light of wisdom, which is the knowledge of divine truth. Therefore the incarnate Word of God had to be perfect in grace and in the wisdom of truth. Hence we read in John 1:14: "The Word was made flesh, and dwelt among us; and we saw His glory, the glory as it were of the only begotten of the Father, full of grace and truth."

214
The fullness of Christ's grace

First we shall deal with the question of the fullness of grace in Christ. In this matter we should observe that the term *grace* may be understood in two senses.

According to one usage, it means "to be pleasing (*gratum*)": we say that someone is in the good graces of another because he is pleasing to him. In another sense, it means that "something is given *gratis*": a person is said to grant a grace to another when he confers *gratis* a benefit on that other.

These two meanings of *grace* are not wholly unconnected. A thing is given *gratis* to another because he to whom it is given is pleasing (*gratus*) to the giver, either simply or in some respect. The recipient is simply pleasing to the giver when he is pleasing to such an extent that the giver associates him with himself in some way.

For those whom we hold dear (*quos gratos habemus*) we attract to ourselves as far as we can, according to the quantity and degree in which they are dear to us. But the recipient is pleasing to the giver only in some respect when he is pleasing to the extent that he receives something from him, although not to the extent that he is taken into association by the donor. Clearly, therefore, everyone who has favor (*qui habet gratiam*) with another has something given to him *gratis*; but not everyone who has something given to him *gratis* is pleasing (*gratus*) to the donor. Hence we ordinarily distinguish between two kinds of grace: one, namely, which is only given *gratis*, and the other which, in addition, makes pleasing (*gratum facit*).

A thing is said to be given *gratis* if it is in no way due. A thing may be due in two ways, either according to nature or according to operation. According to nature, whatever the natural order of a thing requires, is due to it; thus the possession of reason and hands and feet is due to man. According to operation, a thing is due in the way that a recompense is due to a worker. Therefore those gifts are given *gratis* by God to men, which exceed the order of nature and are not acquired by merits. However, even gifts that are conferred by God because of merits sometimes retain the name and character of grace, because the principle of meriting comes from grace, and also because rewards are given over and above what human merits require, as we learn from Romans 6:23: "the grace of God, life everlasting."

Among such gifts, some exceed the capacity of human nature and are not given for merits. However, the fact that a man has these gifts does not prove that he is thereby rendered pleasing to God. Examples are the gifts of prophecy, of working miracles, of knowledge, of teaching, or any other such gifts divinely conferred. By these and like gifts man is not united to God, except, perhaps, by a certain similarity, so far as he shares to some extent in His goodness; but everything is assimilated to God in this way. Yet some gifts do render man pleasing to God and join man to Him. Such gifts are called graces, not only because they are given *gratis* but also because they make man pleasing to God.

The union of man with God is twofold. One way is by affection, and this is brought about by charity, which in a certain sense makes man one with God in affection, as is said in 1 Corinthians 6:17: "He who is joined to the Lord is one spirit." Through this virtue

God dwells in man, according to John 14:23: "If anyone love me, he will keep my word, and my Father will love him, and we will come to him and will make our abode with him." It also causes man to be in God, according to 1 John 4:16: "He that abideth in charity abideth in God, and God in him." By receiving this gratuitous gift, therefore, man is made pleasing to God and is brought so far that by the love of charity he becomes one spirit with God: he is in God and God is in him. Hence in 1 Corinthians 13:1-3, the Apostle teaches that without charity the other gifts do not profit men: they cannot make men pleasing to God unless charity is present.

This grace is common to the saints. So the man Christ, when asking for this grace for His disciples in prayer, begs: "That they may be one," namely, by the bond of love, "as we also are one."[262]

There is another conjunction of man with God that is brought about, not only by affection or inhabitation, but also by the unity of *hypostasis* or person, so that one and the same *hypostasis* or person is both God and man. And this conjunction of man with God is proper to Jesus Christ. We have already spoken at length of this union.[263] In truth, this is a singular grace of the man Christ, that He is united to God in unity of person. Clearly the grace was given *gratis*, for it exceeds the capacity of nature, and besides, there were no merits to precede this gift. But this grace also makes Him supremely pleasing to God, so that the Father says of Him in a totally unique sense: "This is my beloved Son, in whom I am well pleased."[264]

The difference between these two graces seems to be as follows. The grace whereby man is united to God by affection exists in the soul as something habitual, for that union is accomplished through

---

[262] John 17:22.
[263] Cf. chap. 211.
[264] Matt. 3:17; 17:5.

an act of love, and perfect acts issue from habit; consequently some habitual grace is infused into the soul to produce that eminently perfect habit whereby the soul is united to God by love. On the other hand, personal or hypostatic being is constituted, not by any habit, but by the natures to which the *hypostases* or persons pertain. Therefore the union of human nature with God in unity of person is brought about, not by some habitual grace, but by the conjunction of the natures themselves in one person.

The closer any creature draws to God, the more it shares in His goodness and the more abundantly it is filled with gifts infused by Him. Thus he who comes closer to a fire shares to a greater extent in its heat. But there can be no way, nor can any be imagined, by which a creature more closely adheres to God than by being united to Him in unity of person. Therefore, in consequence of the very union of His human nature with God in unity of person, Christ's soul was filled with habitual gifts of graces beyond all other souls. And so habitual grace in Christ is not a disposition for union, but is rather an effect of union.

This appears clearly in the very way of speaking used by the Evangelist when he says, in words previously quoted: "We saw [Him as it were] the only begotten of the Father, full of grace and truth."[265] The man Christ is, indeed, the only-begotten of the Father, inasmuch as the Word was made flesh. The very fact that the Word was made flesh entailed the consequence that He was full of grace and truth. But among things that are filled with any goodness or perfection, the one from which goodness or perfection flows out upon other things is found to be filled to greater repletion (for example, what can shed light on other objects, shines more brilliantly than they). Therefore, since the man Christ possessed

---

[265]John 1:14.

supreme fullness of grace, as being the only-begotten of the Father, grace overflowed from Him to others, so that the Son of God, made man, might make men gods and sons of God, according to the Apostle's words in Galatians 4:4-5: "God sent His Son, made of a woman, made under the Law, that He might redeem them who were under the Law: that we might receive the adoption of sons."

Because of the fact that grace and truth come to others from Christ, it is fitting that He should be the head of the Church. Sensation and movement are, in a way, conveyed from the head to the other members that are conformed to the head in nature. In like manner grace and truth are conveyed from Christ to other men. Hence we are told in Ephesians 1:22f., that God "hath made Him head over all the Church, which is His body." Christ is not the head of men alone; He can also be called the head of the angels, at least with respect to His excellence and influence, if not with respect to conformity of nature in the same species. This is why, before the words just quoted, the Apostle says that God set Him, namely Christ, "on His right hand in the heavenly places, above all principality and power and virtue and dominion."

In accord with this doctrine, a threefold grace is usually pointed out in Christ. The first is the grace of union, whereby the human nature, with no merits preceding, received the gift of being united in person to the Son of God. The second is the singular grace whereby the soul of Christ was filled with grace and truth beyond all other souls. The third is the grace of being head, in virtue of which grace flows from Him to others. The Evangelist presents these three kinds of grace in due order.[266] Regarding the grace of union he says: "The Word was made flesh." Regarding Christ's singular grace he says: "We saw [Him as it were] the only begotten

[266]John 1:14, 16.

of the Father, full of grace and truth." Regarding the grace of being head, he adds: "And of His fullness we all have received."[267]

215
The infinitude of Christ's grace

The possession of infinite grace is restricted to Christ. According to the testimony of John the Baptist, "God doth not give the Spirit by measure" to the man Christ.[268] But to others the Spirit is given in measure, as we read in Ephesians 4:7: "To everyone of us is given grace according to the measure of the giving of Christ." If this refers to the grace of union, no doubt can arise about what is here stated. To other saints is given the grace of being gods or sons of God by participation, through the infusion of some gift. Such a gift, being created, must itself be finite, just as all other creatures are. To Christ, on the contrary, is given, in His human nature, the grace to be the Son of God not by participation but by nature. But natural divinity is infinite. Through that union, therefore, He received an infinite gift. Hence beyond all doubt the grace of union is infinite.

Concerning habitual grace, however, a doubt can be raised as to whether it is infinite. Since such grace is a created gift, we have to acknowledge that it has a finite essence. Yet it can be said to be infinite for three reasons.

First, on the part of the recipient. The capacity of any created nature is evidently finite. Even though it is able to receive an infinite good by way of knowledge and fruition, it does not receive that good infinitely. Each creature has a definite measure of capacity in keeping with its species and nature. This does not prevent the divine power from being able to make another creature with a

---

[267]John 1:16.
[268]John 3:34.

greater capacity; but such a creature would no longer be of the same nature with regard to species. Thus if one is added to three, a different species of number will result. Consequently, when the divine goodness that is bestowed on anyone does not completely exhaust the natural capacity of his nature, we judge that what is given to him has been apportioned according to some measure. But when the whole of his natural capacity is filled up, we conclude that what he receives is not parceled out to him according to measure. For although there is a measure on the part of the recipient, there is no measure on the part of the giver, who is ready to give all; if a person, for instance, takes a pitcher down to the river, he finds water at hand without measure, although he himself receives with measure because of the limited size of the vessel. In this way Christ's habitual grace is finite in its essence, but may be said to be given infinitely and not according to measure, because as much is given as created nature is able to receive.

Secondly, grace may be said to be infinite on the part of the gift itself that is received. Surely we realize that there is nothing to prevent a thing that is finite in its essence, from being infinite by reason of some form. Infinite according to essence is that which possesses the whole fullness of being; this, of course, is proper to God alone, who is being itself. But if we suppose that there is some particular form not existing in a subject (e.g., whiteness or heat), it would not, indeed, have an infinite essence, for its essence would be confined to a genus or species; but it would possess the entire fullness of that species. With respect to the species in question, it would be without limit or measure because it would have whatever could pertain to that species. But if whiteness or heat is received into some subject, the latter does not always possess everything that necessarily and invariably pertains to the nature of that form, but does so only when the form is possessed as perfectly as it can be (i.e., when the manner of possessing is equal to the thing's capacity for being possessed). In this way, then, Christ's habitual grace was finite in its essence, but is said to have been without limit and measure because Christ received all that could pertain to the nature of grace. Other men do not receive the whole: one man receives grace in this measure, another in that. "There are diversities of grace," as we learn from 1 Corinthians 12:4.

In the third place, grace may be called infinite on the part of its cause. For in a cause is contained, in some way, its effect. Therefore, if a cause with infinite power to influence is at hand, it is able to influence without measure and, in a certain sense, infinitely; for example, if a person had a fountain capable of pouring forth water infinitely, he could be said to possess water without measure and, in a sense, infinitely. In this way Christ's soul has grace that is infinite and without measure, owing to the fact that it possesses, as united to itself, the Word who is the inexhaustible and infinite principle of every emanation of creatures.

From the fact that the singular grace of Christ's soul is infinite in the ways described, we readily infer that the grace which is His as head of the Church is also infinite. For the very reason that He possesses it, He pours it forth. And since He has received the gifts of the Spirit without measure, He has the power of pouring forth without measure all that pertains to the grace of the head, so that His grace is sufficient for the salvation — not of some men only — but of the whole world, according to 1 John 2:2: "And He is the propitiation for our sins; and not for ours only, but also for those of the whole world"; and, we may add, *of many worlds*, if such existed.

216
The fullness of Christ's wisdom

We treat next of the fullness of wisdom in Christ. In this matter, the first point that comes up for consideration is the truth that since

Christ has two natures, the divine and the human, whatever pertains to both natures must be twofold in Christ, as was stated above.[269] But wisdom appertains to both the divine nature and the human nature. The assertion of Job 9:4: "He is wise in heart and mighty in strength," is spoken of God. At times Scripture also calls men wise, whether with reference to worldly wisdom, as in Jeremiah 9:23: "Let not the wise man glory in his wisdom," or with reference to divine wisdom, as in Matthew 23:34: "Behold, I send to you prophets and wise men and scribes."[270] Hence we must acknowledge a twofold wisdom in Christ, conformably with His two natures: uncreated wisdom, which pertains to Him as God, and created wisdom, which pertains to Him as man.

Inasmuch as Christ is God and the Word of God, He is the begotten Wisdom of the Father, as 1 Corinthians 1:24 indicates: "Christ the power of God and the wisdom of God." For the interior word of any intellectual being is nothing else than the conception of wisdom. And since, as we said above,[271] the Word of God is perfect and is one with God, He must be the perfect conception of the wisdom of God the Father.

Consequently, whatever is contained in the wisdom of God the Father as unbegotten is contained wholly in the Word as begotten and conceived. And so we are told, in Colossians 2:3, that in Him (namely, in Christ), "are hid all the treasures of wisdom and knowledge."

Indeed, even as man, Christ has a twofold knowledge. The one is godlike, whereby He sees God in His essence and other things in God (just as God Himself, by knowing Himself, knows all other things). Through this vision God Himself is happy, as is every

---

[269]Cf. chap. 212.

[270]RSV: Matt. 23:33.

[271]Cf. chaps. 41, 43, 52.

rational creature admitted to the perfect fruition of God. Thus, since we hold that Christ is the author of man's salvation, we must also hold that such knowledge as befits the author of salvation pertains to the soul of Christ.

But a principle must be immovable and must also be preeminent in power. Hence that vision of God in which men's beatitude and eternal salvation consist, ought to be found to be more excellent in Christ than in others, and, indeed, ought to be found in Him as in an immovable principle.

The difference between what is movable and what is immovable comes to this: movable things, so far as they are movable, do not possess their proper perfection from the beginning, but acquire it in the course of time; but immovable things, as such, always possess their perfections from the first moment of their existence. Accordingly, Christ, the author of man's salvation, should rightly have possessed the full vision of God from the very beginning of His Incarnation; propriety would not allow Him to have attained to it in the course of time, as other saints do.

It was also appropriate that that soul which was united to God more closely than all others should be beatified by the vision of God beyond the rest of creatures. Gradation is possible in this vision, according as some see God, the cause of all things, more clearly than others.

The more comprehensively a cause is known, the more numerous are the effects that can be discerned in it. For a more perfect knowledge of a cause entails a fuller knowledge of its power, and there can be no knowledge of this power without a knowledge of its effects, since the magnitude of a power is ordinarily gauged from its effects.

This is why, among those who behold the essence of God, some perceive more effects in God Himself or more exemplars of the divine works than do others who see less clearly. It is because of this fact that lower angels are instructed by higher angels, as we have previously observed.[272]

Accordingly, the soul of Christ, possessing the highest perfection of the divine vision among all creatures, clearly beholds in God Himself all the divine works and the exemplars of all things that are, will be, or have been; and so He enlightens not only men, but also the highest of the angels. Hence the Apostle says, in Colossians 2:3, that in Christ "are hid all the treasures of wisdom and knowledge" of God; and in Hebrews 4:13 he points out that "all things are naked and open to His eyes."

Of course the soul of Christ cannot attain to a comprehension of the divinity. For, as we said above,[273] a thing is comprehended by knowledge when it is known to the full extent that it is knowable. Any object is knowable to the degree that it is a being and is true; but the divine being is infinite, as likewise is its truth. Therefore God is infinitely knowable. But no creature can know infinitely, even if what it knows is infinite. Hence no creature can comprehend God by seeing Him. But Christ's soul is a creature, and whatever in Christ pertains exclusively to His human nature is created. Otherwise the nature of Christ's humanity would not differ from the nature of His divinity, which alone is uncreated. However, the *hypostasis* or person of the Word of God, which is one in two natures, is uncreated. For this reason we do not call Christ a creature, speaking absolutely, because the *hypostasis* is connoted by the name of Christ. But we do say that the soul of Christ or the body of Christ is a creature. Therefore Christ's soul does not comprehend God, but Christ comprehends God by His uncreated wisdom. Our Lord had this uncreated wisdom in mind when, speaking of His knowledge of comprehension, He said in

[272] Cf. chap. 126.
[273] Cf. chap. 106.

Matthew 11:27: "No one knoweth the Son but the Father; neither doth anyone know the Father but the Son."

In this respect we note that comprehension of a thing's essence and comprehension of its power are of the same nature; a thing is able to act so far as it is a being in act. Therefore, if Christ's soul is incapable of comprehending the essence of the divinity, as we have shown is the case, it cannot comprehend the divine power.

But it would comprehend the divine power if it knew all that God is able to accomplish and the ways in which He can produce His effects. But this is impossible. Therefore Christ's soul does not know all that God can do, nor all the modes of activity open to Him.

However, since Christ, even as man, is placed by God the Father over every creature, it is fitting that in His vision of the divine essence He should perceive with full knowledge all things that in any way have been wrought by God. In this sense the soul of Christ is said to be omniscient, for it has complete knowledge of all things that are, will be, or have been. Among the other creatures that see God, some enjoy, in their vision of God, a more perfect knowledge, others a less perfect knowledge, of these effects.

In addition to this knowledge, whereby things are known by the created intellect in the vision of the divine essence itself, there are other kinds of cognition by which a knowledge of things comes to creatures. The angels, besides "morning" knowledge, whereby they know things in the Word, also have "evening" knowledge, whereby they know things in their proper natures.[274]

This kind of knowledge pertains to men in one way, in keeping with their nature, and to angels in another way. For men, consistent with the order of nature, derive the intelligible truth of things

---

[274]See the *Summa*, Ia, q. 58, a. 6; St Augustine, *De Genesi ad litteram*, IV, 22-24 (*PL*, XXXIV, 312f.).

from their senses, as Dionysius observes,[275] in such a way that the intelligible species in their intellects are abstracted from phantasms under the action of the agent intellect.

But angels acquire knowledge of things through an influx of divine light. In the same way that things themselves come forth into being from God, representations or likenesses of things are imprinted on the angelic intellect by God. In men and angels alike, however, over and above the knowledge of things they have by nature, there is found a certain supernatural knowledge of divine mysteries, about which angels are enlightened by angels, and men, for their part, are instructed by prophetic Revelation.

Accordingly, since no perfection vouchsafed to creatures may be withheld from Christ's soul, which is the most excellent of creatures, a threefold knowledge is fittingly to be attributed to Him, in addition to the knowledge whereby He beholds the essence of God and all things in that essence.

One kind of knowledge is experimental, as in other men, so far as Christ knew some things through the senses, in keeping with His human nature. A second kind of knowledge is divinely infused, granted to Christ so that He might know all truths to which man's natural knowledge extends or can extend. The human nature assumed by the Word of God ought not to have been lacking in any perfection whatever, since through it the whole of human nature was to be restored. But everything that exists in potency is imperfect before it is reduced to act. Therefore the human intellect is in potency to the intelligibles which man can know naturally. Hence the soul of Christ received knowledge of all such objects through species divinely infused: the entire potency of His human intellect was reduced to act.

---

[275] *De divinis nominibus*, VII, 3 (PG, III, 885); cf. St Thomas, *Expositio super Dionysium de divinis nominibus, lect.* VII (ed. Mandonnet, II, 374).

Furthermore, since Christ in His human nature was not only the restorer of our nature, but was also the fountainhead of grace, He was endowed with a third kind of knowledge whereby He knew most perfectly all that can pertain to the mysteries of grace, which transcend man's natural knowledge, although they are known by men through the gift of wisdom or through the spirit of prophecy. The human intellect is in potency with regard to the acquisition of such knowledge, even though an agency belonging to a higher sphere is required to reduce it to act. When there is question of knowing natural things, the mind is reduced to act by the light of the agent intellect; but it acquires knowledge of these mysteries through divine light.

This discussion clearly shows that the soul of Christ reached the highest degree of knowledge among all creatures as regards the vision of God, whereby the essence of God is seen, and other things in it. The same is true as regards knowledge of the mysteries and also as regards knowledge of things naturally knowable. Consequently Christ could not advance in any of these three kinds of knowledge.

But obviously He knew sensible things more and more perfectly with the passing of time, as He gained experience of them through the bodily senses. Therefore Christ could advance only with respect to experimental knowledge. That He actually did so we learn from Luke 2:52: the boy "advanced in wisdom and age."

However, this can also be understood in another way, so that Christ's increase of wisdom would mean, not that He Himself became wiser, but that wisdom increased in others, in the sense that they were more and more instructed by His wisdom.

This was done for a good reason: that He might show that He was like other men. If He had made a display of His perfect wisdom at a tender age, the mystery of the Incarnation might well have seemed phantastic.

217
The matter of Christ's body

The foregoing exposition clearly indicates the way the formation of Christ's body ought to have taken place. God could, indeed, have fashioned Christ's body from the dust of the Earth or from any other matter, in the way He fashioned the body of our first parent. But this would not have been in keeping with the restoration of man, which is the reason why the Son of God assumed flesh, as we have pointed out.[276] The nature of the human race, which was derived from the first parent and which was to be healed, would not have been so well restored to its pristine honor if the victor over the Devil and the conqueror of death, under which the human race was held captive because of the sin of the first father, had taken His body from some other source. The works of God are perfect, and what He means to restore He brings to perfection. He even adds more than had been taken away: through Christ the grace of God has abounded more than the offense of Adam, as the Apostle teaches.[277] Hence it was fitting that the Son of God should assume a body from the nature propagated by Adam.

Moreover, the mystery of the Incarnation becomes profitable to men by faith. Unless men believed that He who appeared in the guise of a man was the Son of God, they would not follow Him as the author of salvation. This was the case with the Jews, who drew upon themselves damnation rather than salvation from the mystery of the Incarnation, because of their unbelief. In order, therefore, that this ineffable mystery might more readily be believed, the Son of God disposed all things in such a way as to show that He was a true man. This would not have seemed to be so if He had

---

[276]Cf. chap. 200.
[277]Romans 5:15, 20.

taken His bodily nature from some other source than from human nature. Fittingly, therefore, He assumed a body stemming from the first parent.

Furthermore, the Son of God, made man, brought salvation to the human race, not only by conferring the remedy of grace but also by giving an example that cannot be ignored. Doubts may be raised about the teaching and the life of any other man because of a defect in his human knowledge and his mastery of truth. But what the Son of God teaches is believed without hesitation to be true and what He does is accepted without misgiving as good. In Him we ought to have an example of the glory we hope for and of the virtue whereby we may merit it. In both instances the example would have been less telling if He had taken His bodily nature from another source than that from which the rest of men receive theirs. Otherwise, if we tried to persuade a man that he should endure sufferings as Christ endured them, and that he should hope to rise as Christ rose, he could allege as an excuse the different condition of his body. Therefore, to give greater effectiveness to His example, Christ ought to have assumed His bodily nature from no other source than from the nature that comes down from the first parent.

218
The formation of Christ's body

Nevertheless the body of Christ could not becomingly have been fashioned in human nature in the same way as the bodies of other men are formed. Since He assumed this nature for the purpose of cleansing it from sin, He ought to have assumed it in such a way that He would incur no contagion of sin. Men incur Original Sin by the fact that they are begotten through the active human power residing in the male seed. This implies pre-existence, according to seminal principle, in Adam the sinner. Just as the first man would have transmitted Original Justice to his posterity along with the transmission of nature, so he actually transmitted Original Sin by transmitting nature; and this is brought about by the active power of the male seed. Hence the body of Christ ought to have been formed without male seed.

Moreover, the active power of the male seed operates naturally, and so man, who is begotten of male seed, is brought to perfection, not at once, but by definite processes. For all natural things advance to fixed ends through fixed intermediary stages. But Christ's body ought to have been perfect and informed by a rational soul at its very assumption; for a body is capable of being assumed by the Word of God so far as it is united to a rational soul, even though it was not at first perfect with regard to its full measure of quantity. Accordingly, the body of Christ ought not to have been formed through the power of the male seed.

219
The cause of the formation of Christ's body

Since the formation of the human body is naturally effected by the male seed, any other way of fashioning the body of Christ was above nature. God alone is the author of nature, and He works supernaturally in natural things, as was remarked above.[278] Hence we conclude that God alone miraculously formed that body from matter supplied by human nature. However, although every action of God in creation is common to the three divine persons, the formation of Christ's body is, by a certain appropriation, attributed to the Holy Spirit. For the Holy Spirit is the love of the Father and the Son, who love each other and us in Him. Since God decreed that

---

[278]Cf. chaps. 96, 136.

His Son should become incarnate because of "His exceeding charity wherewith He loved us," as the Apostle says in Ephesians 2:4, the formation of Christ's flesh is fittingly ascribed to the Holy Spirit.

Besides, the Holy Spirit is the author of all grace, since He is the first in whom all gifts are given *gratis*. But the taking up of human nature into the unity of a divine person was a communication of superabundant grace, as is clear from what was shown above.[279] Accordingly, to emphasize the greatness of this grace, the formation of Christ's body is attributed to the Holy Spirit.

Another reason for the appropriateness of this teaching is the relationship between the human word and spirit. The human word, as existing in the heart, bears a resemblance to the eternal Word as existing in the Father. And as the human word takes voice that it may become sensibly perceptible to men, so the Word of God took flesh that it might appear visibly to men. But the human voice is formed by man's breath or spirit. In the same way the flesh of the Word of God ought to have been formed by the Spirit of the Word.

[279]Cf. chaps. 214, 215.

The Virgin Birth

220
Explanation of the Creed on the conception and birth of Christ

To exclude the error of Ebion[280] and Cerinthus,[281] who taught that Christ's body was formed from male seed, the Apostles' Creed adds: "who was conceived by the Holy Spirit." In place of this, the Creed of the Nicene Fathers says: "He was made flesh by the Holy Spirit" so that we may believe that He assumed true flesh and not a phantastic body, as the Manichaeans claimed.[282] And the Creed of the Fathers adds, "on account of us men" in order to exclude the error of Origen, who alleged that by the power of Christ's Passion even the devils were to be set free.[283]

In the same Creed the phrase "for our salvation" is appended, to show that the mystery of Christ's Incarnation suffices for men's salvation, against the heresy of the Nazarenes, who thought that faith was not enough for human salvation apart from the works of

---

[280] Cf. St. Augustine, *De haeresibus*, 10 (PL, XLII, 27).

[281] Ibid., 8 (PL, XLII, 27).

[282] Cf. St. Augustine, *De haeresibus*, 46 (PL, XLII, 37).

[283] *Peri archon*, I, 6 (PG, XI, 169).

the Law.[284] The words "He came down from Heaven" were added to exclude the error of Photinus,[285] who asserted that Christ was no more than a man and that He took His origin from Mary. In this heresy the false teaching that Christ had an earthly beginning and later ascended to Heaven by the merit of a good life, replaces the truth that He had a heavenly origin and descended to Earth by assuming flesh. Lastly, the words "and He was made man" were added to exclude the error of Nestorius, according to whose contention the Son of God, of whom the Creed speaks, would be said rather to dwell in man than to be man.[286]

221
Christ's birth from a virgin

Since, as we have shown,[287] the Son of God was to take flesh from matter supplied by human nature, and since in human generation the woman provides matter, Christ appropriately took flesh from a woman. This is taught by the Apostle in Galatians 4:4: "God sent His Son, made of a woman." A woman needs the cooperation of a man for the matter that she supplies to be fashioned into a human body. But the formation of Christ's body ought not to have been effected through the power of the male seed, as we said above.[288] Hence that woman from whom the Son of God assumed flesh conceived without the admixture of male seed. Now the more anyone is detached from the things of the flesh, the more he is filled with spiritual gifts. For man is raised up by spiritual goods but

---

[284]Cf. St. Augustine, *De haeresibus*, 9 (*PL*, XLII, 27).
[285]Ibid., 45 (*PL*, XLII, 34).
[286]Cf. chap. 203.
[287]Cf. chap. 217.
[288]Cf. chap. 218.

dragged down by carnal attractions. Therefore, since the formation of Christ's body was to be accomplished by the Holy Spirit, it behooved that woman from whom Christ took His body to be filled to repletion with spiritual gifts, so that not only her soul would be endowed with virtues by the Holy Spirit, but also her womb made fruitful with divine offspring. So her soul had to be free from sin and her body far removed from every taint of carnal concupiscence. And so she had no association with a man at the conception of Christ; nor did she ever have such experience, either before or after.

This was also due to Him who was born of her. The Son of God assumed flesh and came into the world to raise us to resurrection, in which men "shall neither marry nor be married, but shall be as the angels of God in Heaven."[289] This is why He inculcated the doctrine of continence and of virginal integrity, that an image of the glory that is to come might, in some degree, shine forth in the lives of the faithful. Therefore, He did well to extol purity of life at His very birth, by being born of a virgin; and so the Apostles' Creed says that He was "born of the Virgin Mary." In the Creed of the Fathers He is said to have been "made flesh" of the Virgin Mary. This excludes the error of Valentinus and others, who taught that the body of Christ was either phantastic or of another nature and was not taken and formed from the body of the Virgin.[290]

222
The mother of Christ

The error of Nestorius,[291] who refused to acknowledge that Blessed Mary is the Mother of God, is likewise excluded. Both Creeds assert

[289] Matt. 22:30.
[290] Cf. chap. 208.
[291] Cf. chap. 203.

that the Son of God was born or was made flesh of the Virgin Mary. The woman of whom any person is born is called his mother, for the reason that she supplies the matter for human conception. Hence the Blessed Virgin Mary, who provided the matter for the conception of the Son of God, should be called the true mother of the Son of God. As far as the essence of motherhood is concerned, the energy whereby the matter furnished by a woman is formed, does not enter into the question. She who supplied matter to be formed by the Holy Spirit is no less a mother than a woman who supplies matter that is to be formed by the energy latent in male seed. If anyone insists on maintaining that the Blessed Virgin ought not to be called the Mother of God because flesh alone and not divinity was derived from her, as Nestorius contended, he clearly is not aware of what he is saying. A woman is not called a mother for the reason that everything that is in her child is derived from her. Man is made up of body and soul; and a man is what he is in virtue of his soul rather than in virtue of his body. But no man's soul is derived from his mother. The soul is either created by God directly, as the true doctrine has it, or, if it were produced by transplanting, as some have fancied,[292] it would be derived from the father rather than from the mother. For in the generation of other animals, according to the teaching of philosophers,[293] the male gives the soul, the female gives the body.

---

[292] Traducianism was strongly favored by many early Christian writers, among them Tertullian, *De anima*, 19 (*PL*, 11, 681); St. Gregory of Nyssa, *De hominis opificio*, 29 (*PG*, XLIV, 236); Theodore Abucara, *Opusc*. XXXV (*PG*, XCVII, 1589). St. Augustine wavered between it and creationism, because of the difficulty of explaining the transmission of Original Sin. See his letter to Optatus, *epist*. CXC, 2; 15 (*PL*, XXXIII, 857; 862); *Contra Iulianum*, V, 4 (*PL*, XLIV, 794).

[293] Aristotle, *De generatione animalium*, II, 4 (738 b 20; 740 b 24).

Consequently, just as any woman is a mother from the fact that her child's body is derived from her, so the Blessed Virgin Mary ought to be called the Mother of God if the body of God is derived from her. But we have to hold that it is the body of God, if it is taken up into the unity of the person of God's Son, who is true God. Therefore all who admit that human nature was assumed by the Son of God into the unity of His person, must admit that the Blessed Virgin Mary is the Mother of God. But Nestorius, who denied that the person of God and of the man Jesus Christ was one, was forced by logical necessity to deny that the Virgin Mary was the Mother of God.

223
The Holy Spirit is not the father of Christ

Although the Son of God is said to have been made flesh and to have been conceived by the Holy Spirit and of the Virgin Mary, we are not to conclude that the Holy Spirit is the father of the man Christ, even though the Blessed Virgin is called His mother.

The first reason for this is that everything pertaining to the idea of mother is verified in the Blessed Virgin Mary. She furnished the matter to be formed by the Holy Spirit for the conception of Christ, as the idea of motherhood requires. But not all the elements required for the idea of fatherhood are found on the part of the Holy Spirit. The idea of fatherhood requires that the father produce from his nature a son who is of like nature with himself. Therefore if some agent would make a thing that is not derived from its own substance, and would not produce such a thing unto the likeness of its own nature, that agent could not be called the thing's father. We do not say that a man is the father of the things he makes by plying an art, unless perhaps in a metaphorical sense. The Holy Spirit is, indeed, connatural with Christ as regards the divine nature; in this respect, however, He is not the father of Christ, but rather proceeds from Him. With respect to the human nature, the Holy Spirit is not connatural with Christ. For the human nature in Christ is other than the divine nature, as we said above.[294] Nor is anything of the divine nature changed into human nature, as we also said above.[295] Consequently the Holy Spirit cannot be called the father of the man Christ.

Moreover, that which is of greater moment in any son comes from his father, and what is secondary comes from his mother. Thus in other animals the soul is from the father and the body from the mother. In man, of course, the rational soul does not come from the father, but is created by God; yet the power of the paternal seed operates dispositively toward the form. But that which is the greater in Christ, is the person of the Word, who is in no way derived from the Holy Spirit. We conclude, therefore, that the Holy Spirit cannot be called the father of Christ.

224
The sanctification of Christ's mother

As appears from the foregoing exposition, the Blessed Virgin Mary became the mother of God's Son by conceiving of the Holy Spirit. Therefore it was fitting that she should be adorned with the highest degree of purity, that she might be made conformable to such a Son. And so we are to believe that she was free from every stain of actual sin — not only of mortal sin but of venial sin.

Such freedom from sin can pertain to none of the saints after Christ, as we know from 1 John 1:8: "If we say that we have no sin we deceive ourselves, and the truth is not in us." But what is said

---

[294]Cf. chaps. 211, 212.
[295]Cf. chap. 206.

in the Song of Solomon 4:7, "Thou art all fair, O my love, and there is not a spot in thee," can well be understood of the Blessed Virgin, Mother of God.

Mary was not only free from actual sin, but she was also, by a special privilege, cleansed from Original Sin. She had, indeed, to be conceived with Original Sin,[296] inasmuch as her conception resulted from the commingling of both sexes. For the privilege of conceiving without impairment of virginity was reserved exclusively to her who as a virgin conceived the Son of God. But the commingling of the sexes which, after the sin of our first parent, cannot take place without lust, transmits Original Sin to the offspring. Likewise, if Mary had been conceived without Original Sin, she would not have had to be redeemed by Christ, and so Christ would not be the universal redeemer of men, which detracts from His dignity. Accordingly, we must hold that she was conceived with Original Sin, but was cleansed from it in some special way.

Some men are cleansed from Original Sin after their birth from the womb, as is the case with those who are sanctified in Baptism. Others are reported to have been sanctified in the wombs of their mothers, in virtue of an extraordinary privilege of grace. Thus we are told with regard to Jeremiah: "Before I formed thee in the bowels of thy mother I knew thee; and before thou camest forth

---

[296] In contradiction to what St. Thomas says here, the Church in 1854 solemnly defined (as a revealed truth to be believed by all the faithful) that Mary is the *Immaculate Conception*, i.e., that she was not merely *born* without the stain of Original Sin (as St. Thomas maintains) but that she was also *conceived* without it. See Denz., 1641. In fact, the view favored here by St. Thomas, along with most of the great Scholastics of his time, began to be abandoned after Duns Scotus had pointed the way to the solution of the difficulties raised against the Immaculate Conception. Cf. Scotus, III *Sent.*, d. 3, q. 1, nos. 4-8; 15ff.; d. 18, q. un., no. 13 (Vivès, XIV, 160ff.; 171ff.; 683f.).

279

out of the womb I sanctified thee."[297] And in Luke 1:15 the angel says of John the Baptist: "He shall be filled with the Holy Spirit even from his mother's womb." We cannot suppose that the favor granted to the precursor of Christ and to the prophet was denied to Christ's own mother. Therefore we believe that she was sanctified in her mother's womb (that is, before she was born).

Yet such sanctification did not precede the infusion of her soul. In that case she would never have been subject to Original Sin, and so would have had no need of redemption. For only a rational creature can be the subject of sin. Furthermore, the grace of sanctification is rooted primarily in the soul, and cannot extend to the body except through the soul. Hence we must believe that Mary was sanctified after the infusion of her soul.

But her sanctification was more ample than that of others who were sanctified in the wombs of their mothers. Others thus sanctified in the womb were, it is true, cleansed from Original Sin; but the grace of being unable to sin later on, even venially, was not granted to them. The Blessed Virgin Mary, however, was sanctified with such a wealth of grace that thenceforth she was preserved free from all sin: not only from mortal sin, but also from venial sin. Moreover venial sin sometimes creeps up on us unawares, owing to the fact that an inordinate motion of concupiscence or of some other passion arises prior to the advertence of the mind, yet in such a way that the first motions are called sins. Hence we conclude that the Blessed Virgin Mary never committed a venial sin, for she did not experience such inordinate motions of passion. Inordinate motions of this kind arise because the sensitive appetite, which is the subject of these passions, is not so obedient to reason as not sometimes to move toward an object outside the order of reason,

---

[297]Jer. 1:5.

or even, occasionally, against reason; and this is what engenders the sinful impulse. So in the Blessed Virgin the sensitive appetite was rendered so subject to reason by the power of the grace which sanctified it that it was never aroused against reason but always conformed to the order of reason. Nevertheless she could experience some spontaneous movements not ordered by reason.

In our Lord Jesus Christ there was something more. In Him the lower appetite was so perfectly subject to reason that it did not move in the direction of any object except in accord with the order of reason (that is, so far as reason regulated the lower appetite or permitted it to go into action of its own accord). So far as we can judge, a characteristic pertaining to the integrity of the original state was the complete subjection of the lower powers to reason. This subjection was destroyed by the sin of our first parent, not only in himself, but in all the others who contract Original Sin from him. In all of these the rebellion or disobedience of the lower powers to reason, which is called concupiscence (*fomes peccati*), remains even after they have been cleansed from sin by the sacrament of grace. But such was by no means the case with Christ, according to the explanation given above.

In the Blessed Virgin, however, the lower powers were not so completely subject to reason as never to experience any movement not preordained by it. Yet they were so restrained by grace that they were never aroused contrary to reason. Thus, we usually say that after the Blessed Virgin was sanctified, concupiscence remained in her according to its substance, but it was shackled.

225
The perpetual virginity of Christ's mother

If Mary was thus strengthened against every movement of sin by her first sanctification, much more did grace grow in her and much more was concupiscence weakened or even completely uprooted in her, when the Holy Spirit came upon her, according to the angel's word,[298] to form of her the body of Christ. After she had been made the shrine of the Holy Spirit and the tabernacle of the Son of God, we may not believe that there was ever any inclination to sin in her or that she ever experienced any pleasurable feeling of carnal concupiscence. We must view with revulsion the error of Helvidius who, while granting that Christ was conceived and born of the Virgin, asserted that she later bore other sons to Joseph.[299]

Certainly this error finds no support in Matthew's statement about Mary that Joseph "knew her not until she brought forth her first-born Son,"[300] as though he knew her after she gave birth to Christ. The word *until* in this text does not signify definite time but indicates indeterminate time. Sacred Scripture frequently asserts with emphasis that something was done or not done up to a certain time, as long as the issue could remain in doubt. Thus we read in Psalm 109:1: "Sit Thou at my right hand until I make Thy enemies Thy footstool."[301] There could be some doubt whether Christ would sit at the right hand of God as long as His enemies did not seem to be subject to Him; but once we know that they are, no room for doubt could remain. Similarly there could be some doubt as to whether Joseph knew Mary before the birth of God's Son. The Evangelist took pains to remove this doubt, thus giving us to understand beyond all question that she was not known after giving birth.

Nor does the fact that Christ is called *Mary's first-born* give any support to the error, as though she bore other sons after Him. For

---

[298]Luke 1:35.
[299]Cf. St. Jerome, *De perpetua virginitate B. Mariae*, 11 (*PL*, XXIII, 193).
[300]Matt. 1:25.
[301]RSV: Ps. 110:1.

in scriptural usage the son before whom no other is born is called the first-born, even though no other should follow him. This is clear from the case of the first-born sons who according to the Law were consecrated to the Lord and offered to the priests.

Again, the error of Helvidius receives no support from the Gospel narrative that certain individuals are called the *brethren of Christ*, as though His mother had other sons. Scripture is accustomed to apply the name *brethren* to all who belong to the same relationship. For example, Abraham called Lot his *brother*, although Lot was his nephew.[302] In the same way Mary's nephews and other relatives are called Christ's *brethren*, as also are the relatives of Joseph, who was reputed to be the father of Christ.

Accordingly, the Creed states, "who was born of the Virgin Mary." And, indeed, she is called a *virgin* without any qualification, for she remained a virgin before the birth, at the birth, and after the birth of Christ. That there was no impairment of her virginity before and after Christ's birth, is clear from what has been said. More than that: her virginity was not violated even in the act of giving birth. Christ's body, which appeared to the disciples when the doors were closed,[303] could by the same power come forth from the closed womb of His mother. It was not seemly that He, who was born for the purpose of restoring what was corrupt to its pristine integrity, should destroy integrity in being born.

226
The defects assumed by Christ

In assuming human nature for the salvation of man, the Son of God appropriately showed in the nature He assumed, by the perfection

---

[302] Cf. Gen. 11:27; 13:8.
[303] John 20:26.

of its grace and wisdom, what was to be the goal of human salvation. No less appropriately was the human nature assumed by the Word of God characterized by certain conditions befitting the most suitable way of redeeming the human race. The most suitable way was that man, who had perished through his iniquity, should be restored by satisfying justice. But the order of justice requires that the one who has become liable to some punishment by sinning, should be freed by paying the penalty. Since, however, what we do or suffer through our friends, we ourselves are considered in some fashion to do or to suffer (inasmuch as love is a mutual force that in a way makes two lovers one), the order of justice is not violated if a person is set free by the satisfaction his friend offers for him.

By the sin of the first parent, ruin had come upon the entire human race. No punishment undergone by any man could suffice to liberate the whole human race. No worthy satisfaction was available and no satisfaction offered by any mere man was great enough in value to free all men. Similarly, justice would not be fully met if even an angel, out of love for the human race, were to offer satisfaction for it. An angel does not possess infinite dignity, and hence any satisfaction he offered would not be capable of sufficing for indefinitely many people and their sins. God alone is of infinite dignity and so He alone, in the flesh assumed by Him, could adequately satisfy for man, as has already been noted.[304] Therefore it behooved Him to assume a human nature so constituted that in it He could suffer for man what man himself deserved to suffer on account of his sin, and thus offer satisfaction on man's behalf.

However, not every punishment incurred for sin is suitable for making satisfaction. Man's sin comes from the fact that in turning

---

[304] Cf. chap. 200.

to transient goods he turns away from God. And man is punished for sin on both counts. He is deprived of grace and the other gifts by which union with God is effected, and besides this he deserves to suffer chastisement and loss with respect to the object for whose sake he turned away from God. Therefore the order of satisfaction requires that the sinner should be led back to God by punishments that are to be endured in transient goods.

Unfortunately, the punishments which keep man back from God continue to stand in the way of such recall. No one offers satisfaction to God by being deprived of grace or by being ignorant of God or by the fact that his soul is in a state of disorder, even though such afflictions are punishment for sin; man can satisfy only by enduring some pain in himself and by undergoing loss in external goods.

Accordingly, Christ ought not to have assumed those defects which separate man from God, such as privation of grace, ignorance, and the like, although they are punishment for sin. Defects of this kind would but render Him less apt for offering satisfaction. Indeed, to be the author of man's salvation, He had to possess fullness of grace and wisdom, as we pointed out above.[305] Yet, since man by sinning was placed under the necessity of dying and of being subjected to suffering in body and soul, Christ wished to assume the same kind of defects, so that by undergoing death for men He might redeem the human race.

Defects of this kind are common to Christ and to us. Nevertheless they are found in Christ otherwise than in us. For, as we have remarked, such defects are the punishment of the first sin.[306] Since we contract Original Sin through our vitiated origin, we are in consequence said to have contracted these defects. But Christ did

[305] Cf. chap. 213.
[306] Cf. chap. 193.

not contract any stain in virtue of His origin. He accepted the defects in question of His own free will. Hence we should not say that He *contracted* these defects, but rather that he *assumed* them, for that is contracted (*contrahitur*) which is necessarily drawn along with (*cum trahitur*) some other things. Christ could have assumed human nature without such defects, just as He actually did assume it without the defilement of sin; and indeed the order of reason would seem to demand that he who was free from sin should also be free from punishment. Thus it is clear that defects of this sort were not in Him by any necessity either of vitiated origin or of justice. Therefore in Him they were not contracted but were voluntarily assumed.

Yet, since our bodies are subject to the aforesaid defects in punishment for sin — for prior to sin we were immune from them — Christ, so far as He assumed such defects in His flesh is rightly deemed to have borne the likeness of sin, as the Apostle says in Romans 8:3: "God, sending His own Son in the likeness of sinful flesh." Hence Christ's very passibility or suffering is called sin by the Apostle, when he adds that God "hath condemned sin in the flesh," and observes in Romans 6:10: "In that He died to sin, He died once." For the same reason the Apostle uses an even more astonishing expression in Galatians 3:13, saying that Christ was "made a curse for us." This is also why Christ is said to have assumed one of our obligations (that of punishment) in order to relieve us of our double burden, namely, sin and punishment.

We should call to mind, further, that the penal defects afflicting our bodies are of two kinds. Some are common to all men (such as hunger, thirst, weariness after labor, pain, death, and the like). Others, however, are not common to all, but are peculiar to certain individuals (such as blindness, leprosy, fever, mutilation of the members, and similar ills). The difference between these defects is this: common defects are passed on to us from another, namely, our first parent, who incurred them through sin; but personal defects are produced in individual men by particular causes. But Christ had no cause of defect in Himself, either in His soul, which was full of grace and wisdom and was united to the Word of God or in His body, which was excellently organized and disposed, having been fashioned by the omnipotent power of the Holy Spirit. On the contrary, He took upon Himself certain defects by the free decision of His own will, with a view to procuring our salvation.

Accordingly, Christ judged it well to take upon Himself those defects that are handed down from one man to others (namely, the common defects) but not the special defects that arise in individuals from particular causes. Again, since He came chiefly to restore human nature, He fittingly assumed those defects that are found universally in nature. The doctrine thus set forth also makes it clear that, as Damascene points out, Christ assumed our irreprehensible defects (that is, those which are not open to slander).[307] If Christ had taken to Himself a deficiency in knowledge or in grace, or such ills as leprosy or blindness, this would seem to detract from His dignity and might provide men with an occasion for defaming Him. But no such occasion is given by defects attaching to the whole of nature.

[307] St. John Damascene, *De fide orthodoxa*, III, 20 (PG, XCIV, 1081). This passage justifies our translation of the text in St. Thomas: "*Christus assumpsit defectus nostros indetractabiles, id est, quibus detrahi non potest.*" See also the *Summa*, IIIa, q. 14, a. 4: "*indetractibiles, quia defectum scientiae et gratiae non important.*"

Christ's Crucifixion and Resurrection

227
Why Christ willed to die

Evidently, therefore, as we see from this discussion, Christ took some of our defects on Himself, not out of necessity, but for a definite purpose (namely, for our salvation). But every potency and every habit or capacity are ordained toward act as their end. Hence capacity to suffer is not enough for satisfaction or merit apart from actual suffering. A person is called good or evil, not because he is able to perform good or evil actions but because he performs them; praise and blame are duly rendered not for power to act but for acting. To save us, consequently, Christ was not content merely to make our passibility His portion, but He willed actually to suffer that He might satisfy for our sins. He endured for us those sufferings which we deserved to suffer in consequence of the sin of our first parent. Of these the chief is death, to which all other human sufferings are ordered as to their final term. "For the wages of sin is death," as the Apostle says in Romans 6:23.

Accordingly, Christ willed to submit to death for our sins so that, in taking on Himself without any fault of His own the punishment charged against us, He might free us from the death to which we had been sentenced, in the way that anyone would be freed from a debt of penalty if another person undertook to pay the penalty for him. Another reason why He wished to die was that His death might be for us not only a remedy of satisfaction but also a sacrament of salvation, so that we, transferred to a spiritual life, might die to our carnal life, in the likeness of His death. This is in accord with 1 Peter 3:18: "Christ also died once for our sins, the just for the unjust, that He might offer us to God, being put to death indeed in the flesh, but enlivened in the spirit."

Christ also wished to die that His death might be an example of perfect virtue for us. He gave an example of *charity*, for "greater love than this no man hath, that a man lay down his life for his friends."[308] The more numerous and grievous are the sufferings a person does not refuse to bear for his friend, the more strikingly his love is shown forth. But of all human ills the most grievous is death, by which human life is snuffed out. Hence no greater proof of love is possible than that a man should expose himself to death for a friend.

By His death Christ also gave an example of *fortitude*, which does not abandon justice in the face of adversity. Refusal to give up the practice of virtue even under fear of death seems to pertain most emphatically to fortitude. Thus in Hebrews 2:14-15, the Apostle says with reference to Christ's Passion: "That through death He might destroy him who had the empire of death, that is to say, the Devil, and might deliver them who through the fear of death were all their lifetime subject to servitude." In not refusing to die for truth, Christ overcame the fear of dying, which is the reason men for the most part are subject to the slavery of sin.

[308]John 15:13.

Further, He gave an example of *patience*, a virtue that prevents sorrow from overwhelming man in time of adversity. The greater the trials, the more splendidly does the virtue of patience shine forth in them. Therefore an example of perfect patience is afforded in the greatest of evils, which is death, if it is borne without distress of mind. Such tranquillity the prophet foretold of Christ: He "shall be dumb as a lamb before his shearer, and He shall not open His mouth."[309]

Lastly, our Lord gave an example of *obedience*. For the more difficult are the precepts one obeys, the more praiseworthy is the obedience. But the most difficult of all the objects of obedience is death. Hence, to commend the perfect obedience of Christ, the Apostle says, in Philippians 2:8, that He was obedient to the Father even unto death.

228
The death on the Cross

The same reasons reveal why Christ willed to suffer death on the Cross. In the first place, such a death was suitable as a *salutary means of satisfaction*. Man is fittingly punished in the things wherein he has sinned, as is said in Wisdom 11:17: "By what things a man sinneth, by the same also he is tormented." But the first sin of man was the fact that he ate the fruit of the tree of knowledge of good and evil, contrary to God's command. In his stead Christ permitted Himself to be fastened to a tree, so that He might pay for what He did not carry off, as the Psalmist says of Him.[310]

---

[309] Isa. 53:7.

[310] Psalm 58:5: "Neither is it my iniquity, nor my sin, O Lord: without iniquity have I run, and directed my steps" (RSV: Ps. 59:4).

Death on the Cross was also appropriate as a *sacrament*. Christ wished to make clear by His death that we ought so to die in our carnal life that our spirit might be raised to higher things. Hence He Himself says, in John 12:32: "I, if I be lifted up from the Earth, will draw all things to myself."

This kind of death was likewise fitting as an example of *perfect virtue*. Sometimes men shrink no less from a disgraceful kind of death than from the painfulness of death. Accordingly, the perfection of virtue seems to require that a person should not refuse to suffer even a disgraceful death for the good of virtue. Therefore, to commend the perfect obedience of Christ, the Apostle, after saying of Him that He was "obedient unto death," added: "even to the death of the Cross."[311] This sort of death was looked on as the most ignominious of all, in the words of Wisdom 2:20: "Let us condemn him to a most shameful death."

229
The death of Christ

In Christ three substances — the body, the soul, and the divinity of the Word — are joined together in one person. Two of these, the soul and the body, are united to form one nature. Accordingly, at the death of Christ the union between body and soul was dissolved. Otherwise the body would not have been truly dead, since death of the body is nothing else than the separation of the soul from it.

But neither soul nor body was separated from the Word of God, as far as union with the person is concerned. Human nature results from the union of soul and body; hence Christ could not be said to

[311] Phil. 2:8.

be a man during the three days of His death, when His soul remained separated from His body by death. However, as was shown above,[312] on account of the union of the human nature with the Word of God in one person, whatever is said of the man Christ can rightly be predicated also of the Son of God. Consequently, since the personal union of the Son of God both with the soul and with the body of Christ remained in death, whatever is said of either of them could be predicated of the Son of God. Hence the Creed asserts that the Son of God was buried (for the reason that the body united to Him lay in the tomb) and likewise that He descended into Hell (because His soul descended).

We should also recall that the masculine gender designates a person and that the neuter gender designates nature. Thus in speaking of the Trinity we say that the Son is another person (*alius*) than the Father, but not that He is another thing (*aliud*). Accordingly, during the three days of His death the whole (*totus*) Christ was in the sepulcher and in Hell and in Heaven, because of His person which remained united to His flesh reposing in the tomb and to His soul which was emptying Hell, and which continued to subsist in the divine nature reigning in Heaven. But we cannot say that the whole (*totum*) of Christ was in the sepulcher or in Hell, because only a part of the human nature and not the whole of it was in the sepulcher or in Hell.

230
The voluntary character of Christ's death

Christ's death was like our death as regards the essence of death, which consists in the separation of the soul from the body. But in

---

[312]Cf. chap. 211.

another respect the death of Christ was different from ours. We die for the reason that we are subject to death by a necessary law of nature, or in consequence of some violence done to us. But Christ did not die because of any necessity. He gave up His life by His power and His own will, as He Himself attested of His life: "I have power to lay it down, and I have power to take it up again."[313]

The reason for this difference is that physical things are not subject to our will. But the joining of the soul to the body is physical. Hence the fact that the soul remains united to the body or that it is separated from the body, is not subject to our will, but must be brought about by the power of some agent. But whatever was physical in Christ as regards His human nature was completely subject to His will because of the power of His divinity, to which all nature is subject. Therefore Christ had it in His power that so long as He willed, His soul would remain united to His body, and that the instant He willed, the soul would depart from the body. The centurion standing near the Cross of Christ felt the presence of this divine power when he saw Him expire with a loud cry. By this Christ clearly showed that He was not dying like other men, from the breaking down of nature. For men cannot send forth their last breath with a loud cry; in the moment of death they can scarcely move their tongue in a quavering whisper. Hence the fact that Christ died uttering a loud cry gave evidence of the divine power in Him. It was for this reason that the centurion said: "Indeed, this was the Son of God."[314]

Yet we may not aver that the Jews did not kill Christ or that Christ took His own life. For the one who brings the cause of death to bear on a person is said to kill him. But death does not ensue unless the cause of death prevails over nature, which conserves

[313] John 10:18.
[314] Matt. 27:54.

life. Christ had it in His power either to submit His nature to the destructive cause or to resist that influence, just as He willed. Thus Christ died voluntarily, and yet the Jews killed Him.

231
The Passion of Christ as regards his body

Christ wished to suffer not only death, but also the other ills that flow from the sin of the first parent to his posterity, so that, bearing in its entirety the penalty of sin, He might perfectly free us from sin by offering satisfaction. Of these ills, some precede death, others follow death. Prior to the death of the body come natural sufferings (such as hunger, thirst, and weariness) and also sufferings inflicted by violence (such as wounding, scourging, and the like). Christ wished to endure all these sufferings, since they stem from sin. If man had not sinned, he would not have experienced the affliction of hunger or of thirst or of fatigue or of cold, and he would not have had to undergo the sufferings caused by external violence.

Christ bore these sufferings for a different reason from that on account of which other men endure them. In other men there is nothing that can resist these sufferings. But Christ had at His disposal means to withstand evils of this sort: not only the un-created power of His divinity but also the beatitude of His soul, which is so powerful that, as Augustine says, its happiness in its own way flows over into the body.[315] Thus after the resurrection, by the very fact that the soul will be glorified by the vision of God in unrestricted and full fruition, the body united to the glorified soul will be rendered glorious, impassible, and immortal. Therefore, since the soul of Christ enjoyed the vision of God in the

[315] *Epist.* CXVIII, *ad Dioscorum*, 3 (*PL*, XXXIII, 439).

highest degree of perfection, His body should in consequence, so far as the power of this vision is concerned, have been rendered impassible and immortal by an overflowing of glory from the soul to the body. But divine wisdom so disposed matters that Christ's body would suffer at the very time His soul was enjoying the vision of God, with no overflow of glory from the soul to the body. For, as we have said, all that was physical in Christ's human nature was subject to His will.[316] Hence at His good pleasure he could prevent natural redundance from His higher to His lower parts, and so could allow any part to suffer or to do whatever would be proper to it without interference from any other part. This, of course, is impossible in other men.

This also accounts for the fact that during His Passion Christ suffered most excruciating pain of body. For His bodily pain was in no way lessened by the higher joy of His rational soul, just as, conversely, pain of body did not obstruct the joy of His rational soul.

This reveals, too, that Christ alone was both a *viator* and a *comprehensor*.[317] He enjoyed the vision of God, which characterizes the *comprehensor*, but in such a way that His body remained subject to sufferings, which characterizes the wayfarer. And since a wayfarer has power to merit, either for himself or for others, by the good works he performs from the motive of charity, Christ, too, although He was a *comprehensor*, merited both for Himself and for others by His works and sufferings.

For Himself Christ merited, not indeed glory of soul, which He had from the first instant of His conception, but glory of body, which He won by suffering. For us, too, each of His sufferings and

---

[316] Cf. chap. 230.

[317] In other words, Christ alone enjoyed the Beatific Vision, i.e., He was a *comprehensor* while still a wayfarer (*viator*) on Earth.

actions was profitable unto salvation, not only by way of example, but also by way of merit: owing to the abundance of His charity and grace, He could merit grace for us, so that thus the members might receive of the fullness of the head.

Any suffering of His, however slight, was enough to redeem the human race, if the dignity of the sufferer is considered. For the more exalted the person on whom suffering is inflicted, the greater is the injury judged to be; for instance, a greater outrage is committed if one strikes a prince than if one strikes a common man of the people. Consequently, since Christ is a person of infinite dignity, any suffering of His has an infinite value and so suffices for the atonement of infinitely many sins. Yet the redemption of the human race was accomplished, not by this or that slight suffering, but by Christ's death, which, for reasons listed above,[318] He chose to endure to redeem the human race from its sins. For in any purchasing transaction there is required not only a stipulated amount of appreciable commodity, but also the application of the price to the purchase.

232
The possibility of Christ's soul

Since the soul is the form of the body, any suffering undergone by the body must in some way affect the soul. Therefore in that state in which the body of Christ was passible, His soul was passible also.

We may note that the suffering of the soul is of two kinds. One kind of suffering arises from the body, the other from the object that causes suffering; and this can be observed in any one of the faculties. For the soul is related to the body in the same way that a

---

[318]Cf. chap. 227.

part of the soul is related to a part of the body. Thus suffering may be caused in the faculty of sight by some object, as when vision is dimmed by an excessively bright light; suffering can also arise from the organ itself, as when vision is dulled because of an injured pupil.

Accordingly, if the suffering of Christ's soul is regarded as arising from the body, the whole soul suffered when the body suffered. For the soul in its essence is the form of the body; and the faculties, too, are all rooted in the essence of the soul. Consequently, if the body suffers, every power of the soul suffers in some way. But if the suffering of the soul is considered as arising from an object, not every power of Christ's soul suffered (if we understand *suffering* in the proper sense as connoting harm). For nothing that arose from the object of any of these powers could be harmful, since, as we saw above, the soul of Christ enjoyed the perfect vision of God.[319] Thus the higher reason of Christ's soul, which is immersed in the contemplation and meditation of eternal things, embraced nothing adverse or repugnant that could cause it to suffer any harm.

But the sense faculties, whose objects are material things, could receive some injury from the suffering of the body; and so Christ experienced pain of sense when His body suffered. Furthermore, just as laceration of the body is felt by the senses to be injurious, so the inner imagination apprehends it as harmful; hence interior distress follows even when pain is not felt in the body. We assert that suffering of such distress was experienced by the soul of Christ. More than this: not the imagination alone, but also the lower reason apprehends objects harmful to the body; and so, as a result of such apprehension by the lower reason (which is concerned

[319]Cf. chap. 216.

with temporal affairs), the suffering of sorrow could have place in Christ so far as the lower reason apprehended death and other maltreatment of the body as injurious and as contrary to natural appetite.

Moreover, in consequence of love, which makes two persons, as it were, one, a man may be afflicted with sadness not only on account of objects he apprehends through his imagination or his lower reason as harmful to himself, but also on account of objects he apprehends as harmful to others whom he loves. Thus Christ suffered sadness from His awareness of the perils of sin or of punishment threatening other men whom He loved with the love of charity. And so He grieved for others as well as for Himself.

However, although the love of our fellow men pertains in a certain way to the higher reason (inasmuch as our neighbor is loved out of charity for God's sake), the higher reason in Christ could not experience sorrow on account of the defects of His fellow men, as it can in us. For, since Christ's higher reason enjoyed the full vision of God, it apprehended all that pertains to the defects of others as contained in the divine wisdom, in the light of which the fact that a person is permitted to sin and is punished for his sin, is seen to be in accord with becoming order. And so neither the soul of Christ nor of any of the blessed who behold God can be afflicted with sadness by the defects of their neighbors. But the case is otherwise with wayfarers who do not rise high enough to perceive the plan of wisdom. Such persons are saddened by the defects of others even in their higher reason, when they think that it pertains to the honor of God and the exaltation of the Faith that some should be saved who nevertheless are damned.

Thus, with regard to the very things for which He was suffering in sense, imagination, and lower reason, Christ was rejoicing in His higher reason, so far as He referred them to the order of divine wisdom. And since the referring of one thing to another is the proper task of reason, we generally say that Christ's reason, if it is considered as *nature*, shrank from death (meaning that death is naturally abhorrent), but that if it is considered as *reason*, it was willing to suffer death.

Just as Christ was afflicted with sadness, so He experienced other passions that stem from sadness, such as fear, wrath, and the like. Fear is caused in us by those things whose presence engenders sorrow, when they are thought of as future evils; and when we are grieved by someone who is hurting us, we become angry at him.

Such passions existed otherwise in Christ than in us. In us they frequently anticipate the judgment of reason, and sometimes pass the bounds of reason. In Christ they never anticipated the judgment of reason and never exceeded the moderation imposed by reason.

His lower appetite, which was subject to passion, was moved just so far as reason decreed that it should be moved. Therefore Christ's soul could desire something in its higher part that it shrank from in its lower part, and yet there was no conflict of appetites in Him or rebellion of the flesh against the spirit, such as occurs in us owing to the fact that the lower appetite exceeds the judgment and measure of reason.

In Christ this appetite was moved in accordance with the judgment of reason, to the extent that He permitted each of His lower powers to be moved by its own impulse, in keeping with propriety.

In the light of all this we see clearly that Christ's higher reason was completely happy and full of joy in respect to its proper object. On the part of this *object*, nothing that might engender sorrow could arise in Him. But on the part of the *subject* it was full of suffering, as we indicated in the beginning of this chapter. Yet that enjoyment did not lessen the suffering, nor did the suffering prevent the enjoyment, since no overflowing from one power to another took place; each of the powers was allowed to exercise the function proper to it, as we mentioned above.[320]

233
The prayer of Christ

Since prayer manifests desire, the nature of the prayer Christ offered when His Passion was upon Him may be gathered from the different desires He expressed. In Matthew 26:39 He begs: "My Father, if it be possible, let this chalice pass from me. Nevertheless, not as I will, but as Thou wilt." In saying, "Let this chalice pass from me," He indicates the movement of His lower appetite and natural desire, whereby all naturally shrink from death and desire life. And in saying, "Nevertheless not as I will, but as Thou wilt," He gives expression to the movement of His higher reason, which looks on all things as comprised under the ordinations of divine wisdom. The same is the bearing of the added words, "If this chalice may not pass away,"[321] whereby He showed that only those events can occur which take place according to the order of the divine will.

Although the chalice of the Passion did not pass from Him, but He had to drink it, we may not say that His prayer went unheard. For, as the Apostle assures us in Hebrews 5:7, in all things Christ "was heard for His reverence." Since prayer, as we have remarked, is expressive of desire, we pray unconditionally for what we wish unconditionally; and so the very desires of the just have the force of prayer with God, according to Psalm 9:17: "The Lord hath heard the desire of the poor."[322] But we wish unconditionally only what

[320]Cf. chap. 231.
[321]Matt. 26:42.
[322]RSV: Ps. 10:17.

we desire with our higher reason, which alone has the power of assenting to an undertaking.

Christ prayed absolutely that the Father's will might be done, for this was what He wished absolutely. But He did not thus pray that the chalice might pass from Him, because He wished this not absolutely, but according to His lower reason, as we have noted earlier.

234
The burial of Christ

In consequence of sin, other defects, both on the part of the body and on the part of the soul, overtake man after death. With regard to defects on the part of the body, the body returns to the earth from which it was taken.

This defect on the part of the body has two phases in the case of ourselves: it is laid away and it corrupts. It is laid away, inasmuch as the dead body is placed beneath the earth in burial; and it corrupts, inasmuch as the body is resolved into the elements of which it was composed.

Christ wished to be subject to the first of these defects, namely, the placing of His body beneath the earth. But He did not submit to the other defect, the dissolving of His body into dust. Thus Psalm 15:10 says of Him: "Nor wilt Thou give Thy holy one to see corruption,"[323] that is, decay of the body. The reason for this is plain: although Christ's body received matter from human nature, its formation was accomplished not by any human power but by the power of the Holy Spirit. Accordingly, the substance of His matter being what it was, He wished to be subject to the place

---

[323] RSV: Ps. 16:10.

beneath the earth usually given over to dead bodies; for that place which is in keeping with the matter of the predominant element in bodies is rightly assigned to them. But He did not wish the body that had been formed by the Holy Spirit to undergo dissolution, since in this respect He was different from other men.

235
The descent of Christ into Hell

On the part of the soul, death among men is followed, in consequence of sin, by descent into Hell, not only as a place, but as a state of punishment. However, just as Christ's body was buried beneath the earth regarded as a place but not with respect to the common defect of dissolution, so His soul went down to Hell as a place, not to undergo punishment there, but rather to release from punishment others who were detained there because of the sin of the first parent for which He had already made full satisfaction by suffering death.

Hence nothing remained to be suffered after death, and so without undergoing any punishment He descended locally into Hell that He might manifest Himself as the Savior of the living and the dead. For this reason He alone among the dead is said to have been free, since His soul was not subject to punishment in Hell and His body was not subject to corruption in the grave.

When Christ descended into Hell, He freed those who were detained there for the sin of our first parent but left behind those who were being punished for their own sins. And so He is said to have bitten into Hell but not to have swallowed it, for He freed a part and left a part.

The Creed of our Faith touches on the various defects of Christ when it states: "He suffered under Pontius Pilate, was crucified, died and was buried; He descended into Hell."

236
The resurrection of Christ

Since the human race was freed by Christ from the evils flowing from the sin of our first parent, it was fitting that, as He bore our ills to free us from them, the first fruits of man's restoration effected by Him should make their appearance in Him. This was done that Christ might be held up to us as a sign of salvation in two ways. First, we learn from His Passion what we brought down on ourselves by sin and what suffering had to be undergone for us to free us from sin. Secondly, we see in His exaltation what is proposed to us to hope for through Him.

In triumph over death, which resulted from our first parent's sin, Christ was the first of all men to rise to immortal life. Thus, as life first became mortal through Adam's sin, immortal life made its first appearance in Christ through the atonement for sin He offered. Others, it is true, raised up either by Christ or by the prophets, had returned to life before Him; yet they had to die a second time. But "Christ rising again from the dead, dieth now no more."[324] As He was the first to escape the necessity of dying, He is called "the first begotten of the dead"[325] and "the first fruits of them that sleep."[326] Having thrown off the yoke of death, He was the first to rise from the sleep of death.

Christ's resurrection was not to be long delayed, nor, on the other hand, was it to take place immediately after death. If He had returned to life immediately after death, the fact of His death would not have been well established; and if His resurrection had been long delayed, the sign of vanquished death would not have

[324]Rom. 6:9.
[325]Rev. 1:5.
[326]1 Cor. 15:20.

appeared in Him, and men would not have been given the hope that they would be rescued from death by Him. Therefore He put off His resurrection until the third day, for this interval was judged sufficient to establish the truth of His death and was not too long to wither away the hope of liberation. If it had been delayed for a longer time, the hope of the faithful might have begun to suffer doubt. Indeed, on the third day, as though hope were already running out, some were saying: "We hoped that it was He that should have redeemed Israel."[327]

However, Christ did not remain dead for three full days. He is said to have been in the heart of the earth for three days and three nights,[328] according to that figure of speech whereby a part is often taken for the whole. For, since one natural day is made up of a day and a night, Christ is said to have been dead during the whole of any part of a day or a night that is counted while He was lying in death.

Moreover, in the usual practice of Scripture, night is figured in with the following day, because the Hebrews reckon time by the course of the moon, which begins to shine in the evening. Christ was in the sepulcher during the latter part of the sixth day, and if this is counted along with the preceding night, it will be more or less one natural day. He reposed in the tomb during the night following the sixth day, together with the whole of the Sabbath day, and so we have two days. He lay dead also during the next night, which preceded the Lord's Day, on which He rose, and this occurred either at midnight, according to Gregory,[329] or at dawn, as others think.[330] Therefore, if either the whole night, or a part of

---

[327] Luke 24:21 (RSV: Luke 24:20).

[328] See Matt. 12:40.

[329] St. Gregory the Great, *In Evangelia*, II, *hom.* 21 (PL, LXXVI, 1173).

[330] Thus St. Augustine, *De Trinitate*, IV, 6 (PL, XLII, 894).

it together with the Lord's Day following, is taken into our calculation, we shall have the third natural day.

The fact that Christ wished to rise on the third day is not without mysterious significance; for so He was able to show that He rose by the power of the whole Trinity. Sometimes the Father is said to have raised Him up, and sometimes Christ Himself is said to have risen by His own power.

These two statements do not, in fact, contradict each other, for the divine power of the Father is identical with that of the Son and that of the Holy Spirit. Another reason for Christ's resurrection on the third day was to show that the restoration of life was accomplished, not on the first day of the world (that is, under the natural law) nor on the second day (that is, under the Mosaic Law) but on the third day (that is, in the era of grace).

The fact that Christ lay in the sepulcher for one whole day and two whole nights also has its meaning: by the one ancient debt Christ took on Himself (punishment), He blotted out our two ancient debts (sin and punishment) which are represented by the two nights.

237
Qualities of the risen Christ

Christ recovered for the human race not merely what Adam had lost through sin, but all that Adam could have attained through merit. For Christ's power to merit was far greater than that of man prior to sin. By sin Adam incurred the necessity of dying because he lost the power which would have enabled him to avoid death if he had not sinned. Christ not only did away with the necessity of dying, but even gained the power of not being able to die. Therefore His body after the Resurrection was rendered impassible and immortal. Thus Christ's body was not like that of the first man, which had the power not to die, but was absolutely unable to die. And this is what we await in the future life for ourselves.

Furthermore, the mystery of man's Redemption was now accomplished. To enable Christ to achieve that end, the glory of fruition had, in God's dispensation, been restricted to the higher regions of His soul, so that no overflowing to the lower parts and to the body itself would occur, but each faculty would be allowed to do or suffer what was proper to it.

But now the body and the lower powers were wholly glorified by an overflow of glory from the higher regions of the soul. Accordingly, Christ, who before the Passion had been a *comprehensor* because of the fruition enjoyed by His soul and a wayfarer because of the possibility of His body, was now, after the Resurrection, no longer a wayfarer, but exclusively a *comprehensor*.

238
Arguments demonstrating Christ's resurrection

As we stated above, Christ anticipated the general resurrection in order that His own resurrection might bolster up our hope of our own resurrection.[331] To foster our hope of resurrection, Christ's resurrection and the qualities of His risen nature had to be made known by suitable proofs. He manifested His resurrection not to all alike, in the way that He manifested His human nature and His Passion, but only "to witnesses preordained by God"[332] (namely, the disciples whom He had selected to bring about man's salvation). For the state of resurrection, as was mentioned above, belongs to the glory of the *comprehensor*,[333] and knowledge of this

[331] Cf. chap. 236.
[332] Acts 10:41.
[333] Cf. chap. 237.

is not due to all but only to such as make themselves worthy. To the witnesses He had chosen, Christ revealed both the fact of His resurrection and the glory of His risen nature.

He revealed the fact of His resurrection by showing that He, the very one who had died, rose again both in His nature and in His *suppositum*. As regards nature, He showed that He had a true human body when He offered Himself to be touched and seen by the disciples, to whom He said: "Handle and see; for a spirit hath not flesh and bones, as you see me to have."[334] He gave further evidence of the same by performing acts that belong to human nature (such as eating and drinking with His disciples, conversing with them, and walking about). These are the acts of a living man. Of course, such eating was not dictated by necessity. The incorruptible bodies of the risen will have no need of food; there occurs in them no deterioration that has to be repaired by nourishment. So the food consumed by Christ did not become nourishment for His body but was dissolved into preexisting matter. Yet He proved that He was a true man by the fact that He ate and drank.

As regards His *suppositum*, Christ showed that He was the same person who had died, by displaying to His disciples the marks of His death on His body, namely, the scars of His wounds. Thus, in John 20:27 He says to Thomas: "Put in thy finger hither and see my hands; and bring hither thy hand and put it into my side." And in Luke 24:39 He says: "See my hands and feet, that it is I myself."[335] It was by divine dispensation that He kept the scars of His wounds in His body, so that the truth of the Resurrection might be demonstrated by them; for complete integrity is the proper condition of the incorruptible risen body, although we may say that in the case of the martyrs some indications of the wounds

[334]Luke 24:39 (RSV: Luke 24:38).
[335]RSV: Luke 24:38.

they bore will appear with a certain splendor, in testimony of their virtue. Christ further showed that He was the same *suppositum* by His manner of speech and by other familiar actions whereby men are recognized. Thus the disciples knew Him "in the breaking of bread."[336] Also, He openly showed Himself to them in Galilee, where He was accustomed to converse with them.

Christ manifested the glory of His risen nature when He came among them, "the doors being shut,"[337] and when "He vanished out of their sight."[338] For the glory of risen man gives him the power to be seen in glorious vision when he wishes, or not to be seen when he so wishes. The reason why Christ demonstrated the truth of His resurrection and the glory of His risen body by so many proofs, was the difficulty that faith in the Resurrection presents. If He had displayed the extraordinary condition of His glorified body in its full splendor, He would have awakened prejudice against faith in the Resurrection: the immensity of its glory would have excluded belief that it was the same nature. Further, He manifested the truth not only by visible signs, but also by proofs appealing to the intellect, such as when "He opened their understanding so that they might understand the Scriptures,"[339] and showed that according to the writings of the prophets He was to rise again.

239
The twofold life restored in man by Christ

As Christ destroyed our death by His death, so He restored our life by His resurrection. Man has a twofold death and a twofold life.

---

[336]Luke 24:35 (RSV: Luke 24:34).
[337]John 20:26.
[338]Luke 24:31 (RSV: Luke 24:30).
[339]Luke 24:45 (RSV: Luke 24:43).

The first death is the death of the body, brought about by separation from the soul; the second death is brought about by separation from God. Christ, in whom the second death had no place, destroyed both of these deaths in us — that is, the bodily and the spiritual — by the first death He underwent (namely, that of the body).

Similarly, opposed to this twofold death we are to understand that there is a twofold life. One is a life of the body, imparted by the soul, and this is called the *life of nature*. The other comes from God and is called the *life of justice* or the *life of grace*. This life is given to us through faith, by which God dwells in us, according to Habakkuk 2:4: "The just shall live in his faith."

Accordingly, resurrection is also twofold: one is a bodily resurrection, in which the soul is united to the body for the second time; the other is a spiritual resurrection, in which the soul is again united to God. This second resurrection had no place in Christ, because His soul was never separated from God by sin. By His bodily resurrection, therefore, Christ is the cause of both the bodily and the spiritual resurrection in us.

However, as Augustine says in his commentary on St. John,[340] we are to understand that the Word of God raises up souls but that the Word as incarnate raises up bodies. To give life to the soul belongs to God alone. Yet, since the flesh is the instrument of His divinity, and since an instrument operates in virtue of the principal cause, our double resurrection — bodily and spiritual — is referred to Christ's bodily resurrection as cause.

For everything done in Christ's flesh was salutary for us by reason of the divinity united to that flesh. Hence the Apostle, speaking of the resurrection of Christ as the cause of our spiritual resurrection, says, in Romans 4:25, that Christ "was delivered up

---

[340] *In Ioannis evangelium*, XIX, 15f. (*PL*, XXXV, 1552f.).

for our sins and rose again for our justification." And in 1 Corinthians 15:12 he shows that Christ's resurrection is the cause of our bodily resurrection: "Now if Christ be preached, that He rose again from the dead, how do some among you say that there is no resurrection of the dead?"

Most aptly does the Apostle attribute remission of sins to Christ's death and our justification to His resurrection, thus tracing out conformity and likeness of effect to cause. As sin is discarded when it is remitted, so Christ by dying laid aside His passible life, in which the likeness of sin was discernible. But when a person is justified, he receives new life. In like manner Christ, by rising, obtained newness of glory.

Therefore Christ's death is the cause of the remission of our sin: the efficient cause instrumentally, the exemplary cause sacramentally, and the meritorious cause. In like manner Christ's resurrection was also the cause of our resurrection: the efficient cause instrumentally and the exemplary cause sacramentally. But it was not a meritorious cause, for Christ was no longer a wayfarer, and so was not in a position to merit; and also because the glory of the Resurrection was the reward of His Passion, as the Apostle declares in Philippians 2:9ff.

Thus we see clearly that Christ can be called the first-born of those who rise from the dead. This is true not only in the order of time, inasmuch as Christ was the first to rise, as was said above,[341] but also in the order of causality, because His resurrection is the cause of the resurrection of other men; and in the order of dignity, because He rose more gloriously than all others.

This belief in Christ's resurrection is expressed in the words of the Creed: "The third day He arose again from the dead."

---

[341] Cf. chap. 236.

240

The twofold reward of Christ's humiliation: resurrection and ascension

According to the Apostle, the exaltation of Christ was the reward of His humiliation.[342] Therefore a twofold exaltation had to correspond to His twofold humiliation.

Christ had humbled Himself, first, by suffering death in the passible flesh He had assumed; secondly, He had undergone humiliation with reference to place, when His body was laid in the sepulcher and His soul descended into Hell. The exaltation of the Resurrection, in which He returned from death to immortal life, corresponds to the first humiliation. And the exaltation of the Ascension corresponds to the second humiliation. Hence the Apostle says, in Ephesians 4:10: "He that descended is the same also that ascended above all the heavens."

However, as it is narrated of the Son of God that He was born, suffered, was buried, and rose again — not in His divine nature but in His human nature — so also, we are told, He ascended into Heaven, not in His divine nature but in His human nature. In His divine nature He had never left Heaven, as He is always present everywhere. He indicates this Himself when He says: "No man hath ascended into Heaven but He that descended from Heaven, the Son of man who is in Heaven."[343] By this we are given to understand that He came down from Heaven by assuming an earthly nature, yet in such way that He continued to remain in Heaven. The same consideration leads us to conclude that Christ alone has gone up to Heaven by His own power. By reason of His origin, that abode belonged by right to Him who had come down from Heaven. Other men cannot ascend of themselves, but are

[342] Phil. 2:8-9.
[343] John 3:13.

taken up by the power of Christ, whose members they have been made.

As ascent into Heaven befits the Son of God according to His human nature, so something else is added that becomes Him according to His divine nature: namely, that He should sit at the right hand of His Father. In this connection we are not to think of a literal right hand or a bodily sitting. Since the right side of an animal is the stronger, this expression gives us to understand that the Son is seated with the Father as being in no way inferior to Him according to the divine nature, but on a par with Him in all things. Yet this same prerogative may be ascribed to the Son of God in His human nature, thus enabling us to perceive that in His divine nature the Son is in the Father Himself according to unity of essence, and that together with the Father He possesses a single kingly throne (that is, an identical power). Since other persons ordinarily sit near kings (namely, ministers to whom kings assign a share in governing power) and since the one whom the king places at his right hand is judged to be the most powerful man in the kingdom, the Son of God is rightly said to sit at the Father's right hand even according to His human nature, as being exalted in rank above every creature of the heavenly kingdom.

In both senses, therefore, Christ properly sits at the right hand of God. And so the Apostle asks, in Hebrews 1:13: "To which of the angels said He at any time: sit on my right hand?"

We profess our faith in this ascension of Christ when we say in the Creed: "He ascended into Heaven, and sitteth at the right hand of God the Father."

The Last Judgment

241
Christ as judge

We clearly gather from this that by the Passion and death of Christ and by the glory of His resurrection and ascension, we are freed from sin and death, and have received justice and the glory of immortality — the former in actual fact, the latter in hope.

All these events we have mentioned (the Passion, death, Resurrection, and Ascension) were accomplished in Christ according to His human nature. Therefore we must conclude that Christ has rescued us from spiritual and bodily evils, and has put us in the way of spiritual and eternal goods, by what He suffered or did in His human nature.

He who acquires goods for people also, in consequence, distributes the same to them. But the distribution of goods among many requires judgment, so that each may receive what corresponds to his degree.

Therefore Christ, in the human nature in which He has accomplished the mysteries of man's salvation, is fittingly appointed by God to be judge over the men He has saved. We are told that this is so in John 5:27: "He [the Father] hath given Him [the Son] power to do judgment, because He is the Son of man."[344] There is also another reason. Those who are to be judged ought to see the judge. But the sight of God, in whom the judicial authority resides, in His own proper nature is the reward that is meted out in the Judgment. Therefore the men to be judged — the good as well as the wicked — ought to see God as judge, not in His proper nature, but in His assumed nature. If the wicked saw God in His divine nature, they would be receiving the very reward of which they had made themselves unworthy.

Furthermore, the office of judge is a suitable recompense by way of exaltation, corresponding to the humiliation of Christ, who was willing to be humiliated to the point of being unjustly judged by a human judge. To give expression to our belief in this humiliation, we say explicitly in the Creed, that He suffered under Pontius Pilate. Therefore this exalted reward of being appointed by God to judge all men, the living and the dead, in His human nature, was due to Christ, according to Job 36:17: "Thy cause hath been judged as that of the wicked. Cause and judgment Thou shalt recover."

Moreover, since this judicial power pertains to Christ's exaltation, as does the glory of His resurrection, Christ will appear at the Judgment, not in humility — which belonged to the time of merit — but in the glorious form that is indicative of His reward. We are assured in the Gospel that "they shall see the Son of man coming in a cloud with great power and majesty."[345] And the sight of His glory will be a joy to the elect who have loved Him; to these is made the promise in Isaiah 33:17, that they "shall see the King in His beauty." But to the wicked this sight will mean confusion and lamentation, for the glory and the power of the judge will bring grief and dread to those who fear damnation. We read of this in

[344]RSV: John 5:26.
[345]Luke 21:27.

Isaiah 26:11: "Let the envious people see and be confounded, and let fire devour Thy enemies."

Although Christ will show Himself in His glorious form, the marks of the Passion will appear in Him, not with disfigurement, but with beauty and splendor, so that at the sight of them the elect, who will perceive that they have been saved through the sufferings of Christ, will be filled with joy; but sinners, who have scorned so great a benefit, will be filled with dismay. Thus we read in Revelation 1:7: "Every eye shall see Him, and they also that pierced Him. And all the tribes of the Earth shall bewail themselves because of Him."

242

All judgment is given to the Son

Since the Father "hath given all judgment to the Son," as is said in John 5:22,[346] and since human life even at present is regulated by the just judgment of God — for it is He who judges all flesh, as Abraham declared in Genesis 18:25 — we cannot doubt that this judgment, by which men are governed in the world, pertains likewise to the judicial power of Christ. To Him are directed the words of the Father reported in Psalm 109:1: "Sit Thou at my right hand, until I make Thy enemies Thy footstool."[347] Christ sits at the right hand of God according to His human nature, inasmuch as He receives His judicial power from the Father. And this power He exercises even now before all His enemies are clearly seen to lie prostrate at His feet. He Himself bore witness to this fact shortly after His resurrection, in Matthew 28:18: "All power is given to me in Heaven and on Earth."

[346]RSV: John 5:21.
[347]RSV: Ps. 110:1.

There is another judgment of God whereby, at the moment of death, everyone receives as regards his soul the recompense he has deserved. The just who have been dissolved in death remain with Christ, as Paul desired for himself;[348] but sinners who have died are buried in Hell.

We may not suppose that this division takes place without God's judgment, or that this judgment does not pertain to the judicial power of Christ, especially as He Himself tells His disciples in John 14:3: "If I shall go and prepare a place for you, I will come again and will take you to myself, that where I am, you also may be." To be taken in this way means nothing else than to be dissolved in death, so that we may be with Christ; for, as is said in 2 Corinthians 5:6, "while we are in the body we are absent from the Lord."

However, since man's recompense is not confined to goods of the soul but embraces goods of the body (which is again to be resumed by the soul at the resurrection) and since every recompense requires judgment, there has to be another judgment by which men are rewarded for what they have done in the body as well as for what they have done in the soul. This judgment, too, belongs rightfully to Christ, in order that, as He rose and ascended into Heaven in glory after dying for us, He may also by His own power cause the bodies of our lowliness to rise again in the likeness of His glorified body, and may transport them up to Heaven whither He has preceded us by His ascension, thus opening the way before us, as had been foretold by Micah.[349] This resurrection of all men will take place simultaneously at the end of the world,

---

[348] Cf. Phil. 1:23.

[349] Mic. 2:13: "For he shall go up that shall open the way before them: they shall divide, and pass through the gate, and shall come in by it; and their king shall pass before them, and the Lord at the head of them."

as we have already indicated.[350] Therefore this judgment will be a general and final judgment, and we believe that Christ will come a second time, in glory, to preside at it.

In Psalm 35:7[351] we read: "Thy judgments are a great deep"; and in Romans 11:33 the Apostle exclaims: "How incomprehensible are His judgments!" Each of the judgments mentioned contains something profound and incomprehensible to human knowledge. In the first of God's judgments, by which the present life of mankind is regulated, the time of the judgment is, indeed, manifest to men, but the reason for the recompenses is concealed, especially as evils for the most part are the lot of the good in this world, while good things come to the wicked. In the other two judgments of God the reason for the requitals will be clearly known, but the time remains hidden, because man does not know the hour of his death, as is noted in Ecclesiastes 9:12: "Man knoweth not his own end"; and no one can know the end of this world. For we do not foreknow future events, except those whose causes we understand. But the cause of the end of the world is the will of God, which is unknown to us. Therefore the end of the world can be foreseen by no creature, but only by God, according to Matthew 24:36: "Of that day and hour no one knoweth; no, not the angels of Heaven, but the Father alone."

In this connection, some have found an occasion for going astray in the added words, "nor the Son," which are read in Mark 13:32.[352] They contend that the Son is inferior to the Father, on

---

[350]Cf. chap. 154.

[351]RSV: Ps. 36:6.

[352]Thus Arius and Eunomius. Cf. St. Athanasius, Contra Arianos, III, 26 (PG, XXVI, 380); St. Hilary, De Trinitate, IX, 2 (PL, X, 282); St. Ambrose, De fide, V, 16 (PL, XVI, 688); St. Jerome, In evangelium Matthaei, IV, on chap. 24:36 (PL, XXVI, 181).

the score that He is ignorant of matters which the Father knows. The difficulty could be avoided by replying that the Son is igno-rant of this event in His assumed human nature, but not in His divine nature, in which He has one and the same wisdom as the Father or, to speak with greater propriety, He is wisdom itself intellectually conceived. But the Son could hardly be unaware of the divine judgment even in His assumed nature, since His soul, as the Evangelist attests,[353] is full of God's grace and truth, as was pointed out above.[354] Nor does it seem reasonable that Christ, who has received the power to judge "because He is the Son of man"[355] should be ignorant in His human nature of the time appointed for Him to judge. The Father would not really have given all judgment to Him, if the judgment of determining the time of His coming were withheld from Him.

Accordingly, this text is to be interpreted in the light of the usual style of speech found in the Scriptures, in which God is said to know a thing when He imparts knowledge of that thing, as when He said to Abraham, in Genesis 22:12: "Now I know that thou fearest God." The meaning is not that He who knows all things from eternity began to know at that moment, but that He made known Abraham's devotedness by that declaration. In a similar way the Son is said to be ignorant of the day of Judgment, because He did not impart that knowledge to the disciples, but replied to them (as we see in Acts 1:7): "It is not for you to know the times or moments which the Father hath put in His own power." But the Father is not ignorant in this way, since in any case He gave knowledge of the matter to the Son through the eternal generation. Some authors extricate themselves from the difficulty

[353]John 1:14.
[354]Cf. chap. 213.
[355]John 5:27 (RSV: John 5:26).

in fewer words, saying that Mark's expression is to be understood of an adopted son.[356]

However that may be, the Lord wished the time of the future Judgment to remain hidden, that men might watch with care so as not to be found unprepared at the hour of Judgment. For the same reason He also wished the hour of each one's death to be unknown. For each man will appear at the Judgment in the state in which he departs from this world by death. Therefore the Lord admonishes us in Matthew 24:42: "Watch ye therefore, because you know not what hour your Lord will come."

243
The universality of the Judgment

According to the doctrine thus set forth, Christ clearly has judicial power over the living and the dead. He judges both those who are living in the world at present and those who pass from this world by death. At the Last Judgment, however, He will judge the living and the dead together. In this expression *the living* may be taken to mean the just who live by grace and *the dead* may be taken to mean sinners who have fallen from grace. Or else by *the living* may be meant those who will be found still alive at the Lord's coming and by *the dead* those who have died in previous ages.

We are not to think that certain of the living will be judged without ever having undergone death of the body, as some have argued.[357] For in 1 Corinthians 15:51, the Apostle says clearly:

---

[356] St. Gregory of Tours, *Historia Francorum*, I, *prol.* (PL, LXXI, 163); Peter Comestor, *Historia scholastica: In evangelia*, 142 (PL, CXCVIII, 1611).

[357] St. John Chrysostom, *In Epistolam primam ad Corinthios, hom.* XLII, 2 (PG, LXI, 364); St. Jerome, *Epist.* LIX, 3 (PL, XXII, 587); *Epist.* CXIX, 7 (PL, XXII, 971). Cf. St. Augustine, *Epist.* CXCIII, 4 (PL, XXXIII, 872).

"We shall all indeed rise again." Another reading has: "We shall indeed sleep" (that is, we shall die); or, according to some books, "We shall not indeed all sleep," as Jerome notes in his letter to Minervius on the resurrection of the body.[358] But this variant does not destroy the force of the doctrine under discussion. For a little previously the Apostle had written: "As in Adam all die, so also in Christ all shall be made alive."[359] Hence the text which reads: "We shall not all sleep," cannot refer to death of the body, which has come down to all through the sin of our first parent (as is stated in Romans 5:12), but must be interpreted as referring to the sleep of sin, concerning which (in Ephesians 5:14) we are exhorted: "Rise, thou that sleepest, and arise from the dead: and Christ shall enlighten thee."

Accordingly, those who are found alive at the Lord's coming will be marked off from those who have died before, not for the reason that they will never die, but because in the very act by which they are taken up "in the clouds to meet Christ, into the air"[360] they will die and immediately rise again, as Augustine teaches.[361]

In discussing this matter, we must take cognizance of the three phases which, apparently, constitute a judicial process. First, someone is haled into court; secondly, his cause is examined; and thirdly, he receives sentence.

As to the first phase, all men — good and evil, from the first man down to the very last — will be subject to Christ's judgment, for, as we are told in 2 Corinthians 5:10, "We must all be manifested before the judgment seat of Christ." Not even those who

---

[358] *Epist.* CXIX, 2 (*PL,* 967).

[359] 1 Cor. 15:22.

[360] 1 Thess. 4:16 (RSV: 1 Thess. 4:17).

[361] *Retractationes,* II, 33 (*PL,* XXXII, 644).

have died in infancy, whether they were baptized or not, are exempt from this universal law, as is explained by the Glossary on this text.[362]

With regard to the second phase (namely, the examination of the case), not all, either of the good or of the wicked, will be judged. A judicial investigation is not necessary unless good and evil actions are intermingled. When good is present without admixture of evil, or evil without admixture of good, discussion is out of place. Among the good there are some who have wholeheartedly despised temporal possessions and have dedicated themselves to God alone and to the things that are of God. Accordingly, since sin is committed by cleaving to changeable goods in contempt of the changeless Good, such souls exhibit no mingling of good and evil. This is not to imply that they live without sin, for in their person is asserted what we read in 1 John 1:8: "If we say that we have no sin, we deceive ourselves." Although certain lesser sins are found in them, these are, so to speak, consumed by the fire of charity, and so seem to be nothing. At the Judgment, therefore, such souls will not be judged by an investigation of their deeds.

On the other hand, those who lead an earthly life and in their preoccupation with things of this world use them, not indeed against God, but with excessive attachment to them, have a notable amount of evil mixed up with the good of faith and charity, so that the element predominating in them cannot easily be perceived. Such souls will undergo judgment by an examination of their merits.

Similarly, with reference to the wicked, we should recall that the principle of approach to God is faith, according to Hebrews 11:6: "He that cometh to God must believe." Therefore in him

---

[362] Walafrid Strabo, *Glossa ordinaria* (PL, CXIV, 558).

who lacks faith there is found nothing of good which, mixed with evil, might render his damnation doubtful. And so such a one will be condemned without any inquiry into merits. Again, he who has faith but has no charity and, consequently, no good works, possesses, indeed, some point of contact with God. Hence an examination of his case is necessary, so that the element predominating in him,[363] whether good or evil, may clearly emerge. Such a person will be condemned only after an investigation of his case. In the same way an earthly king condemns a criminal citizen after hearing him, but punishes an enemy without any hearing.

Lastly, regarding the third phase of a judgment (pronouncement of the sentence), all will be judged, for all will receive glory or punishment according to the sentence. The reason is given in 2 Corinthians 5:10: "That every one may receive the proper things of the body, according as he hath done, whether it be good or evil."

244

The procedure and place of the Judgment

We are not to suppose that judicial examination will be required in order that the judge may receive information, as is the case in human courts; for "all things are naked and open to His eyes," as we are told in Hebrews 4:13. The examination is necessary for the purpose of making known to each person, concerning himself and others, the reasons why each is worthy of punishment or of glory, so that the good may joyfully acknowledge God's justice in all things and the wicked may be roused to anger against themselves.

Nor should we imagine that this examination is to be conducted by verbal discussion. Endless time would be required to

---

[363] Vivès: *"in isto"*; Mandonnet et al.: *"in Christo."*

recount the thoughts, words, and deeds — good or evil — of each person. Therefore Lactantius was deceived when he suggested that the day of Judgment would last a thousand years.[364] Even this time would scarcely be enough, as several days would be required to complete the judicial process for a single man in the manner proposed. Accordingly, the divine power will bring it about that in an instant everyone will be apprised of all the good or evil he has ever done, for which he is to be rewarded or punished. And all this will be made known to each person, not only about himself, but also about the rest. Hence, wherever the good is so much in excess that the evil seems to be of no consequence or vice versa, there will seem, to human estimation, to be no conflict between the good and the evil. This is what we meant when we said that such persons will be rewarded or punished without examination.[365]

Although all men will appear before Christ at that Judgment, the good will not only be set apart from the wicked by reason of meritorious cause, but will be separated from them in locality. The wicked, who have withdrawn from Christ in their love of earthly things, will remain on Earth; but the good, who have clung to Christ, will be raised up into the air when they go to meet Christ, that they may be made like Christ not only by being conformed to the splendor of His glory, but by being associated with Him in the place He occupies. This is indicated in Matthew 24:28: "Wheresoever the body shall be, there also shall the eagles (by which the saints are signified) be gathered together." According to Jerome, instead of *body* the Hebrew has the significant word *joatham*,[366]

---

[364] *Divinae institutiones*, VII: *De beata vita*, 24 (PL, VI, 808).

[365] Cf. chap. 243.

[366] *In evangelium Matthaei*, IV (PL, XXVI, 179). St. Thomas here misreads *ptoma* (corpse), which occurs in the Greek Matthew and is quoted by Jerome, for some fancied Hebrew or Aramaic word.

which means "corpse," to commemorate Christ's Passion, whereby Christ merited the power to judge and men who have been conformed to His Passion are admitted into the company of His glory, as we are told by the Apostle in 2 Timothy 2:12: "If we suffer, we shall also reign with Him."

This is the ground for our belief that Christ will come down to judge somewhere near the place of His Passion, as is intimated in Joel 3:2: "I will gather together all nations and will bring them down into the valley of Josaphat; and I will plead with them there." This valley lies at the foot of Mount Olivet, from which Christ ascended into Heaven. For the same reason, when Christ comes for the Judgment, the sign of the Cross and other signs of the Passion will be displayed, as is said in Matthew 24:30: "And then shall appear the sign of the Son of man in Heaven," so that the wicked, looking upon Him whom they have pierced, will be distressed and tormented, and those who have been redeemed will exult in the glory of their Redeemer. And as Christ is said to sit at God's right hand according to His human nature (inasmuch as He has been lifted up to share in the most excellent goods of the Father), so at the Judgment the just are said to stand at Christ's right, as being entitled to the most honorable place near Him.

245
The role of the saints in the Judgment

Christ will not be the only one to judge on that day; others will be associated with Him. Of these, some will judge only in the sense of serving as a basis for comparison. In this way the good will judge the less good, or the wicked will judge the more wicked, according to Matthew 12:41: "The men of Nineveh shall rise in judgment with this generation and shall condemn it." And some will judge by giving their approval to the sentence; in this way all the just shall judge, according to Wisdom 3:7-8: "The just . . . shall judge nations." But some will judge with a certain judicial power delegated to them by Christ, having "two-edged swords in their hands," as is indicated in Psalm 149:6.

This last kind of judicial power the Lord promised to the Apostles (in Matthew 19:28) when He said: "You who have followed me, in the regeneration, when the Son of man shall sit on the seat of His majesty, you also shall sit on twelve seats, judging the twelve tribes of Israel." We are not to conclude from this that only the Jews who belong to the twelve tribes of Israel will be judged by the Apostles, for by the twelve tribes of Israel are understood all the faithful who have been admitted to the Faith of the patriarchs. As for infidels, they will not be judged, but have already been judged.

Similarly, the twelve Apostles who walked with Christ during His earthly life are not the only ones who will judge. Judas assuredly will not judge, and Paul, on the other hand, who labored more than the rest, will not lack judicial power, especially as he himself says in 1 Corinthians 6:3: "Know you not that we shall judge angels?" This dignity pertains properly to those who have left all to follow Christ, for such was the promise made to Peter in answer to his question in Matthew 19:27: "Behold, we have left all things and have followed Thee; what therefore shall we have?" The same thought occurs in Job 36:6: "He giveth judgment to the poor."

And this is reasonable, because, as we said, the investigation will deal with the actions of men who have used earthly things well or ill.[367] Correctness of judgment requires that the mind of the judge should be unswayed by those matters about which he has to

---

[367]Cf. chap. 243.

judge; and so the fact that some have their minds completely detached from earthly things gives them title to judicial authority.

The announcing of the divine commandments also contributes to the meriting of this dignity. In Matthew 25:31 we read that Christ will come to judge accompanied by angels (that is, by preachers), as Augustine suggests in a work on penance.[368] For they who have made known the precepts of life ought to have a part in examining the actions of men regarding the observance of the divine precepts.

The persons mentioned will judge by cooperating in the task of revealing to each individual the cause of the salvation or damnation both of himself and of others, in the way that higher angels are said to illuminate the lower angels and also men.

We profess that this judicial power belongs to Christ when we say, in the Apostles' Creed: "From thence He shall come to judge the living and the dead."

246
The foregoing teachings comprised in articles of Faith

Having reviewed the doctrines pertaining to the truth of the Christian Faith, we should advert to the fact that all the teachings thus set forth are reduced to certain articles: twelve in number, as some think, or fourteen, according to others.

Faith has to do with truths that surpass the comprehension of reason. Hence, whenever a new truth incomprehensible to reason is proposed, a new article is required. One article pertains to the divine unity. For, even though we prove by reason that God is one, the fact that He governs all things directly or that He wishes to be

---

[368] *Sermo* 351, *De utilitate agendae poenitentiae* (PL, XXXIX, 1544).

worshiped in some particular way, is a matter relating to Faith. Three articles are reserved for the three divine persons. Three other articles are formulated about the effects produced by God: creation, which pertains to nature; justification, which pertains to grace; and reward, which pertains to glory. Thus seven articles altogether are devoted to the divinity.

Concerning the humanity of Christ, seven more are proposed. The first is on the incarnation and conception of Christ. The second deals with the nativity, which involves a special difficulty because of our Lord's coming forth from the closed womb of the Virgin. The third article is on the death, Passion, and burial; the fourth on the descent into Hell; the fifth on the Resurrection; the sixth on the Ascension; and the seventh treats of Christ's coming for the Judgment. And so there are fourteen articles in all.

Other authorities, reasonably enough, include faith in the three persons under one article, on the ground that we cannot believe in the Father without believing in the Son and also in the Holy Spirit (the bond of love uniting the first two persons). However, they distinguish the article on the Resurrection from the article on eternal reward. Accordingly, there are two articles about God; one on the unity; the other on the Trinity. Four articles deal with God's effects: one with creation; the second with justification; the third with the general resurrection; and the fourth with reward. Similarly, as regards belief in the humanity of Christ, these authors comprise the conception and the nativity under one article; and they also include the Passion and death under one article. According to this way of reckoning, therefore, we have twelve articles in all.

And this should be enough on Faith.

HOPE

The second part
of
LIGHT OF FAITH:
THE COMPENDIUM OF THEOLOGY

Introduction

1
Necessity of the virtue of hope

The Prince of the Apostles has left us an admonition urging us to render an account not only of our faith, but also of the hope that is in us.[369] In the first part of the present work we have briefly set forth the teaching of Christian faith. We now turn to the task of undertaking, in compendious fashion, an exposition of the truths pertaining to hope.

We should recall that in one kind of knowledge, man's desire can come to rest. We naturally desire to know truth, and when we do know it, our craving in this direction is satisfied. But in the knowledge of faith man's desire never comes to rest. For faith is imperfect knowledge: the truths we accept on faith are not seen. This is why the Apostle calls faith "the evidence of things that appear not."[370]

---

[369] See 1 Pet. 3:15: "But sanctify the Lord Christ in your hearts, being ready always to satisfy everyone that asketh you a reason of that hope which is in you."

[370] Heb. 11:1.

Accordingly, even when we have faith, there still remains in the soul an impulse toward something else, namely, the perfect vision of the truth assented to in faith, and the attainment of whatever can lead to such truth. As we pointed out above, among the various teachings of faith there is one according to which we believe that God exercises providence over human affairs.[371] In consequence of this belief, stirrings of hope arise in the soul of the believer that by God's help he may gain possession of the goods he naturally desires, once he learns of them through faith. Therefore, as we mentioned at the very beginning,[372] next after faith, the virtue of hope is necessary for the perfection of Christian living.

2
Prayer and hope

In the order of Divine Providence, each being has assigned to it a way of reaching its end in keeping with its nature. To men, too, is appointed a suitable way, that befits the conditions of human nature, of obtaining what they hope for from God. Human nature inclines us to have recourse to petition for the purpose of obtaining from another, especially from a person of higher rank, what we hope to receive from him. So prayer is recommended to men, that by it they may obtain from God what they hope to secure from Him.

But the reason why prayer is necessary for obtaining something from a man is not the same as the reason for its necessity when there is question of obtaining a favor from God. Prayer is addressed to man, first, to lay bare the desire and the need of the petitioner, and secondly, to incline the mind of him to whom the prayer is addressed to grant the petition. These purposes have no place in

[371] Cf. *supra*, chaps. 123, 143.
[372] Cf. chap. 1.

the prayer that is sent up to God. When we pray we do not intend to manifest our needs or desires to God, for He knows all things. The Psalmist says to God: "Lord, all my desire is before Thee"[373] and in the Gospel we are told: "Your Father knoweth that you have need of all these things."[374] Again, the will of God is not influenced by human words to will what He had previously not willed. For, as we read in Numbers 23:19, "God is not a man, that He should lie, nor as the son of man, that He should be changed"; nor is God moved to repentance, as we are assured in 1 Kings 15:29.[375] Prayer, then, for obtaining something from God, is necessary for man on account of the very one who prays, that he may reflect on his shortcomings and may turn his mind to desiring fervently and piously what he hopes to gain by his petition. In this way he is rendered fit to receive the favor.

Yet a further difference between the prayer offered to God and that addressed to man is to be marked. Prayer addressed to a man presupposes a certain intimacy that may afford the petitioner an opportunity to present his request. But when we pray to God, the very prayer we send forth makes us intimate with Him, inasmuch as our soul is raised up to God, converses with Him in spiritual affection, and adores Him in spirit and truth. The familiar affection thus experienced in prayer begets an inducement in the petitioner to pray again with yet greater confidence. And so we read in Psalm 16:6: "I have cried to Thee"[376] (that is, in trusting prayer) "for Thou, O God, hast heard me"; as though, after being admitted to intimacy in the first prayer, the Psalmist cries out with all the greater confidence in the second.

[373] Ps. 37:10 (RSV: Ps. 38:9).
[374] Matt. 6:32.
[375] RSV: 1 Sam. 15:29.
[376] RSV: Ps. 17:6.

Therefore, in prayer to God, perseverance or repetition of our supplication is not unseemly, but is acceptable to God. Indeed, "we ought always to pray and not to faint," as we learn from Luke 18:1. Our Lord, too, invites us to pray, for He said: "Ask, and it shall be given you . . . knock, and it shall be opened to you."[377] But in prayer addressed to man, persistence in begging becomes irritating.

[377]Matt. 7:7.

Hope and Prayer

Since, beyond faith, hope is also necessary for salvation, our Savior, who inaugurated and perfected our faith by instituting the sacraments, thought it well to carry us to a living hope by giving us a prayer that mightily raises up our hope to God. God Himself taught us what we should ask of Him. He would not urge us to pray unless He were determined to hear us; no one asks another for a favor without hope in him, and he asks only what he hopes for. So in teaching us to ask God for benefits, Christ exhorts us to hope in God and shows us what to hope for by telling us what to request.

We shall consider the petitions in the Lord's Prayer, noting all that relates to Christian hope. We shall indicate the person in whom we ought to hope (and why) and what to expect from Him. Our hope should be anchored in God to whom we are to pray, as Psalm 61:9 says: "Trust in Him" (i.e., God) "all ye congregation of people; pour out your hearts before Him"[378](i.e., in prayer).

---

[378]RSV: Ps. 62:8.

4

Why we must pray to God for what we hope

The reason why we must hope in God is chiefly the fact that we belong to Him, as effect belongs to cause. God does nothing in vain, but always acts for a definite purpose. Every active cause has the power of producing its effect in such a way that the effect will not be wanting in whatever can advance it toward its end. This is why, in effects produced by natural causes, nature is not found to be deficient in anything that is necessary, but confers on every effect whatever goes into its composition and is required to carry through the action whereby it may reach its end. Of course, some impediment may arise from a defect in the cause, which then may be unable to furnish all this.

A cause that operates intellectually not only confers on the effect, in the act of producing it, all that is required for the result intended, but also, when the product is finished, controls its use, which is the end of the object. Thus a smith, in addition to forging a knife, has the disposition of its cutting efficiency. Man is made by God somewhat as an article is made by an artificer. Something of this sort is said in Isaiah 64:8: "And now, O Lord, Thou art our Father and we are clay, and Thou art our Maker."

Accordingly, just as an earthen vessel, if it were endowed with sense, might hope to be put to good use by the potter, so man ought to cherish the hope of being rightly provided for by God. Thus we are told in Jeremiah 18:6: "As clay is in the hand of the potter, so are you in my hand, O house of Israel."

The confidence which man has in God ought to be most certain. As we just intimated, a cause does not refrain from rightly controlling its product unless it labors under some defect. But no defect or ignorance can occur in God because "all things are naked and open to His eyes," as is said in Hebrews 4:13. Nor does He lack power, for "the hand of the Lord is not shortened that it cannot save," as we read in Isaiah 59:1. Nor is He wanting in good will, for "the Lord is good to them that hope in Him, to the soul that seeketh Him," as we are reminded in Lamentations 3:25. Therefore the hope with which a person trusts in God does not confound him that hopes, as is said in Romans 5:5.

We should also bear in mind that, while Providence watches solicitously over all creatures, God exercises special care over rational beings. For the latter are exalted to the dignity of God's image, and can rise to the knowledge and love of Him, and have dominion over their actions, since they are able to discriminate between good and evil. Hence they should have confidence in God, not only that they may be preserved in existence in keeping with the condition of their nature — for this pertains also to other creatures — but that, by avoiding evil and doing good, they may merit some reward from Him. We are taught a salutary lesson in Psalm 35:7: "Men and beasts Thou wilt preserve"[379] (that is, God bestows on men and irrational creatures alike whatever pertains to the sustaining of life). And then the Psalmist adds, in the next verse: "But the children of men shall put their trust under the covert of Thy wings,"[380] indicating that they will be protected by God with special care.

We should observe, further, that when any perfection is conferred, an ability to do or acquire something is also added. For example, when the air is illuminated by the sun, it has the capacity to serve as a medium for sight; and when water is heated by fire it can be used to cook — and it could hope for this if it had a mind. To man is given, over and above the nature of his soul, the perfection of grace, by which he is made a partaker in the divine

[379]RSV: Ps. 36:6.
[380]Ps. 35:8 (RSV: Ps. 36:7).

nature, as we are taught in 2 Peter 1:4.[381] As a result of this, we are said to be regenerated and to become sons of God, according to John 1:12: "He gave them power to be made the sons of God." Thus raised to be sons, men may reasonably hope for an inheritance, as we learn from Romans 8:17: "If sons, heirs also." In keeping with this spiritual regeneration, man should have a yet higher hope in God, namely, the hope of receiving an eternal inheritance, according to 1 Peter 1:3-4: "God . . . hath regenerated us unto a lively hope, by the resurrection of Jesus Christ from the dead, unto an inheritance incorruptible, undefiled, and which cannot fade, reserved in Heaven for you."

Through this "spirit of adoption" that we receive, we cry: "*Abba* (Father)," as is said in Romans 8:15. Hence our Lord began His prayer by calling upon the Father, saying, "Father," to teach us that our prayer must be based on this hope. By uttering the name, "Father," man's affection is prepared to pray with a pure disposition, and also to obtain what he hopes for. Moreover, sons ought to be imitators of their parents. Therefore he who professes that God is his Father ought to try to be an imitator of God, by avoiding things that make him unlike God and by earnestly praying for those perfections that make him like to God. Hence we are commanded in Jeremiah 3:19: "Thou shalt call me *Father* and shalt not cease to walk after me." If, then, as Gregory of Nyssa reminds us,[382] you turn your gaze to worldly affairs or seek human honor or the filth of passionate craving, how can you (who lead such a corrupt life) call the source of incorruption your Father?

---

[381] "By whom he hath given us most great and precious promises; that by these you may be made partakers of the divine nature; flying the corruption of that concupiscence which is in the world."

[382] *De oratione dominica*, II (PG, XLIV, 1144).

5

Why we are to say "our Father," not "my Father"

He who looks on himself as a son of God, ought, among other things, to imitate our Lord especially in His love, as we are urged to do in Ephesians 5:1-2: "Be ye therefore followers of God as most dear children, and walk in love." God's love is not restricted to any individual, but embraces all in common; for God loves "all things that are," as is said in Wisdom 11:25. Most of all He loves men, according to Deuteronomy 33:3: "He hath loved the people." Consequently, in Cyprian's words, "our prayer is public and is offered for all; and when we pray, we do not pray for one person alone, but for the whole people, because we are all together one people."[383] Or, as Chrysostom says, "Necessity forces us to pray for ourselves, but fraternal charity impels us to pray for others."[384] This is why we say, "our Father," and not simply "my Father."

At the same time we should remember that, although our hope rests chiefly on God's help, we can aid one another to obtain more easily what we ask for. St. Paul says, in 2 Corinthians 1:10-11: God will "deliver us, you helping withal in prayer for us." And in James 5:16 we are exhorted: "Pray one for another, that you may be saved." For, as Ambrose reminds us, "many insignificant people, when they are gathered together and are of one mind, become powerful, and the prayers of many cannot but be heard."[385] This agrees with Matthew 18:19: "If two of you shall consent upon Earth concerning anything whatsoever they shall ask, it shall be done to them by my Father who is in Heaven."[386] Therefore we do

---

[383] *Liber de oratione dominica*, VIII (PL, IV, 524).

[384] Pseudo-Chrysostom, *In evangelium Matthaei, hom.* XIV (PG, LVI, 711).

[385] Ambrosiaster, *In epistolam ad Romanos*, XV (PL, XVII, 177).

[386] RSV: Matt. 18:18.

not pour forth our prayers as individuals, but with unanimous accord we cry out, "our Father."

Let us also reflect that our hope reaches up to God through Christ, according to Romans 5:1-2: "Being justified therefore by faith, let us have peace with God, through our Lord Jesus Christ, by whom also we have access through faith into this grace wherein we stand, and glory in the hope of the glory of the sons of God." Through Him who is the only-begotten Son of God by nature, we are made adopted sons: "God sent His Son . . . that we might receive the adoption of sons," as is said in Galatians 4:4-5. Hence, in acknowledging that God is our Father, we should do so in such a way that the prerogative of the Only-begotten is not disparaged. In this connection Augustine admonishes us: "Do not make any exclusive claims for yourself. In a special sense, God is the Father of Christ alone and is the Father of all the rest of us in common. For the Father begot Him alone, but created us."[387] This, then, is why we say: "our Father."

6

God's power to grant our petitions

When hope is abandoned, the reason is usually to be found in the powerlessness of him from whom help was expected. The confidence characteristic of hope is not wholly grounded on the mere willingness to help professed by him on whom our hope rests: power to help must also be present.

We sufficiently express our conviction that the divine will is ready to help us when we proclaim that God is our Father. But to

---

[387] *Sermo* LXXXIV, which is among the sermons wrongly attributed to St. Augustine (*PL*, XXXIX, 1907). The passage is taken from St. Ambrose, *De sacramentis*, V, 19 (*PL*, XVI, 451).

exclude all doubt as to the perfection of His power, we add: "who art in Heaven." The Father is not said to be in Heaven as though He were contained by Heaven. On the contrary, He encompasses Heaven in His power, as is said in Ecclesiasticus 24:8: "I alone have compassed the circuit of Heaven." Indeed, God's power is raised above the whole immensity of Heaven, according to Psalm 8:2: "Thy magnificence is elevated above the heavens."[388] And so, to strengthen the confidence of our hope, we hail the power of God which sustains and transcends the heavens.

This same phrase removes a certain obstacle that may stand in the way of our prayer. Some people act as though human affairs were subjected to a deterministic fatalism imposed by the stars, contrary to what is commanded in Jeremiah 10:2: "Be not afraid of the signs of Heaven, which the heathens fear." If this error had its way, it would rob us of the fruit of prayer. For if our lives were subjected to a necessity decreed by the stars, nothing in our course could be changed. In vain we should plead in our prayer for the granting of some good or for deliverance from evil. To prevent this error from undermining confidence in prayer, we say: "who art in Heaven," thus acknowledging that God moves and regulates the heavens. Accordingly, the assistance we hope to obtain from God cannot be obstructed by the power of heavenly bodies.

In order that prayer may be efficacious at the court of God, man must ask for those benefits which he may worthily expect from God. Of old some petitioners were rebuked: "You ask and receive not, because you ask amiss."[389] Anything suggested by earthly wisdom rather than by heavenly wisdom, is asked for in the wrong spirit. And so Chrysostom assures us that the words, "who art in Heaven," do not imply that God is confined to that locality, but

---

[388]RSV: Ps. 8:1.
[389]James 4:3.

rather indicate that the mind of him who prays is raised up from the Earth and comes to rest in that celestial region.[390]

There is another obstacle to prayer or confidence in God that would deter one from praying. This is the notion that human life is far removed from Divine Providence. The thought is given expression in the person of the wicked in Job 22:14: "The clouds are His covert, and He doth not consider our things, and He walketh about the poles of Heaven"; also in Ezechiel 8:12: "The Lord seeth us not, the Lord hath forsaken the Earth."

But the Apostle Paul taught the contrary in his sermon to the Athenians, when he said that God is "not far from every one of us; for in Him we live and move and are."[391] That is, our being is preserved; our life is governed; and our activity is directed by Him. This is confirmed by Wisdom 14:3: "Thy providence, O Father, governeth" all things from the beginning. Not even the most insignificant of living things are withdrawn from God's Providence, as we are told in Matthew 10:29-30: "Are not two sparrows sold for a farthing? And not one of them shall fall on the ground without your Father. But the very hairs of your head are all numbered." Men are placed under the divine care in a yet more excellent way, so that in comparison with them the Apostle could ask: "Doth God take care for oxen?"[392] The meaning is not that God has no concern at all for such animals but that He does not take care of them in the same way He does of men, whom He punishes or rewards in accordance with their good or evil actions, and whom He foreordains to eternal life. This is why, in the words quoted from Matthew, our Lord says: "The very hairs of your head

---

[390] In Matthaeum, hom. XIX, 4 (PG, LVII, 278).
[391] Acts 17:27-28.
[392] 1 Cor. 9:9.

are all numbered," thus indicating that everything belonging to man is to be recovered at the resurrection.

Consequently all diffidence should be banished from our lives. For, as our Lord adds in the same context: "Fear not, therefore; better are you than many sparrows."[393] This clarifies the passage we called attention to above:[394] "The children of men shall put their trust under the covert of Thy wings."[395]

Although God is said to be near to all men by reason of His special care over them, He is exceptionally close to the good who strive to draw near to Him in faith and love, as we are assured in James 4:8: "Draw nigh to God, and He will draw nigh to you." Confirmation of this is found in Psalm 144:18: "The Lord is nigh unto all men that call upon Him: to all that call upon Him in truth."[396] Indeed, He not only draws nigh to them; He even dwells in them through grace, as is intimated in Jeremiah 14:9: "Thou, O Lord, art among us."

Therefore, to increase the hope of the saints, we are bidden to say: "who art in Heaven" — that is, *in the saints*, as Augustine explains.[397] For, as the same doctor adds, the spiritual distance between the just and sinners seems to be as great as the spatial distance between Heaven and Earth.[398] To symbolize this idea, we turn toward the east when we pray, because it is in that direction that heaven rises. The hope of the saints and their confidence in

---

[393] Matt. 10:31.

[394] Cf. chap. 4.

[395] Ps. 35:8 (RSV: Ps. 36:7).

[396] RSV: Ps. 145:18.

[397] *De sermone Domini in monte*, II, 5 (*PL*, XXXIV, 1276). Cf. St. Thomas, *Expositio orationis dominicae* (Vivès, XXVII, 185): "The saints are called the heavens, according to Psalm 18:2: 'The heavens show forth the glory of God' " (RSV: Ps. 19:1).

[398] Ibid., col. 1277.

prayer are increased by the divine nearness, and also by the dignity they have received from God, who through Christ has caused them to be heavens, as is indicated in Isaiah 51:16: "That Thou mightest plant the heavens and found the Earth." He who has made them heavens will not withhold heavenly goods from them.

7

Objects of hope

Having treated of the truths that lead men to hope in God, we must go on to inquire what are the blessings we ought to hope to receive from Him. In this connection we should observe that hope presupposes desire. Before a thing can be hoped for, it must first be desired. Things that are not desired are not said to be objects of hope; rather they are feared or even despised. Secondly, we must judge that what is hoped for is possible to obtain; hope includes this factor over and above desire. True, a man can desire things he does not believe he is able to attain; but he cannot cherish hope with regard to such objects. Thirdly, hope necessarily implies the idea that the good hoped for is hard to get: trifles are the object of contempt rather than of hope. Or, if we desire certain things and have them, as it were, to hand, we are not deemed to hope for them as future goods, but to possess them as present to us.

We should further note that among the difficult things a person hopes to obtain, there are some he hopes to get through the good offices of another and some that he hopes to acquire through his own efforts. The difference between these two classes of goods comes to this: to obtain the things he hopes to acquire by himself, a man employs the resources of his own power; to obtain what he hopes to receive from another, he has recourse to petition.

If he hopes to receive such a benefit from a man, his request is called *simple petition;* if he hopes to obtain a favor from God, it is called *prayer*, which, as Damascene says, "is a petition addressed to God for suitable goods."[399]

However, the hope a man places in his own powers or in another man does not pertain to the *virtue* of hope; that virtue is limited to the hope he has in God. Hence we are told in Jeremiah 17:5: "Cursed be the man that trusteth in man, and maketh flesh his arm"; and a little farther on (17:7): "Blessed be the man that trusteth in the Lord, and the Lord shall be his confidence." This shows us that the goods our Lord teaches us to ask for in His prayer are to be regarded as possible, yet not easy to get; access to them is afforded by God's help and not by human power.

8

The first petition: desire for perfect knowledge of God

In this connection we must heed the order of desire, as regulated by charity, so that a corresponding order of goods to be hoped and asked for from God may be established. The order of charity requires us to love God above all things. And so charity moves our first desire in the direction of the things that are of God. But desire has to do with future good, and nothing in the future can accrue to God, considered as He is in Himself, since He is eternally the same. Therefore our desire cannot bear on things that belong to God as they are considered in themselves: we may not entertain the idea that God can acquire some goods He does not already possess. Rather, our love regards these goods in such a way that we love them as existing. However, we can desire, with respect to God, that He who exists forever great in Himself, may be magnified in the thoughts and reverence of all men.

---

[399] "*Oratio est petitio decentium a Deo.*" *De fide orthodoxa*, III, 24 (PG, XCIV, 1089).

This is not to be dismissed as impossible. For, since man was made for the very purpose of knowing God's greatness, he would seem to have been created in vain if he were unable to attain to the perception of this attribute, contrary to what is said in Psalm 88:48: "Hast Thou made all the children of men in vain?"[400] If this were the case, the desire of nature, whereby all men naturally desire to know something of the divine perfections, would be fruitless. Indeed, no man is completely deprived of knowledge of God, as we are taught in Job 36:25: "All men see Him." Yet such knowledge of God is hard to obtain; indeed, it is beyond all human power, according to Job 36:26: "Behold, God is great, exceeding our knowledge."

Accordingly, knowledge of God's greatness and goodness cannot come to men except through the grace of divine Revelation, as we are told in Matthew 11:27: "No one knoweth the Son but the Father; neither doth any one know the Father but the Son, and he to whom it shall please the Son to reveal Him." Therefore Augustine says, in his commentary on John, that no one knows God unless He who knows manifests Himself.[401]

To some extent God makes Himself known to men through a certain natural knowledge, by imbuing them with the light of reason and by giving existence to visible creatures, in which are reflected some glimmerings of His goodness and wisdom, as we read in Romans 1:19: "That which is known of God" — that is, what is knowable about God by natural reason — "is manifest in them" (namely, is disclosed to pagan peoples). "For God hath manifested it unto them," through the light of reason and through the creatures He has put in the world. The Apostle adds: "For the invisible things of Him, from the creation of the world, are clearly

[400] RSV: Ps. 89:47.
[401] *In Ioannis evangelium*, LVIII, 3 (*PL*, XXXV, 1793).

seen, being understood by the things that are made; His eternal power also and divinity."[402]

But this knowledge is imperfect because not even creatures can be perfectly comprehended by man and also because creatures are unable to represent God perfectly, since the excellence of the cause infinitely surpasses its effect. Therefore in Job 11:7 the question is put: "Peradventure thou wilt comprehend the steps of God, and wilt find out the Almighty perfectly?" And in Job 36:25, after affirming, "All men see Him," the speaker adds, "every one beholdeth afar off."

As a result of the imperfection of this knowledge, it happened that men, wandering from the truth, erred in various ways concerning the knowledge of God to such an extent that, as the Apostle says in Romans 1:21-23, some "became vain in their thoughts, and their foolish heart was darkened; for, professing themselves to be wise, they became fools, and they changed the glory of the incorruptible God into the likeness of the image of a corruptible man and of birds and of fourfooted beasts and of creeping things."

To recall men from this error, God gave them a clearer knowledge of Himself in the Old Law, through which men were brought back to the worship of the one God. Thus the truth is announced in Deuteronomy 6:4: "Hear, O Israel, the Lord our God is one Lord." But this information about God was wrapped up in the obscurities of figurative language, and was confined within the limits of one nation, the Jewish people, as is indicated in Psalm 75:2: "In Judea God is known; His name is great in Israel."[403]

In order that true knowledge of God might spread throughout the whole human race, God the Father sent the only-begotten

---

[402] Rom. 1:20.
[403] RSV: Ps. 76:1.

Word of His majesty into the world, that through Him the entire world might come to a true knowledge of the divine name. Our Lord Himself began this work among His disciples, as He tells us in John 17:6: "I have manifested Thy name to the men whom Thou hast given me out of the world." But His intention in imparting knowledge of the Deity was not limited to the disciples; He wished this knowledge to be promulgated through them to the whole world. This is why He adds the prayer: "That the world may believe that Thou hast sent me."[404] He carries on His task without intermission through the Apostles and their successors; by their ministry men are brought to the knowledge of God, to the end that the name of God may be held in benediction and honor throughout the entire world, as was foretold in Malachi 1:11: "From the rising of the sun even to the going down, my name is great among the Gentiles, and in every place there is sacrifice, and there is offered to my name a clean oblation."

When we say in our prayer, "hallowed be Thy name," we ask that the work thus begun may be brought to completion. "In making this petition," says St. Augustine, "we do not mean to imply that the name of God is not holy, but we ask that it may be regarded by all men as holy; that is, that God may become so well known that men will not judge anything to be holier."[405] Among the various indications that make the holiness of God known to men, the most convincing sign is the holiness of men, who are sanctified by the divine indwelling. Gregory of Nyssa asks: "Who is so bereft of the finer sensibilities as not, on beholding the spotless life of believers, to glorify the name that is invoked by those who lead such a life?"[406] The Apostle speaks in like vein, in

---

[404] John 17:21.
[405] *De sermone Domini in monte*, II, 5 (*PL*, XXXIV, 1277).
[406] *De oratione dominica*, III (*PG*, XLIV, 1153).

1 Corinthians 14:24-25. After saying: "If all prophesy, and there come in one that believeth not, or an unlearned person, he is convinced of all," he adds: "And so, falling down on his face, he will adore God, affirming that God is among you indeed."

Therefore, as Chrysostom points out, in teaching us the words, "hallowed be Thy name," our Lord also bids us, when we pray, to ask that God may be glorified by our lives.[407] The sense of the prayer is this: "Grant us so to live, that all men may glorify Thee through us."[408]

God is sanctified or hallowed in the minds of other men through us, to the extent that we are sanctified by Him. Hence when we say: "hallowed be Thy name," we pray, as Cyprian remarks, that God's name may be hallowed in us.[409] Following the lead of Christ, who says: "Be holy, because I am holy,"[410] we beg that we, who have been sanctified in Baptism, may persevere in the state in which we began.

Furthermore we pray daily to be sanctified in order that we, who daily fall, may wash away our sins by a constant process of purification.

This petition is put first because, as Chrysostom observes, he who would offer a worthy prayer to God should ask for nothing before the Father's glory, but should make everything come after the praise of Him.[411]

---

[407] *In Matthaeum*, hom. XIX, 4 (PG, LVII, 279).

[408] Vivès: "*Ita fac nos vivere, Ut per nos te universi glorificent*"; Mandonnet: "*Ita fac nos vivere, ut nos te et universi glorificent*." The Vivès reading is preferred as agreeing better with the context.

[409] *Liber de oratione dominica*, XII (PL, IV, 527).

[410] See Lev. 11:44; cf. 1 Pet. 1:16.

[411] *Loc. cit.*

9

The second petition: prayer for participation in God's glory

After desiring and praying for the glory of God, man is led to desire and ask that he may be given a share in divine glory. And so the second petition is worded: "Thy kingdom come." In discussing this petition, we shall follow the same procedure as we observed in treating of the preceding petition. We shall consider, first, that we do right to desire the kingdom of God; secondly, that man can attain to the possession of this kingdom; thirdly, that he can attain to it not by his own powers, but only with the help of divine grace. And then, in the fourth place, we must inquire into the sense in which we pray that the kingdom of God may come.

As to the first point, we should note that to every being its own good is naturally desirable. Hence good is conveniently defined as that which all desire. The proper good of any being is that whereby it is brought to perfection. We say that a thing is good inasmuch as it reaches its proper perfection. On the other hand, a thing lacks goodness so far as it is lacking in its proper perfection. Consequently each thing seeks its own perfection, and so man, too, naturally desires to be perfected. And, since there are many degrees of human perfection, that good chiefly and primarily comes under man's desire which looks to his ultimate perfection. This good is recognized by the sure sign that man's natural desire comes to rest in it. For, since man's natural desire always inclines toward his own good which consists in some perfection, the consequence is that as long as something remains to be desired, man has not yet reached his final perfection.

Something can thus remain to be desired in two ways. The first is when the thing desired is sought for the sake of something else: when it is obtained, desire cannot cease, but must be borne along toward that other object. The second is when a thing does not suffice to provide what man desires. For instance, a meager portion of food is not enough to sustain nature, and so does not satisfy natural appetite.

Consequently that good which man chiefly and mainly desires must be of such a nature that it is not sought for the sake of something else and that it satisfies man. This good is commonly called *happiness*, inasmuch as it is man's foremost good: we say that certain people are happy because we believe that everything goes well with them. It is also known as *beatitude*, a word that stresses its excellence. It can also be called *peace*, so far as it brings quiet; for cessation of appetite appears to imply interior peace. This is indicated in the words of Psalm 147:14: "Who hath placed peace in thy borders."

We see clearly that man's happiness or beatitude cannot consist in material goods. The first reason for this is that such goods are not sought for their own sake, but are naturally desired because of something else. They are suitable for man by reason of his body. But man's body is subordinated to his soul as to its end. For the body is the instrument of the soul that moves it, and every instrument exists for the good of the art that employs it. Furthermore, the body is related to the soul as matter is related to form. But form is the end of matter, just as act is the end of potency. Consequently man's final happiness does not consist in riches or in honors or in health and beauty or in any goods of this kind.

The second reason why happiness is not to be found in material goods is that such goods cannot satisfy man. This is clear on many scores. In the first place, man has a twofold appetitive power: one intellectual, the other sensitive. Consequently he has a twofold desire. But the desire of the intellectual appetite veers chiefly toward intelligible goods, which exceed the competency of material goods. Secondly, material goods, as being the lowest in the order of nature, do not contain all goodness but possess only a portion of goodness, so that one object has this particular aspect of goodness (for example, the power to give pleasure) while another object has a different advantage (for instance, the power to cause bodily well-being) and so on of the rest. In none of them can the human appetite, which naturally tends toward universal good, find complete satisfaction. Nor can full satisfaction be found even in a large number of such goods, no matter how much they may be multiplied, for they fall short of the infinity of universal good. Thus we are assured in Ecclesiastes 5:9 that "a covetous man shall not be satisfied with money."[412] Thirdly, since man by his intellect apprehends the universal good that is not circumscribed by space or time, the human appetite, consistently with the apprehension of the intellect, desires a good that is not circumscribed by time. Hence man naturally desires perpetual stability. But this cannot be found in material things, which are subject to corruption and many kinds of change. Therefore the human appetite cannot find the sufficiency it needs in material goods. Accordingly, man's ultimate happiness cannot consist in such goods.

Moreover, since the sense faculties have bodily activities (inasmuch as they operate through bodily organs which exercise their functions on corporeal objects), man's ultimate happiness cannot consist in the activities of his sensitive nature (for example, in certain pleasures of the flesh). The human intellect, too, has some activity with reference to corporeal things, for man knows bodies by his speculative intellect and manages corporeal things by his practical intellect. And so man's ultimate happiness and perfection cannot be placed in the proper activity of the speculative intellect or of the practical intellect that deals with material things.

---

[412]RSV: Eccles. 5:10.

Likewise, such happiness is not found in that activity of the human intellect whereby the soul reflects on itself. There are two reasons for this. In the first place the soul, considered in its own nature, is not beatified. Otherwise it would not have to labor for the attainment of beatitude. Therefore it does not acquire beatitude from the mere contemplation of itself. In the second place, happiness is the ultimate perfection of man, as was stated above. Since the perfection of the soul consists in its proper activity, its ultimate perfection is to be looked for on the plane of its best activity, and this is determined by its best object, for activities are specified according to their objects. But the soul is not the best object to which its activity can tend. For it is aware that something exists that is better than itself. Hence man's ultimate beatitude cannot consist in the activity whereby he makes himself or any of the other higher substances the object of his intellection, as long as there is something better to which the action of the human soul can turn. Man's activity may extend to any good whatever, for the universal good is what man desires, since he apprehends universal good with his intellect. Therefore, whatever may be the degree to which goodness extends, the action of the human intellect, and hence also of the will, reaches out toward it in some way. But good is found supremely in God, who is good by His very essence and is the source of every good. Consequently man's ultimate perfection and final good consist in union with God, according to Psalm 72:28: "It is good for me to adhere to my God."[413]

This truth is clearly perceived if we examine the way other things participate in being. Individual men all truly receive the predication *man* because they share in the very essence of the species. None of them is said to be a man on the ground that he

---

[413]RSV: Ps. 73:28.

shares in the likeness of some other man, but only because he shares in the essence of the species. This is so even though one man brings another to such participation by way of generation, as a father does with regard to his son. Now beatitude or happiness is nothing else than perfect good. Therefore all who share in beatitude can be happy only by participation in the divine beatitude, which is man's essential goodness, even though one man may be helped by another in his progress toward beatitude. This is why Augustine says in his book, *De vera religione*, that we are beatified not by beholding the angels, but by seeing the Truth in which we love the angels and are happy along with them.[414]

Man's spirit is carried up to God in two ways: by God Himself, and by some other thing. It is borne up to God by God Himself when God is seen in Himself and is loved for Himself. It is raised up by something else when the soul is elevated to God by His creatures, according to Romans 1:20: "The invisible things of Him . . . are clearly seen, being understood by the things that are made."

Perfect beatitude cannot consist in a person's movement toward God through the agency of something else. For, first, since beatitude denotes the ultimate term of all human actions, true and perfect happiness cannot be found in that which is of the nature of change in the direction of the end rather than of a final term. Knowledge and love of God through the medium of something other than God is brought about by a certain movement of the human mind, as it advances through one stage to another. True and perfect beatitude, therefore, is not discovered in this process.

Secondly, if man's beatitude consists in the adhering of the human mind to God, perfect beatitude must require a perfect adhering to God. But the human mind cannot adhere perfectly to

---

[414]*De vera religione*, LV, 110 (*PL*, XXXIV, 170).

God through the medium of any creature, whether by way of knowledge or by way of love. All created forms fall infinitely short of representing the divine essence. Objects pertaining to a higher order of being cannot be known through a form belonging to a lower order. For example, a spiritual substance cannot be known through a body, and a heavenly body cannot be known through one of the elements. Much less can the essence of God be known through any created form. Yet, just as we gain a negative insight into higher bodies from a study of lower bodies (thus learning, for instance, that they are neither heavy nor light) and just as we conceive a negative idea about angels from a consideration of bodies (judging that they are immaterial or incorporeal), so by examining creatures we come to know not what God is, but rather what He is not. Likewise, any goodness possessed by a creature is a definite minimum in comparison with the divine goodness, which is infinite goodness. Hence the various degrees of goodness emanating from God and discerned in things, which are benefits bestowed by God, fail to raise the mind to a perfect love of God. Therefore true and perfect beatitude cannot consist in the adherence of the mind to God through some alien medium.

Thirdly, according to right order, things that are less familiar become known through things that are more familiar. Likewise, things that are less good are loved because of their relation to things that have greater goodness. Thus, as God is the first truth and supreme goodness, and is eminently knowable and lovable in Himself, the order of nature requires that all things should be known and loved through Him. So if the mind of any person has to be brought to the knowledge and love of God through creatures, this results from his imperfection. Accordingly, such a one has not yet achieved perfect beatitude, which excludes all imperfection.

We conclude, therefore, that perfect beatitude consists in the direct union of the spirit with God in knowledge and love. In the same way that a king has the office of directing and governing his subjects, that tendency predominates in man which is the norm for regulating everything else in him. This is why the Apostle warns in Romans 6:12: "Let not sin therefore reign in your mortal body." So, since the notion of perfect beatitude requires that God be known and loved in Himself so that the soul embraces other objects only through Him, God reigns truly and perfectly in the good. Thus we are told in Isaiah 49:10: "He that is merciful to them shall be their shepherd, and at the fountains of waters He shall give them drink." In other words, by Him they shall be refreshed with the most excellent goods, of whatever kind they may be.

We should recall, further, that the intellect understands all it knows by means of a certain likeness or form. In a similar way the external organ of sight perceives a stone by means of a form of the stone. Consequently the intellect cannot behold God as He is in His essence by means of a created likeness or form that would represent the divine essence. For we are aware that an object belonging to a higher order of being cannot be represented, so far as its essence is concerned, by a likeness pertaining to a lower order. Thus a spiritual substance cannot, if there is question of its essence, be understood by means of any bodily likeness. And so, as God transcends the whole order of creation much more than a spiritual substance excels the order of material things, He cannot be seen in His essence through the medium of a corporeal likeness.

The same truth is quite evident if we but reflect on what the vision of a thing in its essence implies. He who apprehends some property pertaining essentially to man does not perceive the essence of man (just as a person who knows what an animal is, but does not know what rationality is, fails to understand the essence of man). Any perfection predicated of God belongs to Him essentially. But no single created likeness can represent God with respect to all the perfections predicated of Him. For in the created intellect the likeness whereby man apprehends the life of God differs from the likeness whereby he apprehends God's wisdom, and so on with regard to justice and all the other perfections that are identical with God's essence. So the created intellect cannot be informed by a single likeness representing the divine essence in such a way that the essence of God can be seen therein. And if such likenesses are multiplied, they will be lacking in unity, which is identical with God's essence. Consequently the created intellect cannot be raised so high by a single created likeness (or even by many of them) as to see God as He is in Himself, in His own essence. In order, therefore, that God may be seen in His essence by a created intellect, the divine essence must be perceived directly in itself and not through the medium of some likeness.

Such vision requires a certain union of the created intellect with God. In the first chapter of his book, *De divinis nominibus*, Dionysius observes that when we arrive at our most blessed end and God appears, we shall be filled with a superintellectual knowledge of God.[415] The divine essence, however, has this exclusive characteristic, that our intellect can be united to it without the medium of any likeness. The reason is that the divine essence itself is its own existence or *esse*, which is true of no other form.

Knowledge requires the presence of some form in the intellect; so, if any form that exists by itself (e.g., the substance of an angel) cannot inform an intellect and yet is to be known by the intellect of another, such knowledge has to be brought about by some likeness of the thing informing the intellect. But this is not necessary in the case of the divine essence, which is its own existence.

Accordingly, the soul that is beatified by the vision of God is made one with Him in understanding. The knower and the known

---

[415] Pseudo-Dionysius, *De divinis nominibus*, I, 4 (PG, III, 592).

must somehow be one. And so, when God reigns in the saints, they too reign along with God. In their person are uttered the words of Revelation 5:10: "(Thou) hast made us to our God a kingdom and priests, and we shall reign on the Earth." This kingdom, in which God reigns in the saints and the saints reign with God, is called the Kingdom of Heaven, according to Matthew 3:2: "Do penance, for the Kingdom of Heaven is at hand." This is the same manner of speaking as that whereby presence in Heaven is ascribed to God — not in the sense that He is housed in the material heavens but to show forth the eminence of God over every creature, in the way that Heaven towers high above every other material creature, as is indicated in Psalm 112:4: "The Lord is high above all nations, and His glory above the heavens."[416]

The beatitude of the saints is called the Kingdom of Heaven, therefore, not because their reward is situated in the material heavens but because it consists in the contemplation of supercelestial nature. This is also the reason for the statement about the angels in Matthew 18:10: "Their angels in Heaven always see the face of my Father who is in Heaven." Hence Augustine, in his explanation of the passage in Matthew 5:12 ("Your reward is very great in Heaven") says in his book, *De sermone Domini in monte:* "I do not think that *Heaven* here means the loftier regions of this visible world. For our reward . . . is not to be in evanescent things. I think that the expression *in Heaven* refers rather to the spiritual firmament, where eternal justice dwells."[417]

This ultimate good, which consists in God, is also called *eternal life*. The word is used in the sense in which the action of the animating soul is called *life*. Hence we distinguish as many kinds of life as there are kinds of action performed by the soul, among

[416]RSV: Ps. 113:4.
[417]*Lib.* I, 5 (*PL*, XXXIV, 1236).

which the action of the intellect is supreme; and, according to the Philosopher, the action of the intellect is life.[418] Furthermore, since an act receives species from its object, the vision of the divinity is called eternal life, as we read in John 17:3: "This is eternal life: that they may know Thee, the only true God."

The ultimate good is also known as *comprehension* (*comprehensio*), a word suggested by Philippians 3:12: "I follow after, if I may by any means apprehend" (*comprehendam*). The term is not, of course, used in the sense according to which *comprehension* implies enclosing; for what is enclosed by another is completely contained by it as a whole. The created intellect cannot completely see God's essence, in such a way, that is, as to attain to the ultimate and perfect degree of the divine vision, and so to see God to the extent that He is capable of being seen. For God is knowable in a way that is proportionate to the clarity of His truth, and this is infinite. Hence He is infinitely knowable.

But infinite knowledge is impossible for a created intellect, whose power of understanding is finite. God alone, therefore, who knows Himself infinitely well with the infinite power of His intellect, comprehends Himself by completely understanding Himself.

Nevertheless, comprehension is promised to the saints, in the sense of the word *comprehension* that implies a certain grasp. Thus when one man pursues another, he is said to apprehend (*dicitur comprehendere*) the latter when he can grasp him with his hand. Accordingly, "while we are in the body," as we read in 2 Corinthians 5:6-7, "we are absent from the Lord; for we walk by faith and not by sight." And so we press on toward Him as toward some distant goal. But when we see Him by direct vision we shall hold Him present within ourselves. Thus in the Song of Solomon 3:4,

[418] Aristotle, *Metaphysics*, XII, 7 (1072b 27).

the spouse seeks him whom her soul loves; and when at last she finds him she says: "I held him, and I will not let him go."

The ultimate good we have been speaking of contains perpetual and full joy. Our Lord was thinking of this when He bade us, in John 16:24: "Ask and you shall receive, that your joy may be full." Full joy, however, can be gained from no creature, but only from God, in whom the entire plenitude of goodness resides. And so our Lord says to the faithful servant in Matthew 25:21: "Enter thou into the joy of thy Lord," that you mayest have joy of thy Lord, as is indicated in Job 22:26: "Then shalt thou abound in delights in the Almighty." Since God rejoices most of all in Himself, the faithful servant is said to enter into the joy of his Lord inasmuch as he enters into the joy wherein his Lord rejoices, as our Lord said on another occasion when He made a promise to His disciples: "And I dispose to you, as my Father hath disposed to me, a kingdom, that you may eat and drink at my table in my kingdom."[419] Not that the saints, once they have been made incorruptible, have any use for bodily foods in that final state of good; no, by *the table* is meant rather the replenishment of joy that God has in Himself and that the saints have from Him.

This fullness of joy must be understood not only of the object of rejoicing, but also with reference to the disposition of him who rejoices. In other words, the object of the rejoicing must be present, and the entire affection of the joyful person must be centered on the cause of the joy. As we have shown, in the vision of the divine essence, the created spirit possesses God as present; and the vision itself sets the affections completely on fire with divine love. If any object is lovable so far as it is beautiful and good, as Dionysius remarks in *De divinis nominibus*,[420] surely God, who is

---

[419]Luke 22:29-30.
[420]*Cap.* IV, 10 (PG, III, 708); also 13 and 14 (PG, III, 712).

the very essence of beauty and goodness, cannot be gazed at without love. Therefore perfect vision is followed by perfect love. Gregory observes in one of his homilies on Ezechiel: "The fire of love which begins to burn here on Earth, flares up more fiercely with love of God when He who is loved is seen."[421] Moreover, joy over an object embraced as present is keener the more that object is loved; consequently that joy is full, not only because of the object that gives joy, but also on the part of him who rejoices. This joy is what crowns human beatitude. Hence Augustine writes in his *Confessions* that happiness is joy in truth.[422]

Another point to consider is this: as God is the very essence of goodness, He is the good of every good. Therefore all good is beheld when He is beheld, as the Lord intimated when He said to Moses: "I will show thee all good."[423] So if God is possessed, all good is possessed, as is suggested in Wisdom 7:11: "All good things came to me together with her" (i.e., with Wisdom). In that final state of good, when we see God, we shall have a full abundance of all goods; and so our Lord promises the faithful servant in Matthew 24:47 that "He shall place him over all His goods."

Since evil is opposed to good, the presence of all good requires the utter banishment of evil. Justice has no participation with injustice, and light has no fellowship with darkness, as we are told in 2 Corinthians 6:14. In that final state of good, therefore, those who possess all good will not only have a perfect sufficiency, but they will enjoy complete serenity and security as a result of their freedom from all evil, according to Proverbs 1:33: "He that shall hear me, shall rest without terror and shall enjoy abundance without fear of evils."

[421] Gregory the Great, *In Ezechielem homiliae*, II, 2 (*PL*, LXXVI, 954).
[422] *Lib.* X, 23 (*PL*, XXXII, 793).
[423] Exod. 33:19.

A further result is that absolute peace will reign in Heaven. Man's peace is blocked either by the inner restlessness of desire (when he covets what he does not yet possess) or by the irksomeness of certain evils which he suffers or fears he may suffer. But in Heaven there is nothing to fear. Restlessness of craving will end, because of the full possession of all good. Every external cause of disturbance will cease, because all evil will be absent. The perfect tranquillity of peace will be enjoyed there. Isaiah 32:18 alludes to this: "My people shall sit in the beauty of peace" (i.e., the perfection of peace). To show the cause of peace the Prophet adds: "And in the tabernacles of confidence" (for confidence will reign when the fear of evils is abolished) "and in wealthy rest" (which refers to the overflowing abundance of all good).

The perfection of this final good will endure forever. It cannot fail through any lack of the goods which man enjoys, for these are eternal and incorruptible. We are assured of this in Isaiah 33:20: "Thy eyes shall see Jerusalem, a rich habitation, a tabernacle that cannot be removed." The cause of this stability is given in the next verse (33:21): "Because only there our Lord is magnificent." The entire perfection of that state will consist in the enjoyment of divine eternity.

Similarly, that state cannot fail through the corruption of the beings existing there. These are either naturally incorruptible, as is the case with the angels, or they will be transferred to a condition of incorruption, as is the case with men. "For this corruptible must put on incorruption," as we are informed in 1 Corinthians 15:53. The same is indicated in Revelation 3:12: "He that shall overcome, I will make him a pillar in the temple of my God."

Nor can that state fail by reason of the turning away of man's will in disgust. The more clearly God, the essence of goodness, is seen, the more He must be loved; and so enjoyment of Him will be desired ever more keenly, according to Ecclesiasticus 24:29: "They that eat me shall yet hunger, and they that drink me shall yet thirst." For this reason the words of 1 Peter 1:12, "on whom the angels desire to look," were spoken of the angels who see God.

That state will not be overthrown by the attack of an enemy, for no disturbing interference of any evil will be found there, as we read in Isaiah 35:9: "No lion shall be there" (that is, no assaulting devil) "nor shall any mischievous beast" (that is, any evil man) "go up by it nor be found there." Hence our Lord says of His sheep, in John 10:28: "They shall not perish forever, and no man shall pluck them out of my hand."

Furthermore, that state cannot come to an end as a result of the banishment of some of its inhabitants by God. No one will be expelled from that state on account of sin, which will be simply non-existent in a place where every evil will be absent; hence we are told in Isaiah 60:21: "Thy people shall be all just." Again, none will be exiled for the purpose of urging them on to greater good, as happens at times in this world when God withdraws spiritual consolations even from the just and takes away other of His benefits, in order that men may seek them with greater eagerness and may acknowledge their own powerlessness. That state is not one of correction or progress, but is a life of final perfection. This is why our Lord says in John 6:37: "Him that cometh to me, I will not cast out." Therefore that state will consist in the everlasting enjoyment of all the goods mentioned, as is said in Psalm 5:12: "They shall rejoice forever, and Thou shalt dwell in them."[424] Consequently the kingdom we have been discussing is perfect happiness, for it contains all good in changeless abundance. And, since happiness is naturally desired by men, the kingdom of God, too, is desired by all.

---

[424]RSV: Ps. 5:11.

10
The possibility of reaching the kingdom

We must go on to show that man can reach that kingdom. Other-wise it would be hoped for and prayed for in vain. In the first place, the divine promise makes this possibility clear. Our Lord says, in Luke 12:32: "Fear not, little flock, for it hath pleased your Father to give you a kingdom." God's good pleasure is efficacious in carrying out all that He plans, according to Isaiah 46:10: "My counsel shall stand, and all my will shall be done." For, as we read in Romans 9:19: "Who resisteth His will?" Secondly, an evident example shows that attainment of the kingdom is possible.[425]

---

[425] The *Compendium theologiae* breaks off at this point. His untimely death prevented St. Thomas from finishing the book. His opusculum, *Expositio orationis dominicae*, though it is probably a *reportatio*, gives us an idea of the plan he very likely would have followed in completing Part II of the *Compendium*. Part III, on the virtue of charity, was to have developed the theme indicated in the opening chapter of the present work, that we should carry out God's will through love.

BIOGRAPHICAL NOTE

———————

St. Thomas Aquinas

(1225-1274)

Scholar *and* saint! Certainly it's a rare combination today, but Thomas Aquinas was both. He devoted his life to comprehending God's Revelation — through reason, contemplation, and prayer — and to living in conformity with the call of that Revelation.

Born of an illustrious, politically prominent family in Naples, St. Thomas was educated at the famous Monte Cassino Abbey and at the University of Naples. In 1244, against the wishes of his family, he entered the Dominican Order. The Dominicans sent Thomas to the University of Paris to study with the renowned Aristotelian scholar, Albert the Great. In 1252, Thomas began his teaching career which involved him in every major intellectual debate of the time. Through many formal academic disputations, through his preaching, and in over one hundred written volumes, St. Thomas gave his reason unreservedly to the service of Christian Revelation. Relying heavily on the Greek philosopher Aristotle, Thomas showed that Christian faith is credible, defensible, and intelligible.

Moreover, St. Thomas's prodigious scholarship nurtured his own spiritual development. He prayed intensely and was known to suffer the terrible spiritual trials and to receive the sublime consolations of the true ascetic and contemplative.

St. Thomas died on March 7, 1274 at the age of fifty. He was canonized in 1323 and proclaimed a Doctor of the Universal Church in 1567.

In his encyclical *Æterni Patris* (August 4, 1879), Pope Leo XIII called on all men to "restore the golden wisdom of St. Thomas and to spread it far and wide for the defense and beauty of the Catholic Faith, for the good of society, and for the advantage of all sciences."

DETAILED LIST OF TOPICS

Detailed List of Topics

FAITH

Author's Introduction

THE DIVINE TRINITY

God

The Holy Trinity

Creation from Nothing

The Human Soul

God's Activity in Creating

Christ's Incarnation

The Virgin Birth

BIBLIOGRAPHY

BIBLIOGRAPHY

In the following listings, *PL* (*Patrologia latina*) stands for J. P. Migne, *Patrologiae cursus completus*, series *latina*, 221 vols. (Paris, 1844-64). *PG* (*Patrologia graeca*) stands for J. P. Migne, *Patrologiae cursus completus*, series *graeca*, 161 vols. (Paris, 1857-66).

Abelard, Peter. *Sic et non* (*PL*, CLXXVIII).
Albert the Great, St. *Opera omnia*, ed. A. Borgnet, 38 vols.
      (Paris: Vivès, 1890-99).
Ambrose, St.
    De fide (*PL*, XVI).
    De sacramentis (*PL*, XVI).
Ambrosiaster. *In epistolam ad Romanos* (*PL*, XVII).
Anaxagoras. Fragment 12. *See* Diels.
Aristotle. *Opera*, ed. Academia Regia Borussica, 5 vols. in 6
      (Berlin: G. Reimer, 1831-70).
Athanasius, St.
    Contra Apollinarium (*PG*, XXVI).
    Contra Arianos (*PG*, XXVI).
    De synodis (*PG*, XXVI).
Augustine, St.
    De civitate Dei (*PL*, XLI).
    Confessiones (*PL*, XXXII).

De doctrina christiana (PL, XXXIV).

Epistolae (PL, XXXIII).

De Genesi ad litteram (PL, XXXIV).

De haeresibus (PL, XLII).

In Ioannis evangelium (PL, XXXV).

Contra Iulianum (PL, XLIV).

Retractationes (PL, XXXII).

De sermone Domini in monte (PL, XXXIV).

Sermones (PL, XXXIX).

De Trinitate (PL, XLII).

De vera religione (PL, XXXIV).

Averroes. *Aristotelis Stagiritae libri omnes cum Averrois Cordubensis variis in eosdem commentariis*, 11 vols. (Venice: Juntas, 1550-52).

Avicenna. *Opera in lucem redacta ac nuper quantum ars niti potuit per canonicos emendata* (Venice, 1508).

Bernard, St. *In cantica* (PL, CLXXXIII).

Boethius.

Commentaria in Porphyrium (PL, LXIV).

De consolatione philosophiae (PL, LXIII).

De persona et duabus naturis (PL, LXIV).

Bonaventure, St. *Opera omnia*, 10 vols. (Quaracchi: Ex typographia Collegii S. Bonaventurae, 1882-1902).

Busse, A. (ed.). *Porphyrius, Isagoge et in Categorias commentarium* (in *Commentaria in Aristotelem graeca*, 23 vols. [Berlin: G. Reimer, 1882-1909]), Vol. IV. 1887.

Cicero. *De divinatione, De fato, Timaeus*, ed. O. Plasberg, W. Ax (Leipzig: Teubner, 1938).

Cyprian, St. *Liber de oratione dominica* (PL, IV).

Denzinger, H., and Bannwart, C. *Enchiridion symbolorum*, 21st-23rd ed. by J. P. Umberg (Freiburg: Herder, 1937).

Diels, H. *Die Fragmente der Vorsokratiker*, 3 vols. (Berlin: Weidmann, 1922).

Dionysius (the Pseudo-Areopagite).
De coelesti hierarchia (PG, III).
De divinis nominibus (PG, III).

Empedocles. Fragment 126. *See* Diels.

Gilbert de la Porrée.
In librum de praedicatione trium personarum (PL, LXIV).
In librum de Trinitate (PL, LXIV).

Gregory the Great, St.
Dialogi (PL, LXXVII).
In evangelia (PL, LXXVI).
In Ezechielem homiliae (PL, LXXVI).
Moralia (PL, LXXV).

Gregory of Nyssa, St.
De hominis opificio (PG, XLIV).
De oratione dominica (PG, XLIV).

Gregory of Tours, St. *Historia Francorum* (PL, LXXI).

Hilary, St. *De Trinitate* (PL, X).

Hippolytus. *Philosophumena* (PG, XVI; Pseudo-Origen, *Contra haereses*).

Irenaeus, St. *Adversus haereses* (PG, VII).

Jerome, St.
Epistolae (PL, XXII).
In evangelium Matthaei (PL, XXVI).
De perpetua virginitate B. Mariae (PL, XXIII).

John Chrysostom, St.
In epistolam primam ad Corinthios (PG, LXI).
In Matthaeum (PG, LVII).

John Damascene, St. *De fide orthodoxa* (PG, XCIV).

Julian of Toledo. *Prognosticon* (PL, XCVI).

Lactantius. *Divinae institutiones* (PL, VI).

Leo the Great, St.
    Epistolae (PL, LIV).
    Sermones (PL, LIV).

Leo II, St. *Epistolae* (PL, XCVI).

Longpré, E. "De B. Virginis maternitate et relatione ad Christum," *Antonianum*, VII (1932), 289-313.

Macrobius. *In Somnium Scipionis;* in *Macrobius*, ed. F. Eyssenhardt (Leipzig: Teubner, 1893).

Mansi, J. D. *Sacrorum Conciliorum nova et amplissima collectio*, 53 vols. in 60 (Paris, Arnhem, and Leipzig: Welter, 1901-27).

Motte, A. R. "Un chapitre inauthentique dans le *Compendium Theologiae* de S. Thomas," *Revue Thomiste*, XLV (1939), 749-53.

Origen. *Peri archon* (PG, XI). Also known as *De principiis*.

Peter Comestor. *Historia scholastica* (PL, CXCVIII).

Peter Lombard. *Libri IV sententiarum*, 2nd ed., 2 vols. (Quaracchi: Ex typographia Collegii S. Bonaventurae, 1916).

Plato. *Opera*, ed. J. Burnet, 5 vols. in 6 (Oxford: Clarendon Press, 1900-1907 and later reprintings).

Porphyry. *Isagoge: De specie*. See Busse.

Pseudo-Chrysostom. *In evangelium Matthaei* (PG, LVI).

Pseudo-Dionysius. See Dionysius, the Pseudo-Areopagite.

Pseudo-Origen. See Hippolytus.

Scotus, John Duns. *Opera omnia*, 26 vols. (Paris: Vivès, 1891-95).

Strabo, Walafrid. *Glossa ordinaria* (PL, CXIII and CXIV).

Tertullian.
    Adversus Valentinianos (PL, II).
    De anima (PL, II).

Theodore of Mopsuestia. *Fragmentum de Incarnatione* (PG, LXVI).

Theophylact. *In evangelium Marci* (*PG*, CXXIII).

Thomas Aquinas, St.

    Opera omnia, ed. E. Fretté and P. Maré, 34 vols. (Paris: Vivès, 1871-80).

    Opera omnia, iussu edita Leonis XIII, Vols. I-XV (Rome: R. Garroni, 1882-1930).

    Opuscula omnia, ed. P. Mandonnet, 5 vols. (Paris: Lethielleux, 1927).

    In Metaphysicam Aristotelis commentaria, ed. M. R. Cathala, 3rd. ed. (Turin: Marietta, 1935).

    Summa theologiae, Vols. I-V (Ottawa: Impensis Studii generalis O. Pr., 1941-45).

    De unitate intellectus contra Averroistas, ed. L. W. Keeler (Rome: Apud aedes Pont. Universitatis Gregorianae, 1936).

Vigilius Tapsensis. *Contra Arianos dialogus* (*PL*, LXII).

INDEX

_____

Index